ADVANCE PRAISE FOR NEOBUGARRÓN:

"This book documents a rarely discussed figure within the twists and turns of male-male sex. Straddling the divides between homo- and heterosexual, active and passive, the *bugarrón* was an ostensibly heterosexual man who had sex with other men as a masculine dominant. The *neobugarrón* is Soto-Crespo's name for the commodification of gay male sex through this figure within neoliberalism. The book is a fascinating read for everyone interested in sex, pleasure, and capital."

—Jack Halberstam, author of *Female Masculinity*

"This book makes generous work of situating itself in critical and scholarly contexts that contribute to a wide variety of ongoing conversations. Soto-Crespo's case studies of practicing sex workers and close readings of a range of cultural texts make this book both unique and powerfully interdisciplinary."

—Ricardo L. Ortiz, author of *Cultural Erotics in Cuban America*

"Soto-Crespo sets the stage for a complete rethinking of nonidentitarian, anomalous sexual practices in the Caribbean. Striking the right balance between rigor and provocativeness, gruesomeness and levity, and ambition and evidence, his book is destined to become a canonical work."

—Melba Vélez Ortiz, author of *Maatian Ethics in a Communication Context*

NEOBUGARRÓN

ABNORMATIVITIES: QUEER/GENDER/EMBODIMENT
Scott Herring, Series Editor

NEOBUGARRÓN

HETEROFLEXIBILITY, NEOLIBERALISM, AND LATIN/O AMERICAN SEXUAL PRACTICE

Ramón E. Soto-Crespo

THE OHIO STATE UNIVERSITY PRESS
COLUMBUS

Copyright © 2023 by The Ohio State University.
All rights reserved.

Library of Congress Cataloging-in-Publication data available online at https://catalog.loc.gov
LCCN: 2023019295
Identifiers: ISBN 978-0-8142-1551-7 (hardback); ISBN 978-0-8142-5885-9 (paperback); ISBN 978-0-8142-8308-0 (ebook)

Cover design by Susan Zucker
Text composition by Stuart Rodriguez
Type set in Minion Pro

*For Leo Bersani (1931–2022),
who once asked me: "Is* bugarrón *like trade?"
This book is my answer.*

CONTENTS

List of Illustrations	ix
Preface	xi
Acknowledgments	xvii
INTRODUCTION	1
CHAPTER 1 — Anthropologies of Lust: Deployment of *Bugarrón* Surveillance	16
CHAPTER 2 — The *Neobugarrón*: A Lesson in Neoliberalism and Biopolitics	46
CHAPTER 3 — *Bugarrón* Cinema: A Disturbance in the Field of Vision	84
CHAPTER 4 — *Mundo Cruel*: The *Neobugarrón* in Literature	122
CONCLUSION	155
Bibliography	157
Filmography	167
Index	169

ILLUSTRATIONS

FIGURE 2.1	Drawing of a *bugarrón* ("Josué")	48
FIGURE 2.2	Typical online representation of *neobugarrón*	48
FIGURE 2.3	*Bugarrón* social photo ("Ismael")	66
FIGURE 2.4	*Bugarrón* social photo ("Javier")	69
FIGURE 2.5	Elio Rodríguez's *Tropical, 2*	77
FIGURE 2.6	Josephine Baker in a banana skirt	78
FIGURE 2.7	Carmen Miranda and Don Ameche in *That Night in Rio*	79
FIGURE 2.8	Carmen Miranda	79
FIGURE 2.9	Alberto Korda's *Guerrillero Heroico*	80
FIGURE 2.10	Suitberto Goire's *La Fuerza de Tu Mirada Nos Guía*	81
FIGURE 2.11	Elio Rodríguez's *La Leyenda del Macho*	82

PREFACE

This book is about a sexual practice hiding in plain sight in the Americas. Its practitioners refer to themselves as *hombres* or *hombres normales*. The term designates a heterosexually identified man who has sex with other men, adopting the role exclusively of top (or insertive) in sexual encounters. By always performing the "active" role, an *hombre normal* continues to be included under the umbrella of heterosexuality, according to a sex-gender logic that equates penetration with masculinity/heterosexuality and being penetrated with femininity/homosexuality. The fact that he has sex with other men but is still regarded as heterosexual makes an *hombre normal* incompatible with the modern sexual-identity categories that we inherit from the late nineteenth-century. *Hombres normales* introduce a conundrum into the homo/heterosexual logic similar to the "thousands of aberrant sexualities" or "minor perverts" that in Foucault's *History of Sexuality, Vol. 1* (1978) appear to "produce more species, even where there [is] no order to fit them into" (43–44).

Normal men are not exclusively heterosexual. For a long time, skeptics have perceived this self-understanding of *normal* men as a trick by those who want to hold on to heterosexual privilege while experiencing same-sex practices "on the side." But I suggest that we may have missed their cue. The identification with *normal* men may not attest simply to self-deception. *Hombre normal* or *hombre* may be a category in itself. Not only is this the name these men use to refer to themselves when questioned as to a particular sexual practice, but it is also consistent with an understanding of heterosexuality that Alfred A. Kinsey referred to as a "continuum" or "continuity of gradations" (*Sexual Behavior* 639). *Normal* men inhabit a gradation on the heterosexual continuum somewhere between exclusive heterosexuality and bisexuality. They are what Ritch Savin-Williams and Zhana Vrangalova call "mostly heterosexual" or heteroflexible ("Mostly Heterosexual" 67). It is in this space between standard categories (heterosexuality and bisexuality) that *normal* men thrive. Because their sexual practices place them in neither one nor the other acknowledged sexual "identity," *normal* men are beyond the "radical condensation of sexual categories" (Sedgwick, *Epistemology* 9). Their sexual practice makes them not fit into the categories established in the homo/hetero divide. As nonexclusively heterosexual men who enjoy sex with other men, *hombres normales* stand for a type of sexual practice largely unaccounted for, ever since the solidification of accepted sexual practices. This solidification is what Foucault calls "subjects of a 'sexuality'" (*Use of Pleasure* 4).

NEOBUGARRÓN[1] traces the discursive presence and transformative masks of *hombres normales*. These human subjects are perceived as "minor objects" in the larger discourse of sexual genealogy because they fall in between the interpretive layers of "identities" or ideal categories. From their graded in-between location, *normal* men challenge heteronormativity by identifying with a heterosexual "identity" that may not be a social ideal. In this way, they can be interpreted as nonidentitarian because their idea of *normal* men does not match society's ideal of a heterosexually exclusive "identity." In sexuality, the ideal tends to be sustained by the self-confessed exclusive. As such, *hombres* are not exclusively heterosexual men or exclusively straight men, but they also are not bisexual. Bisexuality they understand as either entailing reciprocity of sexual penetration or as embodying the passive sexual desire of being penetrated. These men show neither of those proclivities and do not consider themselves bisexual. At the same time, they are not gay or homosexual. *Hombres normales* represent a unique sexual gradation. *Hombres normales* are not queer, yet they oppose an exclusively heterosexual ideal. They are not queer because they identify with an expanding sense of normality rather than with nonnormativity. Another way of putting this is that they can be practitioners of a broader sense of normality. As such, *hombres normales* do not fit queer studies frameworks.

I began by referring to *hombres normales* because this is how these practitioners refer to themselves when questioned about their sexual practice. The

---

1. Throughout the text, references to the title of this book are set in roman small caps, while references to the concept or practice of *neobugarrón* are italicized.

term *hombres normales* is also a clever way of hiding in plain sight. However, *hombres normales* is not the term by which they are referred to in the countries where they reside or in the academic scholarship that studies them. Others do not know them as *normal* men. Instead, a slew of names has been devised to categorize *hombres normales*. In Latin America and the Caribbean, *hombres normales* have been categorized as a type; that is to say, the sexual practice has led to the construction of a kind of person. Similar to Foucault's claim in *History of Sexuality, Vol. 1*, where anal and oral sex led to the making of a sodomite, so has *bugarrón* sexual practice led to the making of a *bugarrón* type in Latin America and the Caribbean islands. That is why, in the Caribbean, practitioners of this sexual activity are known as *bugarrones*. A sexual practice has been made into a type. Impossible to reconcile with the categories of homosexuality, bisexuality, and heterosexuality, *bugarrón* sexual practice is considered an anomaly.

The origin of the term *bugarrón* continues to excite speculation among scholars of Latin American and Caribbean male sexuality. Carlos Ulises Decena provides a succinct account of where the word may come from, speculating that it "traveled from the French *bougre*, through the English *bugger* (bugger on?!), to the Spanish *bugarrón*" (*Tacit* 239). *Bugarrón* is the Spanish term used in Puerto Rico, Cuba, and the Dominican Republic, but it is far from the only term employed in Latin America for those heterosexually identified men who have sex with other men. The term for this practice varies from country to country.

In Mexico, *hombres normales* are known as *mayates*. According to Héctor Domínguez-Ruvalcaba, "The word *mayate* . . . comes from *mayatl*, a náhuatl word (the language of the Aztecs) for a species of bright green beetle whose larvae grow in manure. *Mayate* then is an allusion to the colorful proletarian man's dress [bright green], as well as a fecal metonym to describe his sexuality" ("Mayate" 133). Mexico has other names for these "normal men" who have sex with other men. These terms mix sexual practice with class and occupation. For instance, *chichifo* is the term for heterosexually identified sex workers who have sex with other men. *Chacal* is the Mexican term for those *bugarrón* practitioners who come from an uncultured, marginal, or rural background. Over decades, these terms often switch their class and work associations or acquire new meanings.

In Costa Rica, these "normal men" are known as *cacheros*. In Argentina, they are known as *hombres*, from the Spanish *hombre* or "man." And in Colombia, they are known as *chongos*. Scholars have tended to regard these regional or national terms as equivalent. The logic of equivalence represents a process of abstraction where smaller differences are diminished in order to conceptualize commonalities. As José Toro-Alfonso argues: "Whether we call them *cacheros, bugarrones, fletes, bugas* . . . , the individuals described as such are men who have sex with men but who . . . limit themselves to active penetration and domination" ("Vulnerability" 84). The terms are seemingly interchangeable at the level of sexual categorization but more diverse in terms of the racial, ethnic, class stigmas stemming from their local cultures of origin. For this reason, this study focuses on sexual practice across national borders, thus acknowledging that "normal men" belong to a similar sexual gradation in the heterosexual continuum across the Americas. Kinsey's studies of sexual gradation are useful in providing coordinates for understanding how sexual practices work in a continuum. Kinsey's notion of gradation does not seek to provide a truth of desire or of the sexual subject's nature. *Bugarrón* sexual practice becomes more intelligible in terms of gradations, but the "truth" of *bugarrón* sexual practice is not what's at stake here.

This book uses *bugarrón* as the default term in part because it resonates with my upbringing in Puerto Rico. Another reason for preferring *bugarrón* as the default term has to do with its rich discursive presence in Caribbean literature. Very little was known about *bugarrón* during the 1980s when I was growing up in the Caribbean. What we know today of this sexual practice is a result of the HIV/AIDS pandemic and the urgency of viral containment. During the 1990s, there was an international effort to trace all vectors of HIV transmission, one of the most enigmatic of which concerned *bugarrón* sexual practice. It was enigmatic because it did not concern gay men or transvestites. As a result, ethnographies during this period tackled localities and failed to provide a sense of *bugarrón* sexual practice at a regional or hemispheric level. This book examines the discursive production of *bugarrón* sexual practice. It brings the narrow studies into a conversation in order to provide a geographically broad multidisciplinary perspective.

NEOBUGARRÓN focuses on the emergence of *bugarrón* sexual practice in the discourses of knowledge during the late twentieth century, concerned with discovering the origins of the practice. Consistent with a multidisciplinary approach, this book seeks to "identify the accidents, the minute deviations—or conversely, the complete reversals—the errors, the false appraisals, and the faulty calculations" of these discourses (Foucault, "Nietzsche" 374). NEOBUGARRÓN provides an account of a superimposition that displaces concerns for origins. Thus, I emphasize *bugarrón* sexual practice's emergence in modern anthropological, medical, cinematic, and literary discourses. Following Foucault, *emergence* refers here to the moment when a specific phenomenon appears in a disciplinary discourse by being vested with a heightened level of attention, concern, and curiosity that makes it worth studying. In this book, I inspect how *bugarrón* sexual practice is apprehended (or represented) in the works of epidemiologists, anthropologists, fiction writers, and filmmakers in Latin America. While focusing on the cultural transformations that those accounts glossed over (i.e., their errors, mishaps, tentative renderings, deviations), NEOBUGARRÓN finds the gaps in their analyses to be not shortcomings but rather opportunities for thinking through a *bugarrón* practice in transformation. In other words, NEOBUGARRÓN does not seek to fill in the broken linear history of a concept or object but instead provides an account of what Foucault calls the rendering of its dispersal. I emphasize the approaches, challenges, justifications, strategies, and misreadings that studies in anthropology, fiction, cinema, and social media employ. Beyond exploring the way in which *bugarrón* sexual practice managed to become the focus of modern discourses in the late twentieth century, this book's aim is the analysis of a sexual practice's transformation. For just as *normal* men are not what they once were, so the *bugarrón* today is not the *bugarrón* of bygone years.

ACKNOWLEDGMENTS

The writing of this book was made possible by faculty fellowships from the University of Illinois's Humanities Research Institute, the University of Illinois's College Research Board, and the State University of New York at Buffalo's Humanities Institute.

Over the years, I have presented my research in several institutional venues. I am incredibly grateful to the Futures of American Studies at Dartmouth College; the Studies in National and International Development Lecture Series (SNID) at Queens University in Ontario, Canada; and Penn State's Gender and Queer Studies Program. I also thank Sint Marteen University, Universidad de las Palmas, University of Aruba, and Colegio de Mayagüez, where my research was welcomed.

Thanks to friends and colleagues in the profession who, over the years, provided insightful comments on this project: Rachel Ablow, Kevin Arnold, Michael Bérubé, Colleen Boggs, Hamilton Carroll, Elizabeth Dillon, Alison Donell, Geraldine Friedman, Mary Foltz, James A. Godley, Donatella Izzo, John T. Kirby, Rodrigo Lazo, Caroline Levander, Vincent Leitch, Eric Lott, Lisa Lowe, Janet Lyon, Ruth Mack, Carine Mardorossian, Scott Morgensen, Amanda Morrison, Melvin Rahmin, Edwin Reyes-Tineo, Brian Russell Roberts, Diane Rubenstein, Steven Ruszczycky, Aparagita Sagar, Rebecca Sanchez, Leslie Sassone, William Solomon, David Squires, Michelle Stephens, Marcia Stephenson, Deena Weinstein, Erick Walker, and Kari Winter.

One of my writing hubs is Key West, where the late K-West and the current Bourbon Street Club have been a magnet for Caribbean male exotic dancers. Also, I want to thank Marlene Koenig for her inspiring creativity.

At the University of Illinois, my most sincere thanks to those colleagues who have been enthusiastic about this book: Dale Bauer, J. B. Capino, Lucinda Cole, Jane Desmond, Virginia Dominguez, Chris Freeburg, Patricia Gill, Janice Harrington, David L. Hays, Gordon Hutner, Jamie Jones, Robert Markley, Tim Newcomb, Robert Dale Parker, (Dede) Fairchild Ruggles, and Richard Wheeler. I also want to thank the English Department staff at Illinois, who have helped me with matters related to resources and research: Sandra Hardin, Thomas Layman, and Jessalee Williams. I extend special thanks for their kindness and help to Antoinette Burton, Russ Castronovo, Lauren Goodlad, Jack Halberstam, Caroline Levine, Ricardo L. Ortiz, Joseph Valente, Melba A. Velez, and Jane Ward. Their support made a significant impact on the book's progress. I am also very thankful to Donald E. Pease, whose help, excitement, and critical insights have been invaluable. Many thanks to Robert L. Caserio, who has been a supporter and an inspiration.

Special thanks to Argentinian director Marco Berger for his willingness to heed my requests and share his work and impressions. Thanks also to Cuban painter Elio Rodríguez for his amazing art.

This book would not have been written without Tim Dean's suggestions, queries, and challenging argumentation. Thank you.

The editorial staff at The Ohio State University Press merits special recognition. Thanks to the perseverance and commitment of Kristen A. Elias Rowley, the support of the Abnormativities series editor Scott Herring, and the production team at the Press. Special thanks to Elizabeth Zaleski, Stuart Rodríguez, Susan Zucker, Olivia Sergent, and Samara Rafert. Their assistance has been invaluable.

Lastly, I thank for their patience and understanding Elvin, Trisha, Illianis, and Mayrín Soto Crespo, and Irma E. Crespo González.

INTRODUCTION

NEOBUGARRÓN: *Heteroflexibility, Neoliberalism, and Latin/o American Sexual Practice* chronicles the cultural modifications of a distinct male–male sexual practice in Latino/a America and the Caribbean during the twentieth and twenty-first centuries. Historically this practice has been embodied in the figure of the *bugarrón,* an ostensibly heterosexual man who has sex with other men but who is presumed to take the dominant role exclusively. An ambiguous figure, the *bugarrón*—who is neither clearly gay nor simply straight—has for decades eluded comprehension by anthropologists and epidemiologists, as well as by public policy experts in the Americas and around the globe. A host of local terms describe practitioners of *bugarrón* sex in different parts of the Americas: *cacheros* (Costa Rica), *mayates* (Mexico), *hombres normales* (Argentina and Chile), and *bugarrones* (Cuba, Puerto Rico, and the Dominican Republic). During the late 1980s, *bugarrón* sexual practice was problematized in public debates over HIV/AIDS prevention and health risks. Surveillance of *bugarrón* practitioners intensified because they were typically regarded as a troubling vector of HIV transmission between heterosexual and homosexual communities.

My research suggests that this ambiguous entity mutated into what I am calling the *neobugarrón,* a neoliberal market-oriented actor who used the traditional sexual practice as an optimizing strategy for manipulating the forces of globalization during the 1990s. Now, at a crucial historical juncture when some version of LGBTQ rights has been expanded across the Western hemisphere, the *bugarrón* has become a virtually extinct category. *Bugarrón* activity may still take place occasionally, but the term's former signification is disappearing from cultural use. Today, more often than not, the term *bugarrón* refers to men who sell sex to gay tourists. Just as a simulacrum displaces the real, so has the *neobugarrón* displaced the *bugarrón*. I contend that sexual practices that did not develop into a unique sexual "identity" have a history worth documenting, especially as their traces in our contemporary world are disappearing. It is necessary to record this Latin American sexual practice as it is poised on the cusp of extinction. This book chronicles the twists and turns of a failed understanding of male–male sexuality, while also providing an account of how the *neobugarrón* is key for comprehending the relationship between capital and sexuality in the Americas.

EXAMINING THE BIRTH OF A *NEOBUGARRÓN* SUBJECT

My approach complicates current models for understanding the development of sexual subjects by introducing a nonexclusive sexual practice into the mix of contemporary discourses on sexuality, which have become dominated by politicized identities. It thus reopens an area of uncertainty that has been covered over in identitarian discourses. This study of the *bugarrón* widens the focus beyond a risky sexual practice in order to theorize *neobugarrón* as a biopolitical paradox. As Foucault explained, biopolitics is concerned with the management of life and death in contemporary societies. NEOBUGARRÓN considers the *neobugarrón* as an example of a sexual practice that has come to serve as a strategy of neoliberal optimization at the margins of globalization. As neoliberal economic policies privatize public services in Latin America, citizens affected by this shift find themselves forced to improvise ways to make a living. Traditional sexual practices, such as those of the *bugarrón,* become ways to earn an income from the booming tourist industry, which includes sex tourism. At a moment of precarious economic conditions, *bugarrón* sexual practice acquires a lucrative market commodification—the *neobugarrón*. The emergence of the *neobugarrón* in the marketplace signals the disappearance of a traditional *bugarrón* sexual practice. Whereas in the circumscribed world of Havana, Cuba, *neobugarrón* as a "new class of male sex worker" is known as *pinguero*—a man who works with his *pinga* (cock)—this urban connotation is tied to having displaced a traditional *bugarrón* practitioner: "The *pinguero* killed the *bugarrón*" (Hodge, "Colonizing" 631). A lethal shift has taken place: from a sexual practice seeking pleasure to a sexual practice selling the mystique of an "authentic" anomalous pleasure.

This project has been influenced by works in queer studies that analyze shifting sexual arrangements.[1] While queer scholarship has provided some frameworks for understanding a nonexclusive sexual practice in Latin America, *bugarrón* as a discarded sexual type does not fit these interpretive models very well. Instead of arguing that transvaluation of failure into success is something that "queers" excel in doing, this book reconsiders methodological mishaps, ethnographic misreadings, historical gaps, cinematic absences, and their various interpretations as opportunities for thinking discursive blindness. It is necessary to revisit the historical, theoretical, and philosophical work of George Chauncey, Arnold I. Davidson, Michel Foucault, Alfred J. Kinsey, and Eve Kosofsky Sedgwick in order to recover an ethics for interpreting discarded concepts and vanishing ways of thinking about sexual practices. In his lectures *Subjectivity and Truth* (2017), Foucault differentiated anthropology and ethnography from the kind of thinking about sex that drives his project. He argues that his work should be understood as "the history not of sexual behavior, of sexual practices, but of reflection on sexual practices" (188). A historian does not have access to sexual practices themselves, only to discourses that reflect on those practices. Reflecting on sexual practices means for him thinking through "the way in which sexual practices emerge within a cultural or normative consciousness" (188). NEOBUGARRÓN seeks to reflect on the ways in which a *neobugarrón* subjectivity emerges in discourses of the twentieth and twenty-first centuries. Whereas traditionally *bugarrón* stood for a type, a figure, constructed from a sexual practice, *neobugarrón* reflects the self-packaging, or self-making, of a neoliberal subjectivity.

Consider how two ethnographies account for the presence of *bugarrón* sexual practice in the Caribbean. The first, by Antonio de Moya and Rafael García, specifies that in Caribbean countries *bugarrón* is "almost synonymous with being the insertive partner in paid homosexual relations" ("Three Decades" 128).[2] The classification "insertive partner" indicates a "role" in the sexual act and not a subject-forming characteristic. By contrast, the second example claims *bugarrón* subjectivity by drawing a relational correspondence with other sexual types, thus shifting the tension from sexual practice to sexual subject. In *What It Means To Be a Man* (1999), Puerto Rican anthropologist Rafael L. Ramírez provides not only a description of *bugarrón* sexual practice

---

1. I am referring here to works such as Martin Levine's *Gay Macho* (1998), Samuel R. Delany's *Times Square Red, Times Square Blue* (1999), Jack Halberstam's *Female Masculinity* (1998), Carolyn Dinshaw's *Getting Medieval* (1999), Scott Herring's *Queering the Underworld* (2007), Sharon Marcus's *Between Women* (2007), and Heather Love's *Feeling Backwards* (2007).

2. In "Masculine Identity and Sexuality" (2002), Rafael L. Ramírez et al. concur with de Moya by reiterating that *bugarrón* practitioners retain their heterosexuality because "they penetrated their partners" (93).

but also a taxonomy of sexual types as they relate to the construct *bugarrón*: "In contrast to other Puerto Rican masculine types—such as: *straights* (purely heterosexual men), *entendidos* (heterosexual men that are considered similar to a 'fag hag'), *poncas* (men who act heterosexual but are suspected otherwise), *locas del closet* (closeted gay men), and *locas* (gay men)—the *bugarrón* is a sexual subjectivity in its own right" (Ramírez et al. 93–99).[3] For Ramírez, the sexual practice typical of a man who has sex with men emerges from this relational taxonomy as a subject. Even though subjectivity has not been created by a process of self-identification (hermeneutics of the self), Ramírez in this example made traditional *bugarrón* sexual practice into a subject. Is *bugarrón* sexual practice merely a role (insertive) that any man might occupy, or is it a distinct subjectivity? Ramírez's work raises the question: How does *bugarrón* sexual practice acquire subjectivity in the Caribbean? That is precisely the question that NEOBUGARRÓN explores by analyzing diverse works from ethnography to cultural representations of sexual practice. The *bugarrón* archive brings together a disparate set of sources culled from anthropology, health management, cinema, popular fiction, and social media. It engages works dating from the early encounter between anthropology and *bugarrón* sexual practice in the 1990s to its most recent representation in Latin American cinema.

THE CHALLENGES OF A SEXUAL ANOMALY: METHODOLOGY AND ONTOLOGY

NEOBUGARRÓN does not embark on its own ethnographic study of *bugarrón* sexual practice but rather engages ethnographic works on the subject that have been published over the years. By analyzing ethnographic writing as discourses on *bugarrón* sexual practice, NEOBUGARRÓN brings to light complications and mishaps that repeatedly appear in these studies. Similarly, NEOBUGARRÓN provides symptomatic readings of literary and cinematic works that address, directly or indirectly, *bugarrón* sexual practice. Literary criticism and cinema studies provide tools to engage the representation of *bugarrón* sexual practice in films, visual studies, anthropology, and literature. NEOBUGARRÓN traces a genealogy of *bugarrón* sexual practice in each specific medium, but the book should not be mistaken for a cultural history. It is composed of four chapters examining the representation of *bugarronería*. Chapters 1 and 2 provide an account of how the *bugarrón* as an object

---

3. In this book, quotations that contain slurs are retained in order to provide a literal translation and/or illustrate the cited author's mode of self-expression.

of concern came into focus. During the mid-1990s, *bugarrón* sexual practice became the focus of discourses of HIV prevention, anthropology, and surveillance in Latin America, and during the late 1990s, *bugarrón* sexual practice became a matter of interest in the Latin American LGBTQ tourist industry. In these discourses, I trace how *bugarronería* emerges as a nodal point among discourses of risk, sexuality, and HIV/AIDS. Chapters 3 and 4 provide genealogies of two discourses. My study of *bugarrón* sexual practice in literature begins with the analysis of an undeveloped figure of a *bugarrón* practitioner in the work of Patricia Powell and ends with the complex figure of *superbugarrón* in Reinaldo Arenas, thus examining a thread of *bugarrón* fictional representations from minor character to protagonist.

Discourses of knowledge that attempt strict coherence and consistency vis-à-vis their objects of study fail with sexual anomalies. *Bugarrón* sexual practice is not incoherent but, instead, anomalous; it exceeds the conventional rationalization of sexuality as a question of either/or. Yet the challenge comes when *bugarrón* sexual practice achieves a new level of paradox. Because traditional *bugarrón* sex is fast disappearing, I begin with the anthropological works that attempt to track down its practitioners during the 1990s at the peak of the AIDS crisis. During this period, numerous ethnographies were published about *bugarrón* sexual practice with an eye on HIV prevention. While these writings acknowledge that traditional *bugarrón* sexual practice was receding in modernity, its disappearance coincided with the emergence of a new subjectivity to replace it—a neoliberal *bugarrón* subject, or what I call *neobugarrón*. A complication arises when the discourses studied here continue to describe *neobugarrón* as if it were a traditional *bugarrón* sexual practice. NEOBUGARRÓN intervenes in these discourses by elucidating the distinction between traditional *bugarrón* sexual practice and a *neobugarrón* subject.

In *Hybrid Cultures* (1995), Argentine anthropologist Néstor García Canclini warned us that "the least effective cultural politics are those that cling to the archaic and ignore the emergent" (138). For García Canclini, some cultural practices exit modernity while others enter and carve a space within it. We can say, then, that whereas traditional *bugarrón* sexual practice exits modernity, *neobugarrón* subjectivity enters it. *Neobugarrón* emerges undetected through ethnographic discourses of *bugarrón* sexual practice where the cultural shift from *bugarrón* to *neobugarrón* goes unnoticed. *Neobugarrón* subjectivity hides in plain sight by taking on the mantle of the practice it has commodified. This book focuses primarily on the *neobugarrón* and how it came to infiltrate the cultural production of *bugarrón* sexual practice. To tell the story of the traditional *bugarrón* sexual practice is, from my perspective, to provide an account of the emerging *neobugarrón* subject.

HYBRID METHODOLOGY AND THE POLITICS OF HETEROFLEXIBILITY

Following García Canclini, NEOBUGARRÓN adopts a hybrid methodology by sustaining a tension between Foucauldian and non-Foucauldian understandings of sexuality. Although Foucault focuses primarily on discourses about sex, this leads him to examine only previous works on human sexual behavior.[4] In this study, I attempt to weave together Foucauldian discursive approaches with sexological approaches. These two methodologies are in tension especially when examining discourses on the *bugarrón* and when using terms such as *heteroflexibility*. In what follows, I use the nontechnical term *heteroflexibility* to describe sexual fluidity, that is, a proclivity on the part of heterosexual men and women for engaging in same-sex acts.[5] For instance, the male practitioner of heteroflexibility identifies as straight but occasionally engages in insertive sexual practice with members of his own sex without necessarily compromising his heterosexuality. My use of the term heteroflexibility comes from two different sources. The first is Héctor Carrillo and Amanda Hoffman's essay "From MSM to Heteroflexibilities," where the term is defined as an "elastic" category of heterosexuality (934). Unlike the global descriptor men-who-have-sex-with-men (MSM), which, according to Castillo and Hoffman, has become synonymous with *gay*, heteroflexibility more accurately categorizes the sexual practices of a heterosexually identified man who has sex with men.

The second source is Ritch Savin-Williams's essay "An Exploratory Study" (2018), in which he reports that when subjects in his study were allowed to classify themselves in more than one sexual category, some chose to write in "heteroflexible" (21). Savin-Williams's survey uses Kinsey's 0–6 scale to interpret the participant's responses. For Savin-Williams, Kinsey's rethinking of modern American male sexuality inspired a recalibration of our discourse

---

4. Foucault studied the discourse of *scientia sexualis* from Ellis to Kinsey. In his two lectures on sexuality, the Lectures at the University of Clermont-Ferrand (1964) and the Lectures at the University of Vincennes (1969), Foucault refers of the works of Havelock Ellis, Sigmund Freud, Karl Heinrich Ulrich, Richard von Kraft-Ebbing, Paul Julius Moebius, and Magnus Hirschfield. Yet it is Freud who emerges as Foucault's strongest influence. With Freud's *Three Essays on the Theory of Sexuality* (1903), Foucault contends, a particular thinking of the perversions as an object of knowledge began to be reversed. Foucault's interest in *scientia sexualis* extends to covering the most recent studies of the day. It is the work of Kinsey that makes him realize that "now certain things have come to light . . . frequency, in individual members of the majority, of sexual acts that do not conform to the schema" (Foucault, *Sexuality* 53).

5. Lisa Diamond defines "fluidity" as a "situation-dependent flexibility" (*Fluidity* 3). She prefers the term fluidity because it emphasizes "a wider variety of erotic feelings and experiences than would be predicted on the basis of their self-described sexual orientation alone" (10).

on sexuality in contemporary society. This is because Kinsey's study *Sexual Behavior in the Human Male* (1948), documents that "**37 per cent** of the male population had enjoyed **at least some overt homosexual experience** to the point of orgasm, [and] **50 per cent** of the males **who remain single until age 35** have had overt homosexual experience to the point of orgasm" (650; bold in original). The revelation of a higher-than-expected incidence of nonconforming sexual acts leads Kinsey to propose that categories such as heterosexuality and homosexuality (and bisexuality) were perhaps misleading "ideal types" rather than accurate signifiers of sexual truth or identity. In fact, for Kinsey, because homosexual activity "persists on as large a scale as it does . . . it is difficult to maintain the view that psychosexual reactions between individuals of the same sex are rare and therefore abnormal or unnatural" (659).[6] A central consequence of Kinsey's model was the demotion of heterosexual intercourse as the privileged sex act for the modern human male. According to Kinsey's study, those who practice exclusively heterosexual intercourse, and for that matter exclusive homosexual intercourse, are, in fact, fewer in number than those who participate in both.

Following Kinsey, Savin-Williams, Héctor Carrillo, Amanda Hoffman, Marc McCormack, and Tony Silva investigate gradations between the sexual categories of exclusive heterosexuality and bisexuality. What I find interesting about their Kinsey-informed research is not just the discovery of more in-between categories that fall under the general rubric of heterosexuality but also their understanding of a connection between politics and heteroflexibility. If, during his time, Kinsey had to fend off political claims that aligned homosexuality with communism, these twenty-first-century researchers explore the benefits of a different political situation. According to Savin-Williams, a cultural shift has taken place that makes it easier to detect heteroflexible gradations that are usually out of sight. Savin-Williams attributes men's twenty-first-century openness to claiming degrees of in-between sexualities to the "decline of *homohysteria*" ("Exploratory" 25; original italics). As masculinity norms relax, he argues, more individuals "recognize within themselves a degree of same-sex sexuality" (25). Savin-Williams argues that a more inviting, positive cultural context seems necessary for expanding the nonexclusionary scale of heterosexual identification. Contrary to Savin-Williams's Pollyanna viewpoint, NEOBUGARRÓN argues that neoliberalism's market-oriented governmentality is key to the emergence of *neobugarrón* subjectivity. The politics of modern sexual identities in Latin America made a secretly *bugarrón* prac-

---

6. For more on Kinsey's nonexclusive heterosexuality, see Irvine 31–33, Drucker 165–66, and Robinson 116–18.

tice outmoded and ill-fitted.[7] Yet, with neoliberalism, we find in Latin America the repackaging and reappearance of outmoded sexual practices in the new marketplace of *neobugarrón* commodification. Thus, while Kinsey classifies sexual practices in a continuum, Foucault provides a framework for understanding their function in discourses of power/knowledge. In NEOBUGARRÓN, sexual practice and its mutations take precedence over the interpretation of desire. In the next sections, I contextualize *bugarrón* sexual practice in terms of "trade," men on the "down low," "not-gay," and "gay-for-pay."

HETEROFLEXIBILITY AND THE HOMO/HETERO DIVIDE

The connection between cultural shifts and heteroflexibility follows the framing of previous historical accounts of anomalous sexual practices such as "trade." In *Gay New York* (1994), George Chauncey elaborates on types of male sexual practice that existed during the early decades of the twentieth century. He explains that prewar North American sexual culture was more sexually diverse than the one that developed after World War II. With the onset of the Cold War, male sexuality came under increasing surveillance; the Red Scare conditioned US men to follow the straight and narrow path of exclusive heterosexuality so as not to deviate from true "American values." By contrast, the early decades of the twentieth century witnessed a more diverse sexual culture with various male sexual types such as "trade," a term that carries multiple meanings, including "men who insisted on payment for a sexual encounter" and, more broadly, "any 'normal' man who accepted a queer's sexual advances" (Chauncey 16). Given the history of privileging exclusive heterosexuality and the categorization of practices in the West, Chauncey writes, "it is almost impossible today to think about sexuality without imagining that it is organized along an axis of homosexuality and heterosexuality" (12–13). Chauncey here is referring to *The History of Sexuality, Vol. 1*, where Foucault explains that sexuality was constructed, codified, mapped, articulated, and normalized according to certain nodes of knowledge such as the homo/hetero divide.[8] The

---

7. As Richard Parker explains in *Beneath the Equator* (1999), processes of transculturation such as the adoption of terms like *gay* in Latin America point to cultural strategies for reclaiming local uses for concepts once considered foreign (36–50).

8. Foucault did not discuss Latin American sexuality, but in his published lectures there are references to Latin America. The most salient one is found in *Psychiatric Power*, where he discusses the Jesuits' mission in colonial Paraguay and its relation to Jeremy Bentham's panopticon (63–93).

anomalies that exceeded this divide were excluded from the process of categorization. *Bugarrón* sexual practice failed to be included in the homo/hetero divide.[9] Kinsey and twenty-first-century neo-Kinseyan researchers point, in their works, to some of those exclusions that the homo/hetero divide ignored.

Discourses of power and domination not only constructed the idea of sexuality but also manufactured knowledge by "penetrating bodies in an increasingly detailed way" (*History, Vol. 1*, 107). Foucault's elucidation of the homo/hetero divide through which all sexual practices were analyzed points to a dramatic societal shift. In *Epistemology of the Closet* (1990), Sedgwick explains, "many of the major nodes of thought and knowledge in twentieth-century Western culture as a whole are structured—indeed, fractured—by a chronic, now endemic crisis of homo/heterosexual definition" (1). To tackle *bugarrón* sexual practice as one of those anomalies that exceeded the logic of "homo/heterosexual definition" is to turn away from naturalizing categories of mutual exclusion. Heteroflexibility becomes apparent at those historical moments of crisis, such as in neoliberalism with its tendency to reproduce identity categories for human consumption, when the discourses of power/knowledge sustaining the primacy of exclusive heterosexuality diminish in dominance. How can a neoliberal society prioritize exclusive heterosexuality when it embraces a fundamental tenet of producing and consuming ever more commodities and categories? Because *bugarrón* embodies this crisis of definition, it comes across as fundamentally incoherent. It is at these moments of crisis (health, political, economic) where the in-between sexual practices become especially visible. In all its forms, heteroflexibility becomes more easily perceived when political domination retreats and civil society expands. At those moments of state retreat, heteroflexibility shows forth in thorny cases such as trade, *neobugarrón* subjectivity, and men on the down low.

BUGARRONIZING DOWN LOW

In the last decades of the twentieth century, the "down low" would remind US society about the sexual continuum that exists beyond the homo/hetero divide. While in Latin America, *bugarrón* sexual practice became the subject of HIV/AIDS surveillance, in the US, down low became a subject of concern. In "Deconstructing 'Down Low' Discourse" (2005), Layli Phillips explains that

---

9. On the subject of practices excluded from the homo/hetero divide, see also Kahan, *Book* 3–10.

the down low "refers to Black men who secretly have sex with other men while maintaining heterosexual relationships with women and presenting themselves as masculine rather than effeminate" (4). Cultural awareness of a down low sexual practice achieved new heights when Oprah Winfrey interviewed J. L. King about his book on the subject.[10] Yet the meaning associated with the popular sense of down low has managed to erase the term's previous usage. Before it denoted secret same-sex practices between ostensibly heterosexual men, "'down low' infidelity was associated with heterosexual relationships; only later did it begin to connote homosexual sex among men" (Phillips 6). There is evidence of this previous use in popular Rhythm and Blues and rap songs by artists TLC and R. Kelly (Barnshaw and Letukas, "Low Down" 480).

"Maintaining a heterosexual image" is a key component of African American men on the down low (Phillips, "Deconstructing" 6). But this is also the case for Latino men on the down low, as John Barnshaw and Lynn Letukas elucidate in "The Low Down on the Down Low" (2010).[11] Héctor Carrillo and Amanda Hoffman propose a direct connection between down low in white men and heteroflexibility: "The focus on men of colour, and the perception that the down low is an exclusively African American and Latino phenomenon, has often led to reproducing racial stereotypes. By contrast, a majority of the straight-identified men in our study are white, and many are also secretive about their same sex desires and behaviors, which challenges the notion that the so called down low is prevalent exclusively among African American or Latinos" ("Straight" 92). The Black and Latino down low, and white "down low," share traits with *bugarrón* sexual practice—for instance, the proclivity toward secrecy and heterosexual identification (not-gay). Scholarship on these sexual practices often raises questions about their practices being a sexual "identity," thus complicating the theoretical terrain further.[12] Just as we understand men to be "on the down low," not "down low men," so we understand *bugarrón* practitioners as figures, not as self-identified *bugarrón* men. Traditional *bugarrón* sexual practice indicates heteroflexibility; the *neobugarrón*, for his part, signals a transactional heteroflexibility for sale by a male sex worker who has sex with men. In sum, there are no *neobugarrón* men, only *neobugarrón* market-oriented subjects.

---

10. J. L. King and Karen Hunter, *On the Down Low* (2005).
11. See especially Barnshaw and Letukas, "Low Down" 480–81.
12. According to Carrillo and Hoffman, white males on the "down low" find all other categories (heterosexuality, homosexuality, bisexuality) inadequate and "maintain identities as straight men," turning "straight" into a considerably "elastic category" ("From MSM" 927).

NEITHER "NOT-GAY" NOR GAY-FOR-PAY: ARCHAIC HETEROFLEXIBILITY FOR SALE

An insightful perspective on contemporary varieties of male heteroflexibility is found in Jane Ward's *Not Gay* (2015), which offers a new twist on the politics of flexible heterosexuality. Whereas Kinsey's heterosexual spectrum demoted heterosexual intercourse from its position of cultural privilege, Ward discovers that heteroflexibility has been reinterpreted in contemporary times as a form of "hetero-exceptionism" (110). For Ward, "hetero-exceptionism" amounts to a rhetorical strategy "that elevates homosexual encounters out of the troubled waters of gay identity and into the realm of male solidarity" (110). In this reinterpretation, same-sex acts between heterosexual men paradoxically signify proof of their heterosexuality: "Whereby it is presumed that gay men have sex with men for the intrinsic pleasure it brings, . . . straight men have sex with men for largely instrumental reasons (e.g., to meet a suppressed emotional need, to move through a developmental stage, to secure power over women)" (110). Ward's insights introduce a necessary reminder of the fluctuating and changing practices of male sexuality, a perspective in need of constant prompting. Hetero-exceptionism uses what it understands as "gay sex"—that is, sex between men—to bolster the superiority of exclusive heterosexuality. It turns upside down Kinsey's goal of statistically proving how exclusive heterosexuality was a cruel ideal.

Another contemporary practice of heteroflexibility is gay-for-pay. Primarily an exchange of circumscribed sexual services, gay-for-pay is about earning money, not about bolstering exclusive heterosexuality. As some first-hand accounts suggest, gay-for-pay becomes an economic strategy when, for instance, men lose their "new big city job to layoffs" (Rocchi, *Gay-for-Pay* 91). Vince Rocchi's *Gay-for-Pay* (2021) is one of several accounts that provide an inside scoop on how unemployed men use social media, such as Craigslist, to embark on temporary gigs. The need for cash ignites the entrepreneurial spirit. Getting paid for jacking off, receiving oral sex, and having sessions of body worship are options that some men pursue. Yet in gay-for-pay, any connection to a past temporality or an archaic other is missing. The services amount to a practical solution to a financial problem. Since gay-for-pay and not-gay are not vested with the mantle of the archaic, their transactionality stems instead from a specific present situation. By contrast, the *neobugarrón* seduces by reawakening an archaic reality embedded in the mystique of a bygone sexual practice. He sells the idea of an archaic heteroflexibility. Traveling into other cultures for sex tourism is connected to the allure of experiencing a retreating traditional exotic eroticism. In the *neobugarrón* marketplace, the mask of "authenticity" seduces. In contradistinction to the traditional *bugarrón,* who would never self-identify as such, the *neobugarrón* advertises his market subjectivity. As a desired commodity in the neoliberal world of selling pleasures, the *neobugarrón* creatively reproduces "authentic" experiences.

SIMULATION AND NEOLIBERAL SUBJECTIVITY

On the question of neoliberalism, Foucault's writings capture a "classical neoliberalism"—a form of governmentality that, during the late 1970s and early 1980s, was associated with "openness," "progress," and "individual liberties" (Dardot and Laval, *Nightmare* xiii–xiv). Foucault's rethinking of power during this period sustains a space for "the independence of the governed" in relation to those governing (*Birth of Biopolitics* 43); it thus represents a more optimistic vision of neoliberalism than many associate with the term today. Recent critical work on Foucault and neoliberalism, especially by theorists like Pierre Dardot and Christian Laval, contends that neoliberalism for Foucault was a way of "governing economies and societies based on generalized marketization and competition" (*New Way* 12). This rationality generates "an 'accountable' subjectivity by systematically creating competition between individuals" (14). Dardot and Laval point to Foucault's less fatalistic take on neoliberalism when he spotted something peculiar about the contemporary diffusion of power in Western societies.[13] But they also understand neoliberalism as a mode of rationality that has metamorphosed over time: "We are living through a metamorphosis of neoliberalism—and a very dangerous phenomenon it is" (*Nightmare* xiii).

In their view, Foucault detects neoliberalism's silver lining. He turns to thinking through the connections between neoliberal governmentality and "bodies and pleasures." Rethinking power, at a time of increasing neoliberal rollback of state and juridical regulations, represents for Foucault an opportunity for self-creation—an occasion for individuals "to transform themselves, and modify themselves" (Foucault, "Sexuality and Solitude" 177). As he states in an interview with *The Advocate* in 1982: "Sex is not a fatality: it's a possibility for creative life" ("Sex, Power" 163). From that early period of possibility, neoliberalism metamorphosed into what Dardot and Laval describe as a mode

---

13. Unlike Dardot and Laval, most recent work such as Wendy Brown's *In the Ruins of Neoliberalism* (2019), Isabell Lorey's *State of Insecurity* (2015), and Byung-Chul Han's *Psychopolitics* (2017) alert us to neoliberalism's negative side. For instance, Brown tells us that neoliberal rationality "prepared the ground for . . . ferocious anti-democratic forces" (7).

of government that "feeds off the negative reactions it provokes politically" (*Nightmare* xiii). NEOBUGARRÓN understands marketization, competition, optimization, and in some cases survival, as key elements of the sexual capital driving *neobugarrón* subjectivity.[14] In the case of *neobugarrón* sexual practice, self-creation is entangled with a market-oriented strategy. The *neobugarrón* subject is not resistant to "the deployment of sexuality," as Foucault imagined at the end of his *History of Sexuality, Vol. 1*. In a *neobugarrón* subject, "bodies and pleasures" assume the market connotation of commodification.

BRIEF OUTLINE OF THE ARGUMENT

I have organized this study into four chapters, which analyze the anthropological, visual, cinematic, and literary figures of *bugarrón* sexual practice, respectively. Chapter 1, "Anthropologies of Lust: Deployment of *Bugarrón* Surveillance," explains the connection between a surge in ethnographic studies of *bugarrón* sexual practice and the spread of HIV/AIDS in Latin America during the 1990s. At this historical moment, there was burgeoning interest in *bugarrón* sexual practice within the disciplines of anthropology and those associated with public health because *bugarrón* practitioners were regarded as a troubling vector of HIV transmission between heterosexual and homosexual communities. Chapter 1 focuses on the anthropology of Latino American sexual cultures, in tandem with the medical discourses on HIV prevention. It engages anthropological studies such as Annick Prieur's *Mema's House, Mexico City* (1998), Jacobo Schifter's *Lila's House* (1998), and Matthew Gutmann's *Fixing Men* (2007). The chapter illuminates how anthropological and medical works interpreted *bugarrón* sexual practice and traces a global network of *bugarrón* surveillance.

Chapter 2, "The *Neobugarrón*: A Lesson in Neoliberalism and Biopolitics," investigates the transformation of the traditional *bugarrón* into a *neobugarrón* subject. I examine how *bugarrón* sexual practice underwent a change brought about by neoliberalism. As Naomi Klein pointed out in *The Shock Doctrine*

---

14. The work of Dardot and Laval is not the only one exploring Foucault's take on "classical" neoliberalism. Recent publications by Mitchell Dean and Daniel Zamora elaborate on the connection between "classic" neoliberalism and subjectivity in Foucault's works. Dean and Zamora point to the neoliberal rollback as the form of governmentality that for Foucault represented an opportunity to extricate sexuality "from the field of scientific studies in order for it to become a form of self-creation" (*Last Man* 180). In their view, Foucault refers to "bodies and pleasures" as those new venues for "creation, invention and experimentation" (179). Thus, neoliberal governmentality "presented a new understanding of subjectivity" (208). In this context, subjectivity is understood as primarily Foucauldian.

(2007), Latin America has long served as a laboratory of neoliberal economic ideas. Whereas the discourse of anthropology managed to provide some visibility to traditional *bugarrón* sexual practice, and in the process reproduced more complicated sexual anomalies, other technologies of social networking managed to expose a neoliberal *bugarrón* sexual subject. I propose that the *neobugarrón* achieved cultural visibility as a type but one conditioned by financial constraints because the *neobugarrón* becomes a commodity in the neoliberal marketplace of sex tourism. This new visibility complicates how the traditional *bugarrón* sexual practice is understood in the Caribbean. The historical understanding of this traditional sexual practice is being retroactively shaped by the financially driven *neobugarrón*. The chapter elucidates how this visibility also challenges representations of gayness in Latino American visual culture. Finally, I show how the *neobugarrón* sheds light on the interconnections between capitalism and sexuality: contrary to the primary understanding of capital as a homogenizing force, I characterize the *neobugarrón* as an example of capital's capacity for "producing new heterogeneity," to quote Vivek Chibber (*Postcolonial Theory* 244).

Chapter 3, "*Bugarrón* Cinema: A Disturbance in the Field of Vision," pursues the question of *bugarrón* sexual practice's visibility in the cultural arena of cinema. Building on Jacqueline Rose's theory of sexuality as a disruption in the field of vision, the chapter examines visual representation of *bugarrón* sexual practice in Latino American cinema during the late twentieth and early twenty-first centuries, focusing on the recent boom in representations of heteroflexibility in Ricardo de Montreuil's *La mujer de mi hermano* (2005), Marco Berger's *Plan B* (2009), *Absent* (2011), *Hawaii* (2013), and *The Blonde One* (2019), Javier Fuentes-León's *Undertow* (2009), Lorenzo Vigas's *Por Allá [From Afar]* (2015), and José Campusano's *Men of Hard Skin* (2019). It pinpoints the retooling of cinematic techniques by *bugarrón* cinema for the purpose of representing a sexual practice that resists representation.

Chapter 4, "*Mundo Cruel*: The *Neobugarrón* in Literature," provides a genealogy of the literary representation of *bugarrón* sexual practice in Latin American fiction. It analyzes *bugarrón* sexual practice in Reinaldo Arenas's *Antes que anochezca [Before Night Falls]* (1992), Patricia Powell's *A Small Gathering of Bones* (1994), Luis Negrón's *Mundo Cruel* (2010), and David Caleb Acevedo's *Diario de una puta humilde [Diary of a Common Whore]* (2012). The chapter engages *bugarrón* realism in literary representation and explores the structure of antinomies, dyads, and binarisms that function to give a reality effect to *bugarrón* sexual practice in fiction. The focus on realism shows the limits of the representation of *bugarrón* sexual practice, as its translatability into English, for example, leads to erasure in most cases. In other cases, untranslatability forces *bugarrón* sexual practice to be translated as a closeted homosexuality. The chapter engages a politics of translation of *bugarrón* literary references and traces a polysemic definition of *bugarrón* to borderland works such as Manuel Ramos Otero's *La Novelabingo* (1976). Ramos Otero's work, published in New York, provides an account of the previous meaning of *bugarrón*, which can be found in the literary production of mainland Puerto Rican communities. The chapter's final section illuminates how translation misses *bugarrón* sexual practice and how genealogical critique is useful for recovering forgotten nuances in literary works published by authors of the passage to the US mainland.

CHAPTER 1

Anthropologies of Lust

Deployment of Bugarrón *Surveillance*

In 1992 Gilbert Herdt and Shirley Lindenbaum characterized the status of two key discourses of knowledge in the following way: "Where the doctors are privileged in this game, anthropologists are at a disadvantage" (*Time of AIDS* 19). The circumstance was the global spread of the AIDS pandemic and competition between the discourses of power/knowledge addressing the health crisis (*Time of AIDS* 19).[1] Competitiveness, the central tenet of neoliberal economics, and state policies of limited government intervention were influences that affected the sources of funding needed by anthropologists for doing their

---

1. My use of power/knowledge here refers to Foucault's understanding of how discourses, especially those on sexuality, are connected to society's networks of power and their relation to knowledge. Foucault clarifies this intricate connection in *The History of Sexuality, Vol. 1*, where he states that the deployment of sexuality "has its reason in . . . proliferating, innovating, annexing, creating, and penetrating bodies in an increasingly detailed way, and in controlling populations in an increasingly comprehensive way" (107). To put it more succinctly, the deployment of sexuality seeks to exploit "objects of knowledge" as elements "in relations of power" (107). Power/knowledge and the drive to contain the spread of infection were at the heart of anthropological exigency to understand *bugarrón* behavior. World health organizations shared this same level of gravity. These developments in discourses of power/knowledge set the terrain for a closer examination of the works that shape the complicated story of an elusive "traditional" *bugarrón* practice. Accounts of this multifaceted quandary explain how activist ethnographers, HIV/AIDS, globalization, global health organizations, NGOs, and the emergence of gay "identity" in Latin America become imbricated in the capturing of a *bugarrón* practice in an unprecedented global network of institutions of power/knowledge.

ethnographic work. However, with financial support from government health organizations, anthropologists could pursue their research. Urgency and desperation over the global spread of HIV during the 1990s thus led anthropologists worldwide on a quest for face-to-face encounters with practitioners of risky sex in Latin America. For HIV prevention, the World Health Organization defined risky sex as "a calculated exposure to disease or infection" (*Time* 13). Anthropologists concerned with the spread of HIV were in a race to reinvent themselves as more engaged with their subjects; sexual anthropologists looked to have a more significant impact in the research field and an edge on the accumulation of knowledge. At the crossroads of these disciplinary discourses of culture and medicine, we find *bugarrón* sexual practice. Traditionally referred to as *bugarrones* or *cacheros,* these practitioners are nonexclusive heterosexual men who have sex with other men. It was generally believed that these men practiced unprotected sex with their male partners and also at home with their wives.

Here I explore the confluence of disciplinary interests in *bugarrón* sexual practice during the 1990s and how the traditional *bugarrón* practitioner suddenly became the primary target in efforts to prevent the spread of HIV in Latin America. Usually rendered an out-of-sight phenomenon, *bugarrón* sexual practice acquired visibility in ethnography during the HIV/AIDS crisis. Activist ethnographers such as Jacobo Schifter, Héctor Carrillo, Richard Parker, Roger Lancaster, Matthew Gutmann, and Annick Prieur produced new narratives on these practitioners. As a result, HIV/AIDS ethnographies contributed, along with the discourses of health prevention and HIV/AIDS research, to the birth of *bugarrón* sexual practice in the discourses of power/knowledge during the late twentieth century.

From anthropology, health prevention, and the global health security network, we derive a multidisciplinary account of *bugarronería*. By elucidating the connections among a diverse set of academic, health, and anthropological discourses, I analyze the strategies of containment that sought to rein in high-risk *bugarrones*. The guiding questions that propelled their quest for *bugarrón* sexual practice were simple: What are the unknown vectors spreading HIV in populations around the world? How do we know where they are and what they are like? What measures can be put in place to contain their spread? Sexual ethnographies took the leading role in addressing these questions. The anthropologists' diligence in delving into *bugarrón* sexual practice takes us to other insidious questions. First, how can *bugarrón* practitioners be found? And later, what happens to the traditional *bugarrón* in modernity? The competing discourses of global health governance and anthropology would collaborate when performing a thorough inspection of this particular sexual practice. The final section of this chapter addresses two questions that follow: How does *bugarrón* sexual practice become a primary vector in global studies of health and disease prevention? How do *bugarrón* practitioners become the object of global surveillance?

The chapter first analyzes a body of ethnographic work that tackles *bugarrón* sexual practice. Most anthropological works examined here are set in Central America, in Mexico, and along the Mexico–US border. They study *cachero* and *mayate* sexual practices, both consistent with *bugarrón* sexual practice of the Caribbean region. The chapter closes with an analysis of instances where *bugarrón* sexual practice is included in initiatives to surveil elements belonging to the new behavioral concept of men-who-have-sex-with-men (MSM). My pursuit of this behavioral category led me to Elizabeth Pisani's and James Chin's works on the early stages of global health governance at the peak of the AIDS crisis. These two leading epidemiologists exposed the unexpected connections among AIDS, the creation of MSM as an epidemiological catchall concept, and *bugarrón* sexual practice. Their publications bring together two seemingly unconnected accounts: the one articulated by a growing global network of health professionals, and the local accounts of *bugarrón* sexual practice.

HOW TO FIND *BUGARRÓN* PRACTITIONERS: JACOBO SCHIFTER'S BIOPOLITICAL ETHNOGRAPHIES

Among the most revealing of these ethnographies of lust are those of Jacobo Schifter, a Latin American anthropologist whose work shows an unparalleled determination to probe areas of culture beyond the usual parameters of ethnography. Along with the research of Roger Lancaster and Richard Parker, Schifter tracks *bugarrón* sexual practice more thoroughly during the 1990s. But whereas Parker's and Lancaster's work has received critical attention for the analyses of *bugarrón* sexual practice, Schifter's has not received the same level of scrutiny, perhaps because his works provide accounts of unsanitary locations where older men procure the services of younger *cacheros*.

Let me point out the reasons that Schifter's works are important to my research. Not only is his research the least professionalized in the field of sexual culture but also, when examined closely, his works epitomize an unreflective discourse of health management. What distinguishes his approach is his willingness to visit places from which most anthropologists recoil. I find his unrelenting determination unnerving; at the same time, I marvel at his drive and resourcefulness. Schifter exemplifies the figure of an ultimate tracker searching persistently for reckless men-who-have-sex-with-men practicing their risky sex. First, he has identified the riskiest sexual subject in the figure of the *cachero* practitioner, as that heterosexual male who enjoys occasional sexual intercourse with other males and who is solely top, or penetrator, in those situations. As the embodiment of a macho who fucks men, the *cachero* practitioner penetrates and ejaculates without a condom. *Cacheros* are considered the most promiscuous, dangerous, and elusive group in Schifter's account of HIV prevention. In the context of the AIDS crises, the enigmatic and elusive *bugarrón* or *cachero* practitioner has provoked a fundamental change in a Western field of power/knowledge. This shift is best illustrated in Schifter's more salacious ethnographies.

During the early 1990s, the funding for ethnography in Latin America directed toward AIDS prevention came from international health organizations such as the United Nations Program on HIV/AIDS (UNAIDS), a joint venture of the United Nations founded in the mid-1990s that brings together resources of eleven UN system organizations. Funding also came from the World Health Organization (WHO), an international institution in charge of setting global health standards, funding research, and coordinating the worldwide response to global health crises. A third source of funding came from the financial assistance of national governments. Schifter's work received this third type of funding. The Dutch government provided direct support for Schifter's fieldwork in Central America. This funding helped Schifter, in his capacity as regional director of the Latin American Health and Prevention Institute (ILPES), to publish seven books covering the sexual culture of truckers, "pederasts," male sex workers, convicts, teenagers, "transvestites," public sex fetishists, and, most recently, "mongers"; Schifter is the most prolific, accessible, and visible of all Latin America's sexual anthropologists (*Lila's House* 3). In his work, Latin American sexual culture takes the shape of a distinct borderland where divergent epistemologies meet and compete for dominance.

In *Public Sex in a Latin Society* (2000) and *Macho Love: Sex Behind Bars in Central America* (1999), Schifter provides ethnographic accounts of Central American *bugarrón* or *cachero* practitioners. By proposing that *cachero* sexual practice is determined by social class and economic development, Schifter manages to address an undertheorized dimension in studies of sexuality. Indeed, for Schifter, sexuality in Latin America is intricately intertwined with class consciousness and with underdevelopment. Inspecting the life of male sex workers in Costa Rica, he alerts us to one of the most interesting developments of globalization and modernization: the clash between the *chapulines* (or young *cachero* practitioners) and modern gays. If in *Macho Love*, *cachero* practitioners became visible in a situational sense—heterosexual men in prison dealing with the absence of women—in the latter book they are largely understood as resulting from a culture of poverty. In this sense, *cachero* practitioners become visible as a class situational subject: that is, types formed by underdevelopment. This conflicted visibility elaborates the idea that *cachero* practitioners exist because of their economic condition. The implication is that a developed, modern society would make the existence of *cachero* practitioners unnecessary. In modernity, Schifter seems to say, *cachero* sexual practice vanishes. Undoubtedly, *cachero* sexual practice becomes for him a lingering premodern sexual form. Tied to a struggling class, *cacheros* are nevertheless not revolutionary subjects. Critiquing Pat Califia, Schifter argues that public sex in a modern society may be romantically revolutionary, but not in underdeveloped countries, where public sex is a default way of surviving.

Class is not the only determinant for Schifter. He locates the *cachero* practitioner at the heart of the current Central American health crisis. To give the reader a taste of Schifter's studies and their particularity, I would like to discuss one of his most interesting works centered on juvenile prostitution. *Lila's House: Male Prostitution in Latin America* (1998), Schifter's ethnography of male prostitution in Costa Rica, pioneered an area of sexual research that until then had been neglected: "No studies on male prostitution have been published in Costa Rica" (2). This ethnography of the practices of "young men of a lower-middle-class brothel catering to pederasts" develops a first-person narrative, but with an unusually critical glance into Latin American sexual practices (3). Unusual not only because of the sexual practice at hand but also because of the apparently unlocatable sexual identity of the youths in question: "The young men did not appear to fit into the more complex models of bisexuality; they are not sexually attracted to both sexes, . . . they do not participate in the homosexual or bisexual lifestyle. . . . We could say that *cacheros* are only bisexual in terms of their practices, but heterosexual in all other respects" (3–4). In attempting to make sense of these young men's sexual practice, Schifter states that *cacheros,* first, do not show any other "additional [bisexual] characteristics"; second, do not demonstrate a "'dual affective preference,' that is, the desire to have sexual relations with both men and women"; third, do not show any evidence of sexual preferences that are "variable over time"; and fourth, do not provide any indication of either bisexual "sexual fantasies" or "self-identity" (3). He summarizes: "The common denominator of the *cacheros* is that they are men who lead heterosexual lives, but who occasionally have sex with other men, be it for pleasure or for money" (4). Needless to say, *cachero* practitioners do not consider themselves to be a "part of Costa Rica's gay community" (63). Situated at the margins of exclusive heterosexuality and gay identity, *bugarrón* (*cachero*) practitioners see themselves as being part of an inclusive heterosexuality where a specific same-sex practice has been incorporated.

Schifter clarifies further by stating that "there are many kinds of cacheros" and that they include "mature men who prostitute themselves, prisoners who seek out young or effeminate men and those who are fascinated by transvestites or homosexuals—whether effeminate or not" (4). Schifter elaborates by claiming that *cachero* practice, or *cacherismo,* "also includes many other groups of men in search of female substitutes in different environments or contexts, such as coastal areas, banana-growing zones, the police forces, agricultural areas, and other places where there are not many women" (4). From "banana-growing zones" to "police headquarters," *cachero* practitioners become ever-elusive in Schifter's quest.

For *Lila's House,* Schifter interviewed people between the ages of thirteen and twenty-seven who belong to one of many groups within the culture of male prostitution and *cacherismo* in San Jose, Costa Rica (4). The purpose of his study is to "learn about the culture of juvenile prostitution with the aim of implementing an immediate intervention program" (4). His main concern is that these young men are in "danger of being exposed to the AIDS virus and of becoming addicted—if they are not already—to cocaine, crack, or alcohol" (4). His fears are not unfounded, as their practice is risky; furthermore, the establishment Lila's house is in such dereliction that it may well be considered a petri dish for the spread of infectious diseases. The house is a 1920s working-class structure in desperate need of repair located in the middle of a commercial block on the outskirts of San Jose, Costa Rica. When entering the house, Schifter recalls, one is welcomed by "excrement and dog urine that is everywhere" (7). One is also hit by a "penetrating organic odor: sweat, semen, Sanipine (a disinfectant), and used toilet paper on the floor" (8). The beds in the place are everywhere, and they see five or six sexual encounters per day. The bedsheets are changed "'every week or two,'" states Lila, the owner (8). Schifter calculates that the sheets are "normally used for around fifty sexual encounters before being washed" (8). The foul smell of dog excrement forces Schifter to ask Lila about it; his reply is that "the smells and the excrement protect him from possible police raids. 'No cop is going to climb over so much shit'" (9). Unsurprisingly, Lila's house is infested by rodents and cockroaches. A North American client recalls: "I was bent down . . . when I saw a parade of mice and cockroaches. First, one cockroach went by, and then another, and another. Then the mice came out. Three of them in line, one behind the other" (10). The conditions are so extreme that seven puppies die after drinking from the sewer water under the kitchen sink. After paying close attention to the biohazardous conditions of the place, Schifter focuses on the sex.

Observing the sexual dynamics of this brothel, Schifter writes that "homosexual practices do not threaten the young men's 'heterosexuality'" (37). Paying close attention to the dynamics among *cachero* practitioners, Schifter contends, "for sex workers, homosexual practice does not make them gay, or homosexual, or even bisexual.... As long as sexual desire is expressed for the opposite sex and their behavior is masculine, they continue to be male" (56). Fantasy plays a role in this recalcitrant heterosexuality, as *cachero* practitioners confess that "in order to have an erection with a man, most of them admit to closing their eyes and fantasizing that they are with a woman" (72). Yet this requirement for fantasy seems not to apply to oral sex, which is not actually considered sex by *cachero* practitioners: "'Why would I want to imagine anything if I'm getting a blowjob?' Cerebrón [Huge Brain], a *cachero* practitioner, confesses, 'it's not necessary to fantasize when you're getting oral sex, whether it's from a man, women, queer, or the neighborhood calf'" (84). According to Schifter, *cachero* sexual practice seems to be mediated via some porno fantasy, wherein they play the role of porn actor. Expressions such as those verbalized by Cerebrón tell us as much. Beyond the egalitarian viewpoint of his oral sex practice, he states, "Th[e] anus is a vagina ... there is nothing better than sticking your penis in a rectum ... you come faster in a tight ass. When their asshole tightens, you don't care if it's your own grandmother's" (84–87).

However, Schifter notices a change taking place in the late 1990s with the spread of drug addiction in the world of the men who practice *cachero* sex: "The need for money, drugs, or even affection leads them to perform all kinds of practices and exposes them to infection" (112). Creation of a dependency on drugs has altered *cachero* sexual practice. It is in this context that Schifter states: "*Cacheros* feel that their active role [in sex] is disappearing" (102). Schifter ends his account with the prospect of a lost world in which *cachero* practitioners are ghosts of what they once were. The central characteristic that distinguishes *cachero* difference from other sexual practices was fading.[2]

EXITING NATIONAL MODERNITY: THE *BUGARRÓN* HAS WHEELS

At the prospect of a highly hybridized modern Latin America where traditional sexual practices are changing and new practices emerging, where can we find those vestiges of *bugarrón* sexual practice? This is the focus of Schifter's and other's ethnographies on sexual practices on the road. Of Schifter's

---

2. In chapter 2 I explain this shift in *bugarrón* sexual practice, where there is a mutation from a practice driven by the pleasure of sexual penetration to one driven by sexual market demands.

many ethnographies, none is as anxiety-inducing as his study of the truck sex trade between Central American countries and those of the Northern Hemisphere. From the 1990s to the present, the movement of goods and bodies across the US–Mexico border has triggered not only the prospect of trade but also anxiety over jobs, health, and the demographic changes affecting US society. During the 1990s, the Inter-American Highway exemplified the process of neoliberal economic expansion, with the political economies of Panama, Costa Rica, Nicaragua, Guatemala, and El Salvador benefiting from the former North American Free Trade Agreement's deregulation of trade between Mexico, Canada, and the US. Today, the anxiety generated by NAFTA has led to a name change—the US-Mexico-Canada Trade Agreement (USMCA). Concerns over USMCA led to the infamous expansion of the US–Mexico border wall by the disgraced Trump administration and the construction of an archipelago of detention facilities for processing border migrants.

It is not surprising, then, that for Schifter, the Pan-American Highway became a site where more than just goods was being traded. Also referred to as the NAFTA Super Highway or CANAMEX (Canada-American-Mexico Corridor), the Pan-American Highway is a series of main routes such as Interstate 35 and Interstate 29 connecting Mexico, the US, and Canada. Using alarmist rhetoric, Schifter warns of the high-risk sex lives of truckers and their role in the spread of HIV. Not only manufacturing and agricultural goods move across borders but also bodies (legal and illegal) and sexual practices. Under his leadership, a group of researchers during the 1990s interviewed 399 of 5,000 truck drivers who worked in 497 existing truck companies. *Latino Truck Driver Trade* (2001), the result of his anthropological effort, describes "how machismo is suspended for certain periods in the lives of truck drivers, so long as this does not alter the power structure at home" (17). Schifter argues that Latino masculinity shows "an enormous concern for keeping certain spaces, people, and practices separate" and is "characterized by drastic splits between these elements and the prohibition against combining them" (150). It is this compartmentalization that Schifter calls "the main reason [machos] become infected with STD's" (149). The high level of "compartmentalization" and the consequences of its contradictions lead them to "unsafe sex" (149). Compartmentalization creates logical conflict and contradictions resulting in misguided practices. A classic example of this complicated logic is a trucker's reasoning when he tells Schifter that oral sex is actually not sex because "'the mouth doesn't have sexual organs'" (186). The fact that HIV is not spread through oral sex has faded from consideration.

Of all the stories Schifter includes in this exemplary study, the most interesting is the one of Luis—a good-looking young man with light-brown eyes, black hair, and strong arms (26). Luis lives with his wife, Katia, and their son in an inner-city tenement located in the southern part of San Jose, Costa Rica. As one of many truckers who guides the anthropologists, Luis becomes doubly important as a native informant. Schifter's book provides the following account:

> Luis places his hands on my buttocks again. He says nothing, only touches. I do not know what to do. I would like to tell him that I'm married and that I have never had a relationship of this kind. While I wonder how to stop his advances, Luis touches my genitals and feels my interest in him. My erection has betrayed me, revealing a desire that was barely conscious. With no Viagra, no extraneous fantasies, I'm having the kind of erection I haven't had for years.... "I've never been with a man before," I tell him. Luis pretends not to hear, and touches my body all over with his hands and feet, creating different sensations, creating chaos with physical experiences, as if he were still at the wheel of his trailer.... He is not a gay man or a bisexual, or a frustrated homosexual. He is a *cachero*: in Latin America, it is a man who has sex with other men without having a gay identity. It is a mystery to observers from other countries, but one I do not wish to discuss right now. The pain is unbearable. Although he has put Vaseline on the condom (wherever did he find it?), I can't bear his penetration. However, he knows how to distract me with deep kisses, rhythmic masturbation, and a few pinches on my nipples. ... Luis moves with an agility that is something new in my life. He knows how and when to penetrate more slowly. Luis senses these contractions and dances with them, as if he were dancing salsa. (*Latino Truck Driver Trade* 47–48)

Let's take a closer look at this passage because several points in Luis's story help us understand Schifter's approach to a nonexclusive heterosexual sexual practice. First is the narrative's establishing of two ostensibly straight married men engaged in sex with each other. Second is that Luis is the only experienced married man in male-to-male sex. Third is the participant ethnographer's determination that Luis is a *cachero* practitioner: a nonexclusive heterosexual sexual type. Fourth is Schifter's decision to include this description in his nonfiction book, with the proviso that it is a fictionalized account "based on the story of an ethnographer whose fictitious name is Bolívar" (37).

The proper name Bolívar alludes to the historical figure of Simón Bolívar, the leader of South America's wars for independence from Imperial Spain in the early decades of the nineteenth century; in Schifter's narrative, Bolívar becomes a penetrated male, and *cachero* practitioners are more macho than Bolívar. The *cachero* practitioner symbolizes for Schifter the resolute nature of an unsolved divergence. What Schifter does not discuss is the more enigmatic character Bolívar. How does Bolívar fit into this sexual scheme? Is he a penetrated heterosexual but not a *cachero* practitioner? Is Bolívar an example of a different gradation in the male sexual spectrum? Schifter does not refer to a sexual continuum, and this absence makes his examples even more puzzling. Schifter's silence on this issue is felt throughout his study.

Bolívar's location in the narrative raises suspicion about the Manichean character of the distinctions that Schifter and other anthropologists use. The difficulty of placing Bolívar in either Western or Latin American sexual paradigms (without it seeming forced or purely speculative) lends credence to historian Martin Nesvig's claim that Latin American sexualities continue to provide researchers a "complicated terrain" by conjuring at every point the dilemma between "behavior and proscription" (690). Yet we see that Schifter vacillates between a narrow understanding of *cachero* sexual practice and a more open-ended view of it. If he begins with the latter, he sometimes ends up evoking the former. *Bugarrón* sexual practice is beginning to lose its strict definition.

In his own example of Luis, Schifter overlooks the significance of the fact that Luis uses a condom when penetrating Bolívar. The use of a condom indicates that something is afoot here. It is not only that Bolívar is an enigma; it is defying sexual categorization as a type unto itself. The problem with Luis is that he has been conjured as a *bugarrón* practitioner who wears a condom in his impromptu sexual encounter. A condom user, Luis defies the stigma of recklessness and the need for prevention tracking that has driven Schifter's ethnographies from the start. Panic and fantasy have merged not only in the figure of Bolívar but in that of Luis too.

Second, Schifter's view of an epistemological gulf between Western and Latin American perspectives is key to his ethnographic studies because it draws a fundamental distinction between sexual types within society. Schifter's publications not only set the agenda for further studies on sexual subcultures in Latin America but, by being part of the Latin American Institute for Health Education and Prevention, strain even further the already tight tension between academic research and policymaking intervention that frames his methodology. The study of sexual cultures is compromised by the agenda of HIV prevention that propels the writing.

According to Schifter's works, Latin American sexual culture is undergoing a transformation in which the traditional understanding of male sexuality confronts the encroachment of an international gay "identity." Schifter explicitly favors the spread of gay "identity," and his work seeks to influence public policy in favor of the containment of the spread of HIV. Schifter's perspective is consistent with the dominant thinking at the time. In 1997 anthropologist Gilbert Herdt spelled out clearly the mindset behind one of the most successful strategies for tackling the gulf between sexual risk and sexual "identity." He argued, "Both adults and adolescents who engage in sexual behavior are less vulnerable to risk-taking and recklessness that may lead to infection if they are secure in their own identities" (*Sexual Cultures* 19). Herdt voices here what today we may consider a cliché, but in the context of onsite Latin American strategies of prevention, it amounted to a paradigm shift, a new understanding that the "creation of a new context, or cultural milieu," is pivotal for lowering the incidence of high-risk sexual behavior (18). This policy of safety requires an "agency-enhancing sexual/gender identity formation" (18). A shift toward the solidification of sexual "identity" becomes the pillar of a new order to combat the spread of HIV/AIDS. It is this realization, the importance of "identity" as a "new context" for the containment of HIV, that represents the key component in the need for new methods of surveillance. Schifter is not the only anthropologist whose research has been funded with this agenda in mind. Others such as ethnographer and health policymaker Timothy Wright were funded by USAID, the CDC, and Bolivia's Ministry of Health, in Wright's case for his project's "promotion of gay identity—public sexual minorities" in Bolivia ("Gay Organizations" 292). In "Gay Organizations" (2005), he explains the connection among NGOs, international funding, gay identity, and its institutionalization in Latin America as a result of the AIDS crisis. Wright shows how the models used to assess program efficiency paradoxically work against effective disease prevention. Advocating for "ethnographic research sensitive to subculture realities," he condemns the international creation of gay community centers as a strategy by health organizations to reach those identified as part of a "target group" (292). It was their belief that once centers were up and running, they would attract and make possible the recruiting to gay identity of those elements considered *hombres*—that is, the local equivalent of *bugarrones*.

"Identity," tracking, and surveillance became the triumvirate techniques in the implementation phase funded by the global network of power/knowledge.[3]

---

3. Today's discourses of power/knowledge include the Global Health Governance (GHG). As Jeremy Youde explains, GHG formed in response to the AIDS pandemic, when the "resurgence of infectious diseases, and the reconceptualization of health politics undermined some of the traditional structures designed to address cross-border health concerns" (*Global* 2). GHG stands for "the use of formal and informal institutions, rules, and processes by states, intergovernmental organizations, and non-state actors to deal with challenges to health that require cross-border collective action to address effectively" (3). In its overlapping, supposedly "nonhierarchical regimes," it also includes international organizations, civil society groups, and private philanthropic organizations (3). Its primary goals are coordination, cross-border surveillance, and the managing of the infectious disease's connection with "politics, culture, social stratification, and economics" (4). NGOs are included in the GHG assemblage of regimes. According to Jean Grugel, "Since 1992, more than 40 percent of the aid projects cofinanced between the EU and NGOs have been in Latin America" ("Romancing" 87). Writing in 2016, Susan Appe concurs with Grugel's assessment, stating, "The Latin American region in particular has seen the number of informal and formal networks grow at the subnational and national levels. . . . NGO networks in Latin America are salient" ("Networks" 189–90).

Schifter belonged to this specific outlook and proposed measures for resolving the conflict between traditional and modern sexual practices. Despite his identitarian agenda, Schifter's account of a sexual culture in transformation is particularly significant because it emphasizes the conflictual dynamics at the heart of this transition. Nevertheless, the biopolitical dimension of his project, which calls for the management and control of whole populations, is misguided in its attempt to eradicate or resolve the conflict. Latin American sexual culture becomes more interesting in Schifter's work because of what I shall describe as a commingling of mutually exclusive epistemologies of sexuality. Schifter is drawn to find the spaces in society where *bugarrón* sexual practice performs risky sex, yet he demonstrates apprehension at the fact that *bugarrón* practices seem to be disappearing. At the same time, he seems sympathetic to the spread of modern sexual identities as a strategy for containing the spread of HIV. Tracker, chronicler, lamenter, and enabler of modern identities in the Global South, all these roles coalesce in Schifter's writings, making them among the most deceivingly facile ethnographic works published at the height of the AIDS crisis. At stake in Schifter's overall project are the crude realities of illness and death on a continent where, at the end of the twentieth century, underdevelopment makes it impossible to prolong the lives of those infected with HIV.

Schifter recognizes that the *bugarrón* practitioner does not translate easily into the medical *bugarrón* subject. This is because anthropology is able to spot and describe sexual cultures and their practices, but it remains beyond its scope to implement mechanisms of health and safety necessary for the long-term tracking and prevention of HIV. Short of the inducement of adopting a stable and visible gay "identity," the elusive *bugarrón* sexual practice always runs the risk of vanishing into a flexible heterosexuality. Yet for all the hats he wears in his works, Schifter is unaware that *bugarrón* practice has already mutated and that a transformation has already taken place. By giving us an account of the shift of *bugarrón* practitioners seeking pleasure (fiction) and *bugarrón* practitioners selling sex for profit (Lila's *cacheros*), Schifter has revealed this mutation. It is not that *bugarrón* practitioners are mutating but that they have already mutated. In actuality, a *bugarrón* practitioner for sale had already been superimposed. No wonder Schifter feels obligated to represent the traditional *bugarrón* practice in an example conjured from fiction (Luis). The ones monitored in culture are already new *bugarrones*. Luis's example is not a symptom of a conflicting logic but rather the norm of a sexual practice that has changed with the modernization of society. Schifter does not suspect that he is studying a semblance of the tantalizing *bugarrón* sexual practice.

Of interest at this point is the surprising change in the way *gay* and *straight* are being understood. If, in previous decades, gayness was considered dangerous because of its undetectable quality, now it becomes the desired stable visible subject. At the same time, heterosexuality becomes suspect and dangerous because it remains partly invisible to long-term studies of health research. Schifter's example of Luis indicates a misguided direction on health prevention policies. Why track the *bugarrón* practitioner if he already practices those techniques for preventing HIV infection? If, in fact, *bugarrón* practitioners have already gotten the message on health prevention, then the question remains—who hasn't?

RETHINKING SEXUAL CULTURES: ETHNOGRAPHY, MODERNITY, AND *BUGARRÓN* SEXUAL PRACTICE

Although fascinating, misleading, and scandalous, Schifter's works raise the specter that *bugarrón* sexual practice may disappear or mutate into some new behavior. Does modernity render *bugarrón* sexual practice invisible? This question has preoccupied Latin American anthropologists conducting research on HIV prevention. Richard Parker, Roger Lancaster, Annick Prieur, and Héctor Carrillo all have engaged changes in male sexual culture in Latin America with an eye to HIV infection in the region. At the heart of their discussions are not only the spread of HIV but also modernity, the discourses of power/knowledge, and the loss of sexual diversity. In these studies we learn not only what has happened to *bugarrón* sexual practice in modernity but also what *bugarrón* sexual practice has produced through its cultural invisibility. Unexpectedly, some of these ethnographies discover the emergence of hybrid mutations of male sexual practice that appropriate *bugarrón* machismo in a new way. If Schifter confronts the prospect of *cachero* sexual practice disappearing in modernity, this point is modified in Parker's and Carrillo's ethnographies.

In the Brazilian context, Parker explains that the traditional model based on active and passive sexual roles "dominated the sexual landscape throughout the nineteenth and early twentieth centuries" (*Beneath* 36). But, he argues, there has been a dramatic change thanks to what he calls "the global incorporation of Western medical and scientific rationalities" (38). Although homosexuality, heterosexuality, and bisexuality were concepts used by the Brazilian professional classes, "by the mid-twentieth century, these new categories had become central to the medical and scientific discussion of sexual life and had been fully incorporated into the languages of law, government, and organized religion" (38). Parker claims that there has been a top-down dissemination of Western ideas in Latin America, but this top-down, global-to-local dissemination of ideas had to contend with local understandings of sexuality: "[Western] medical or scientific discourses" only gradually began to spread "to more general educated circles over the course of the 1980s" (38). The dissemination of Western categories of sexuality accelerated during the 1980s, Parker argues, "as a direct consequence of the emerging AIDS epidemic" and the resulting discussion of "medical and epidemiological information" within the broader framework of the mass media (39). Parker emphasizes the AIDS epidemic as the major event accelerating the spread of gay "identity" in Latin America.

His insight, that top-down societal changes influence the understanding of sexuality but also sexual cultures themselves, is corroborated by Lancaster's assessment that "new subcultures, new forms of sexual citizenship, and new identities, less beholden to active/passive concepts, have also flourished" ("Tolerance" 265). In Lancaster's view, the old monopoly of passive/active gender role identification suffered a major "breakdown" (265). Lancaster connects *bugarrón* sexual practice to machismo by analyzing the *bugarrón* practitioner's preference for penetrating his sexual partner and consistent refusal to be penetrated in return. The culture of machismo that had dominated local society for decades was changing. According to Lancaster, the field of Latin American sexuality has become "a variegated and inconsistent terrain" (261). But how deeply has modernity altered the field experience for sex researchers who seek to expand the scope of power/knowledge south of the US border? Carrillo's ethnographic study *The Night Is Young* (2002) directly addresses this question. The "inconsistent terrain" of Latin American sexual cultures sways him to rethink his methodology and question a body of knowledge now revealed as preconceived.

Inspired by Parker and Lancaster, Carrillo ventures into the shifting terrain of Latin American sexuality by noting in the opening pages of *The Night Is Young* that his "plan was to study the connections between the social and cultural environment and decisions that Mexicans made about their sexuality and sexual behavior. These topics seemed crucial because of the spreading HIV epidemic in Mexico" (ix). With an eye to the goal of designing "public health interventions that would help reduce sexual HIV risk in Mexico," Carrillo asserts that his book is "a study of Mexican sexual culture . . . and Mexicans' individual sexual identities, desires, ideology, and behavior" (3, 4). Adopting a biopolitical agenda, Carrillo is determined to "help individuals change their sexual behavior and adopt safety measures against HIV" (4). Carrillo's initial viewpoint, of a society split between traditional and modern understandings of sexuality, changes: "The study of HIV prevention, and of contemporary sex and sexuality in Mexico, *had* to be located within these larger debates about modernization and cultural change" (4; original italics).

The question of modernity and development moves to center stage. After an eight-year hiatus studying in the US, Carrillo goes home: "I was returning to Mexico after many years of graduate education and HIV prevention work in the United States" (*Night* ix). Hauling himself from California to Guadalajara, Mexico, Carrillo realizes that the gay framework of his HIV-prevention outlook is at odds with the increasing "hybridization of Mexican sexual culture" (292). *The Night Is Young* shows a preoccupation with modernity's profound impact on traditional sexual practices: "How have [traditional] values changed as the country modernized?"; "How are Mexicans reinterpreting their sexual identities, desires, and behaviors to fit a more contemporary Mexican world?"; and, last, "How [are] ideas about sexuality shaped in Mexico during the twentieth century and how [is] their evolution related to larger process of modernization?" (4). Carrillo transcribes his thoughts on the page in the form of questions, but readers may intuit that exclamation marks might have captured better the anxiety soaking through the pages of his book.

Therefore, he embraced a different direction, one acknowledging that "new values and ideas are in constant interplay with those that preceded them, because the former are not always regarded as a replacement for the latter" (*Night* 292). Carrillo's identity-driven graduate training and his ideas of traditional versus modern sexual practices needed rethinking. His ethnographic position—as both outsider (trained in the US) and insider (born and raised in Mexico)—allowed him to think about the cultural changes affecting Mexican society. *The Night Is Young* claims that Mexicans are constantly "search[ing] for ways to adopt contemporary values while at the same time respecting core traditions" (293). Given the impact of modernity in Mexican society, Carrillo is forced to change his outlook on what amounts to a traditional sexual practice in modern Mexico. But is there a consensus in anthropology that *bugarrón* sexual practice has been transformed by modernity? Gayle Rubin reminds us that Foucault's point about epistemic shifts is not that a complete displacement takes place but that a superimposition occurs (Rubin "Sexual Traffic" 85). The old loses an importance and the new gains. Of all the ethnographies published during this period of ethnographic boom, Annick Prieur's is the one that spots those remaining enclaves of *bugarrón* sexual practice in modernity.

If Parker and Lancaster contend that traditional *bugarrón* sexual practice has mutated under pressure from modern sexual identities, Prieur finds remains of traditional *bugarrón* sexual practice in Mexico's *mayates*. Like Carrillo, Annick Prieur's *Mema's House: On Transvestites, Queens, and Machos* (1998) studies male sexuality in Mexico. Prieur is interested in *mayate* sexual practice, that is, in "a man who looks like a man and has sex with men who are regarded as *homosexuales,* and usually also with women. He is commonly expected to be the active part" (26; original italics). Prieur clarifies that "mayate is first and foremost a term by which those designated as *homosexuales* designate their partners. Only very rarely have I heard any of the men so designated use the term about themselves" (27; original italics).[4] Similar to a *bugarrón,* there is no self-identification that a *mayate* seeks or claims. Like *hombres normales, mayate* is a term that describes a sexual practice, not a subjectivity. Our predisposition to think in terms of identity categories makes it difficult to conceptualize a practitioner of a sexual practice outside the bounds of claiming an "identity." *Mayate* practitioners do not consider themselves homosexuals, instead identifying as *normal* men.

There is another consideration to take into account here, and that is related to what it means to be "active" in a sexual relationship. According to Prieur, "to be a man means to be active, penetrating; to be a *homosexual* means to be passive, penetrated" (198; original italics). As she explains, "To be active with a homosexual partner is subsumed under the more general category of being active, which again characterizes male sexual behavior" (29). Prieur is careful to clarify that *mayate* practitioners consider themselves as "being active," but for them, being active in a sexual relationship with men means something different from being bisexual. Here we encounter another instance of mutually exclusive epistemologies of sexuality. *Mema's House* contributes not only an analysis of *mayates* but also a clarification that bisexuality is also understood differently in certain subcultures in Latin America. Like Schifter, Prieur helps us understand the difference between *mayate* (*bugarrón*) sexual practice and Latin American bisexuality. In fact, Prieur explains that "bisexuality" connotes versatility in the sexual act, that is to say, an expectation of "the changing of roles" and "the trading off between being active and passive" (26). This "trading off" dimension of bisexuality makes its identification difficult for Latin American men who prefer the active role in their sexual relationships.

Prieur's ethnography corroborates Schifter's impression that *cachero* (*mayate*) practitioners have no interest in claiming a sexual identity separate from heterosexuality. More importantly, Prieur makes clear that sexual types "make up a subculture, but not a counterculture" (62). *Mayate* practitioners do not see themselves in "opposition to their surroundings" but as in conformity with the larger context of Mexican gender culture (62). *Mayate* (*bugarrón*)

---

4. The traditional *bugarrón* would never refer to himself as *bugarrón* but as *hombre,* that is, as an ordinary straight man. Today, more often than not, the *bugarrón* is misunderstood as a homosexual man. We find this misunderstanding prevalent in modern Mexico, where Prieur reveals that "in some parts . . . the word *mayate* is actually used to designate a homosexual man" (*Mema's House* 27).

practitioners are present in *Mema's House,* but the practice's visibility is connected to the LGBTQ world. In this way, the term has become part of a semiotics of sexual categorization by LGBTQ culture in modern Mexico. Prieur reveals pockets of *bugarrón* sexual practice that have not disappeared entirely in modernity. Yet their presence has become even more entangled with modern Mexican LGBTQ identities. A shift has taken place thanks to the deployment of modern sexual identity across the Americas.

THE SPECTER OF A *BUGARRÓN* BEYOND BORDERS

The unspoken yet guiding question "Where is the *bugarrón* practitioner?" was answered in the first decade of the twenty-first century when the discourse of medicine began to look at patterns of migration beyond the tracking of truckers across the border. When Parker argues that the *bugarrón* can be found in the "cross-currents of these global processes of change," he is referring to the effects of globalization on Latin American sexual cultures (*Beneath* 2). We could extend his argument to reflect on metropolitan areas in the US, especially those with growing Latino communities. In 2006 the American College of Physicians published in its *Annals of Internal Medicine* a study on the discordance between sexual identity and sexual behavior. Based in New York City, the study focuses on male sexual behavior consistent with *bugarrón* sexual practice. Its results suggest a crosscurrent of globalization following recent migration patterns from the Southern to the Northern Hemisphere. The article explains that "among foreign-born, straight-identified men who have sex with men, 33% were from Latin America; 30% were from the Caribbean; and 32% were from Europe, Asia, or Africa. Approximately 70% of straight-identified men who have sex with men reported being married, which was substantially more than any other identity-behavior group" (Pathela et al., "Discordance" 419). These numbers do not reflect the bisexually identified group that was studied separately.

The study concludes that "men who had sex with men exclusively but self-identified as heterosexual were more likely than their gay-identified counterparts to belong to minority racial or ethnic groups, be foreign-born, have lower education and income levels, and be married" (Pathela et al., "Discordance" 416). What is also of interest is the dramatic difference in risk behavior between gay-identified subjects and heterosexually identified subjects: "Almost 96% of straight-identified men who have sex with men reported having only 1 sex partner in the past year [a regular sex buddy]. . . . [in contrast to] gay-identified men who have sex with men who reported 3 or more partners in the previous year" (420). The overall prevalence of risky sexual behavior was higher for gay men (14%) than for straight men who have sex with men (1%). The authors qualify their findings in the following way: "These straight-identified men who have sex with men, most of whom also have sex with women, will exchange sex with 'gay' men and transvestites but only in the role of the insertive (anal or oral) partner" (423). These findings illuminate a contrary perspective that "straight-identified men who have sex with men may *not* play a substantial role in fueling the current STD and HIV epidemics" (423; my emphasis). Pathela and her co-authors point out that neglect for the well-being of women by the Mexican state, exploitation of women at the border, and the profession of sex worker as last resort are factors that condition this unfortunate situation.

Suppose Pathela and her co-authors' insights are true. In that case, her study casts doubt on the biopolitical motivation behind HIV research in Latin America, compelling us to ask anew: What drives the institutionalization of gay "identity" in the persistent tracking of *bugarrón* sexual practice? It shifts the question from "where is the *bugarrón* practitioner?" to "why track *bugarrón* sexual practice at all?" Was the query "where is the *bugarrón*?" the wrong question to pursue? Pathela and her co-authors' insights also warrant a shift in focus by problematizing further the figure of the married heterosexual condom-bearing *bugarrón* practitioner we encountered in Schifter's truck-driver tale. Schifter's silence on this issue should alert us to a blindness in the anthropological corpus and also to a second absence, invisible yet present, in the medical discourses of health prevention. The fact that the risk of getting infected with HIV is greater for the penetrated male, as Pathela and co-authors hint at, should make us question the rationale for focusing medical research on the tracking of *bugarrón* practice. Even when the discourses of power/knowledge elucidate the space of revenue where *bugarrón* sexual practice takes place, Pathela and her co-authors' essay shifts our attention to a difficult question: Why the fixation on surveilling *bugarrón* sexual practice? Why this legacy of deep concern?

In *Fixing Men* (2007), Matthew Gutmann provides an inside look at a Mexican health facility and nongovernmental organizations in charge of AIDS-prevention treatment in Mexico. *Fixing Men* reveals questionable policy initiatives that justified decades of misplaced surveillance of *bugarrón* practitioners. While doing ethnographic work in Oaxaca on migrant workers returning from and to the US, Gutmann points out that "although health workers acknowledged that by the late 1990s self-identified heterosexuals in Oaxaca were key 'vectors' for the transmission of HIV, in Oaxaca heterosexual transmission of the AIDS virus was said to always follow an 'original' male-male sexual transmission" (70). In this sense, Gutmann argues that the original perception of infection has become engrained as an unchallenged assumption in medical prevention: "The history of AIDS in Mexico is following a pattern common to other lands and peoples: the main vector of transmission early on was through men who had sex with other men" (70). A fixed idea, this original notion has become an unthought body of knowledge in the medical establishment about the most pernicious source of infection for the "general population." As a result, other vectors were not considered to be of great priority. He continues,

> Regardless of their scientific, objectivist pretensions, health care practitioners involved in AIDS care in Oaxaca utilized a variety of culturalist explanations to guide their work. Sexual beliefs and practices associated by these personnel with culture were used to describe and explicate who had AIDS, how they had gotten it, and why they had gotten it. In this sense, then, culture was used as a sheath to enclose and contain the contagion in Oaxaca. In particular, medical employees in Oaxaca were convinced that virtually all men who got infected with HIV did so after having had sex with other men. (77)

Gutmann provides evidence that the culturalist prejudice by medical personnel in speculating on the source of the infection in male–male practices increased when compared with the patients' own accounts of their sexual history. For instance, his investigation revealed that there was a discrepancy in the health personnel's prejudicial misinterpretation of the patients seeking medical attention. Instead of confirming medical prejudice, Gutmann discovered—after having been granted access to patients' sexual history files—that "of the self-identified heterosexuals, more claimed to have had sex with farm animals than with other men" (77). In Mexico, bestiality seemed less stigmatized than homosexuality. Gutmann's study uncovers a cultural blindness on the part of medical experts that seemed to be pervasive: "The medical personnel were convinced that these men were lying. . . . 'Mexican men have sex with other men. They just don't like to admit it'" (77). Gutmann's suspicions increased when he realized that "without exception, men who were convinced that same-sex sex among Mexican men was widespread denied that they themselves had ever partaken" (79). Gutmann's observation is key, as he managed to get firsthand access to discussions in the local COESIDA (Consejo Estatal para la Prevención y Control del SIDA [State Council for AIDS Control and Prevention]) meetings where antiretroviral (ARV) drugs were distributed to a small percentage of the infected population.

In *Fixing Men,* Gutmann addresses issues of "medical profiling," a term he adopts from Charles Briggs and Cara Martin-Briggs's work. The Briggses had discovered a particular type of prejudicial knowledge, one that stuck despite being outdated. In an interesting section, Gutmann explains that

> the conviction among medical practitioners in Oaxaca that homosexual sex was the nearly exclusive vector of transmission of the AIDS virus infecting men was grounded in cultural models—Mexican men like to have sex with other men—and when these cultural explanations seemed too flimsy, the argument for same-sex sex among men relied on earnest physiological "evidence"—anuses, vaginas, mucous, and other bodily fluids. (92)

The perseverance of a misguided culturalist framework for understanding the spread of HIV placed medical efforts head to head with a *bugarrón* sexual practice. Gutmann explains that "cultural assumptions about sexuality and AIDS guide AIDS care in Oaxaca, including the assertion that AIDS is a disease of 'non-heterosexual men,' that is, risk-taking homosexual and bisexual men" (86). As Gutmann states, "such thinking is a way of attributing disease to those who are deemed by some to be outside the cultural bonds of normativity" (87). Gutmann's critique makes the case clear that "AIDS care in the state [of Oaxaca, Mexico] was based on cultural beliefs about male-male sex more than on epidemiological evidence" (98–99).

Gutmann also addresses the involvement of the Mexican state, NGOs, and other multinational organizations in family planning. These agencies and organizations were concerned with analyzing, regulating, and controlling populations in order to "promote economic development in the southern hemisphere through the disarming of the 'population bomb' by lowering birth rates around the globe" (*Fixing Men* 102). Population control, birth-rate control, and fertility rate control were the "population bomb" indices that dictated the allocation of resources. Mortality rate was not a driving factor in the state and its multinational cohorts. The budget allocated to AIDS Oaxaca, Gutmann reveals, was able to cover the ARV drugs for only two hundred people. Those left without health care and medical assistance ran into the thousands. It is for this reason that the office of COESIDA in Oaxaca concealed itself from the public. Because they could not provide services to everybody who needed it, COESIDA's management decided to select, from among the thousands infected, at most two hundred of the few hundred citizens who knew of their existence: "For the thousands of others afflicted with HIV and AIDS in Oaxaca, the clinic remained essentially concealed under a disappearing screen of neoliberal health care reforms and abject poverty" (98). If neoliberal policies allow for the state's retreat from regulating areas of society where experts can do better, then what Gutmann discovers is a different act of neoliberal disappearance.

At the heart of these works describing *bugarrón* surveillance is the problem of neoliberal governmentality that has made the state retreat from direct control over areas of society. In *The Birth of Biopolitics* (2008), Foucault defines these moves by states as a type of government rationality, that is to say, a form of state reasoning or thinking. As a method of rationalization, or of making sense of government and its society, biopolitical states enact policies to the effect of a permanent self-limitation. Foucault makes the case that this internal self-limitation is key to the state's shift from dominance of its citizens to a more enlightened politics of life and population. For enlightened governments, "civil society" represents the thought that the "least" amount of government translates into prosperity for the state (*Birth* 330). The paradox emerges when this minimal government is required to watch over and intervene so that it can "produce, multiply, and guarantee those liberties" that the system needs (330).

On the one hand, as Jessica Whyte reminds us, "the neoliberal right to security is a right for states to beat into submission those who threaten the market order" (*Morals* 25). Those risky elements in society such as *bugarrón* practitioners would have to be made less risky either by regulation, that is, conformity to accepted rights and "identities," or, in some cases, by state neglect ("letting die"; Foucault, *History of Sexuality, Vol. 1*). The self-limiting strategy of neoliberal governance can secure the fundamental inequality of society by withdrawing services from those it considers unworthy to keep alive. Gutmann corroborates this point by explaining the state's culturalist bias against *bugarrón* practitioners. On the other hand, as Nikolas Rose points out, these governments devised schemes for governing at a distance, that is, via techniques of expertise: "schools," "factories," "classrooms," and "hospitals" ("Governing" 38). There must be self-limitation, or small government, but it must be ready to foment the creation of new domains for the "transfer of governmental activity" (Foucault, *Birth* 330). The state, in following the self-limitation rule, has to cede to nongovernmental organizations the management of sectors of its society. In Nikolas Rose's clarification, governmentality no longer needs a direct form of intervention. Instead, it grants relative autonomy to various spaces where techniques of expert knowledge provide regulation and order. In Gutmann's ethnographic study, AIDS Oaxaca fulfills this role. In this way, rational governance refers not to what government does but to what is produced by its liberties.

Governmentality indicates the accomplishments accrued by a government in the spaces where it has made itself absent, and these spaces of nongovernmental control are zones where sexual "identities" become useful as models for social conduct. It is not only the state that abdicates its involvement in control and regulation of certain sections of society as Foucault professes but also institutions that self-limit their visibility or conceal themselves from the public in order to curb demand for scarce resources. Governmentality has saturated all aspects of civil society and increased self-concealment. In Oaxaca, its self-limiting strategies amount to a neoliberal strategy of letting die. In *Fixing Men*, Gutmann reveals a multilayered international system of neglect and concealment. Governmentality and heteroflexibility are two consequential forces in Gutmann's ethnographic study. Their influence is palpable in the negotiating struggles over surveillance, AIDS treatment, medical care, economic survival, and the right to live.

Against a politics of invisibility that ranges from a self-retreated clinic to a network of national and international powers ("multiple layers of influence") guiding the clinics' decisions, Gutmann advocates for "reveal[ing] the underlying assumptions" of this politics of concealment (*Fixing Men* 204). His technique comes straight out of his "ethnographer's toolkit" (202). Gutmann shows that from the late 1990s to the early decades of the twenty-first century, the US cloaked itself under a shroud of concealment and managed to create a market monopoly for the supply of high-priced antiretroviral drugs. This monopoly on medical treatment took place along with the exploitation of a migrant workforce in the farmlands of the US Southwest. Due to these clandestine tactics, Gutmann refers to the US as a "shadow state" looming over the state of Mexico and beyond (98). He explains that when the politics of a shadow state are aligned with local prejudices about the origin of infection in local communities, something like a perfect storm forms. Gutmann's ethnographic study exposes a politics of double concealment. *Fixing Men* uncovers that which had escaped Schifter's ethnographic accounts, that is, the neoliberal transnational machinations of a global network of power/knowledge.

By manipulating prices for antiviral drugs, during the 1990s the US benefited from those impoverished countries south of the border. The mostly uninsured men paying for medical treatment were forced to seek employment as farm workers. This is because local institutions insisted as a matter of policy on withholding health assistance from those they deemed risky. In the estimation of Mexican health officials, men-who-have-sex-with-men were too risky to invest with their scarce supply of antiretroviral drugs. For health agencies, treatment is a separate policy from that of tracking *bugarrón* practitioners. In their belief that Mexican migrant laborers who return from the US are the ones spreading HIV in Mexico, and because they are assumed to be MSM, health agencies refrain from allowing them to benefit from the limited available resources. As it happens, these men are too hot to invest in. Across the board, local prevention organizations and institutions believe that *bugarrón* sexual practice must be tracked down but that practitioners should not be treated. Despite being found worthy of surveillance, *bugarrón* practitioners find themselves unworthy of long-term medical attention.

A self-concealed sexual practice is tracked but not assisted by a self-concealed medical practice in alarm over migrant workers returning from farm facilities in the US. At the same time, US media outlets report citizens being concerned by what they perceive as a sexual risk group spreading HIV across the US–Mexico border. Gutmann points out that these transnational misconceptions hide the fact that a great number of men seem to have become infected with HIV after having sex with female sex workers at the border. As he explains, Mexican farm workers are not ravaging each other in the strawberry fields across the border. Rather, they are having sex with female sex workers in illicit brothels that have spread along the Rio Grande border towns. Much research is needed on this issue, but the uncertainty that it raises, in combination with the culturalist prejudice by health management officials in Oaxaca, casts doubts about persistent rationales for *bugarrón* practitioners' surveillance. According to Gutmann, it is the combination of all these factors—fixed ideas, transnational economic and social pressures, and the dearth of local resources—that contribute to the failed policy of surveillance, resulting in the determination of NGOs, as well as state and health organizations to continue looking in the wrong direction. Concealed and under suspicion is the uncertainty about businesses of heterosexual sex as the main culprit for spreading HIV across the border.[5] As the last section reveals, *bugarrón* sexual practice as a modern "object" of surveillance continues to this day. It is built on a legacy of a misunderstanding that, along with an unprejudiced study of sex at the border, warrants further research. Shifting our focus from the where to the why of surveillance entails redirecting attention from local ethnographies to the growing network of global health governance. There we can find the modern origins of this surveillance.

FROM WHERE TO WHY: UNAIDS AND THE BIRTH OF *BUGARRÓN* SURVEILLANCE

In her essay "Lying Informants" (1987), Wolf Bleek cautions that "anthropological knowledge is predominantly based on what people *say* they do, not on what researchers *see* them doing" (315; original italics). The preoccupation with seeing what they do drove Latin American anthropologist Jacobo Schifter

---

5. On this concern, Gustavo Subero maintains that "the main route of HIV transmission in the Caribbean is heterosexual sex . . . via commercial sex and/or sex tourism" (*Representations* 69).

to the most heinous pockets of Costa Rican society and Central American life during the 1990s. Anthropologists writing at the time—such as Richard Parker, Annick Prieur, and Schifter—benefited from what Elizabeth Pisani called the "HIV surveillance mafia" (*Wisdom* 39). In *The Wisdom of Whores* (2008), Pisani glosses this expression in the following way: "The surveillance mafia was made up of people from lots of different institutions—UNAIDS and WHO of course, but also UNICEF, the US Center[s] for Disease Control, a number of research organizations, some people hijacked from national AIDS programmes and sundry others" (39). The acronym UNICEF refers to the United Nations International Children's Emergency Fund. It is in charge of children's health worldwide and of the distribution of lifesaving vaccines. NGOs are nongovernmental organizations that operate independently of governments. Usually founded by citizens, NGOs aim to tackle social and political issues. Pisani was pivotal in forming this conglomerate of states and NGOs that began tracking the *bugarrón*. She claims to have been one of the originating influencers of this new direction in tackling the spread of HIV. But there is more to Pisani's story that makes it pivotal for understanding the sudden interest in *bugarrón* sexual practice.

Hired by the newly formed UNAIDS in 1996, Pisani turned the agency around. She was recruited for her expertise as an epidemiologist and her previous experience as a journalist in Indonesia, where she worked for the news service Reuters. Her training at the London School of Hygiene and Tropical Medicine, her work as a journalist, and her claimed expertise in surveillance made Pisani a candidate too good not to hire. At UNAIDS she was in charge of synthesizing data on HIV/AIDS collected by many agencies into readable and impact-driven language. Using the term *beating up,* Pisani describes a rhetorical skill that sensationalizes data persuasively enough to raise "billions of dollars for AIDS" (*Wisdom* 12). Through her new role as rhetorical master writer, she managed to reverse an early 1990s slump in AIDS-prevention funding. She provided a narrative in the 1998 UNAIDS report that departed from the stilted bureaucratic language typical of UN writing. Adopting her new rhetorical skills, she highlighted that "[in India] the virus is firmly embedded in the general population, among women whose only risk behaviour is having sex with their own husbands" (28). From a bureaucratic passive voice that had perfected an impenetrable rhetoric, the newly published 1998 UNAIDS report drew attention to itself by its clear, decisive, urgent language. The *New York Times* picked up key phrases from the report, and other news networks disseminated the crucial information that Pisani wanted to underscore. At the heart of her efforts was a clear and urgent message: the "general population" was at risk.

In *Policing Desire* (1987), Simon Watney analyzes the media representations of HIV/AIDS from roughly 1980 to 1986. Although Watney points to

1986 media coverage that underscored at times "strong implications of direct risk and threat to the rest of the population" (139), he also emphasizes that "nothing whatsoever has been done at any official level in either Britain or the United States to challenge the endlessly repeated media association between homosexuality *per se* and Aids" (138; original italics). The media allusion to the general population was not enough. What Pisani accomplished was the certification by an official document, the 1998 UNAIDS report, that the general population was at immediate risk. The instantaneous salability of Pisani's rhetoric was the result of the representative media image she constructed. By conjuring a more specific picture, "innocent housewives," she made relatable the language of an abstract concept, "general population." As a result, just like *wheels* becomes a metonym for *car*, "innocent housewives" became representative of the "general population." We all know and care for a housewife, but we don't know the "general population." The hook worked.

This idea was compounded in the news cycle that ensued, with the formation of a new type of citizen desperately in need of rescue in the fight against the virus—the innocent housewife. Pisani explains: "We argued quite truthfully that men who inject, men who have sex with one another and men who buy sex are likely to pass HIV on to their innocent wives. And then came the sleight of hand. Once innocent wives were infected, we implied, HIV would blaze through the 'general population'" (*Wisdom* 27–28). As she confesses, the statistical figure "came from one small study of women with sexually transmitted infections. Most of these women were probably married to men who visit prostitutes, already a minority in India. They didn't represent the 'general population' in any way. But the way I wrote it pretty much implied that HIV was raging through the faithful wives of India" (28).

The UNAIDS members of Pisani's committee were, as she states, "pretty certain that neither donors nor governments would care about HIV unless we could show that it threatened the 'general population'" (*Wisdom* 28). The construct "innocent housewives," as a new vector to the general population, raised alarms about a disease that could threaten national security. From a mere USD 300 million budget in 1996, the commitment to UNAIDS by countries and international agencies ballooned to a USD 10 billion budget by 2007 (33). Pisani's UNAIDS report changed the global face of AIDS because, she emphasized, "AIDS was no longer about promiscuous queens in rich countries, it was about loyal wives in dirt-poor countries" (34). Pisani's rhetorical recalibration transformed perceptions of the AIDS crisis. She reversed a trend that had stigmatized as irresponsible gay men afflicted by the disease and extended the stigma to those heterosexually identified men who practiced sex with other men. From that moment on, she confesses, "HIV [was] not a disease of the wicked" (34). Instead, HIV became "an affliction of the innocent" (34). As Pisani baldly put it, "AIDS was a growth industry" (34). Pisani's fundraising strategies generated substantial contributions from private foundations and governments but also led to a rapid increase in funding for HIV surveillance of MSM practices worldwide. The claim that "innocent housewives" were being infected and that this represented the gravest risk to the general population made *bugarrón* sexual practice the immediate target of an effort in tracking an understudied, and at the same time overestimated, sexual behavior. The construct of the subjectivity "innocent housewife" has led to the manufacture of the construct MSM as a behemoth inclusive of a range of male same-sex practices. Joining forces with Michael Carael from UNAIDS, Pisani managed to steer the focus of UNAIDS funding toward tracking men's sexual behavior around the globe.

In a review of Pisani's book for the *Journal of the American Medical Association,* the authors emphasize that "by the latter 1990s, scientists and others at UNAIDS knew that HIV was not going to rage through general populations in most of the world, yet the threat of such a scenario was necessary to keep AIDS funding growing" (Green et al., "Review" 2502). Ethnographic, medical, and sociological studies focused on surveilling men's sexual behavior were given special consideration. The goal was unequivocally to change their behavior. Anthropologist Ralph Bolton put it plainly: "We, as anthropologists, have a responsibility to create culture, not merely to interpret it. . . . To create a new sexual culture" ("Rethinking Anthropology" 301). As Christine Stewart highlights, Pisani's book "reveals the uncertainties, the inadequately researched half-truths, the inadequately planned programmes of the international agencies, and the infinite range of the sexual interaction of people that defies categorization" (*"Wisdom"* 744). For John Cleland, writing for the *International Journal of Epidemiology,* Pisani's work amounts to "the most powerful" critique written about "the darker side of the international population-control movement" (1441).

Pisani's narrative was preceded by another account of the misguided efforts undertaken by NGOs and world health organizations. This chronicle was provided by the eminent epidemiologist James Chin, who described his sudden departure in the late 1990s from his post at the Unit of the Global Programme on AIDS (GPA) of the World Health Organization (WHO) in Geneva, Switzerland. In *The AIDS Pandemic* (2007), Chin explains how UNAIDS, "an organization that doesn't deny it is primarily an AIDS advocacy agency—not a scientific or technical agency," provides an "inadequate" account of the pandemic (vii). His narrative underscored his dismay at how HIV/AIDS estimates and projections were "'cooked' or made up" (vii). His version provides corroborating evidence of the exaggerated projections of HIV transmission that Pisani revealed to be "beating up" in *The Wisdom of Whores*. Pisani's success in beating up the rhetoric of AIDS transmission aligns perfectly with Chin's claim that UNAIDS had crossed the line into misinformation. Chin argues that UNAIDS perpetuated "the myth of the great potential for HIV epidemics to spread into 'general' populations" (vi). Appalled by what he considered an "intentionally . . . deliberate exaggeration," Chin "felt obligated" to provide a corrective in his book.

Chin clarifies that his epidemiologically objective assessment is at variance with "the prevailing position of UNAIDS and AIDS program activists" (*AIDS Pandemic* vi). A world expert in "public health surveillance and prevention and control," Chin explains what he calls his "epidemiologically sound conclusion," by which he means that the "vast majority of the world's population do not have sufficient HIV risk behaviors to sustain significant epidemic HIV transmission" (vi). Chin's account corroborates Pisani's confessional tale of concocting a rhetorical exaggeration to raise funds. As in Pisani's version, Chin makes clear that his epidemiological assessment revealed a lower prevalence of infection in the "general population."

In *The AIDS Pandemic in Latin America* (2007), anthropologist Shawn Smallman depicts the quick reconceptualization of an anomalous sexual practice at the time of a global health crisis, where "a plethora of NGOs appeared that received a steady stream of funding from international agencies" (14). In this context, Smallman states, "there were good reasons to be worried about HIV not only in Brazil but also throughout Latin America: an active sex trade, the large number of men having sex with men, the inability of wives to negotiate condom use, . . . and the prejudice that warped the early response to HIV/AIDS" (2). Smallman explains that "men may be married and not think of themselves as being gay, despite the fact that they may engage in regular sex with other men[, so] . . . a new category was created: men-who-have-sex-with-men" (6). The traditional term *bugarrón* became indicative of a primary vector and, as a result, sublated into the term men-who-have-sex-with-men. *Sublation* is used here to describe the process of incorporating a local type into a global umbrella category. I see this process at work with *bugarrón* sexual practice, a practice that challenged modern sexuality and therefore was included in a generic category of analysis at the level of global health governance. In global health networks of power/knowledge during the 1990s, the local term *bugarrón* was incorporated into the epidemiological term MSM. As Pisani had suggested, many of these men "who have anal sex with one another don't think of themselves as gay, and we care about the behavior, not the identity. So it became men-who-have-sex-with-men, or MSM for short"

(*Wisdom* 16). "MSM" became the dumping ground for all sexual anomalies and variations from the heterosexual/homosexual binary (transsexuals, bisexuals, etc.), that is, for those who practiced versatility and reciprocation during sex, and for those who don't. Those "who don't" include the Latin American *bugarrón* practitioner who would refuse to be sexually penetrated. As far as UNAIDS was concerned, no distinctions were made between any of these sexual practices. MSM was the initial step along the path of normalizing sexual anomalies. MSM surveillance accelerated with the massive influx of funds. As the discursive productivity on *bugarrón* sexual practice increased in the discourses of power/knowledge, traditional *bugarrón* sexual practice began dwindling but, more importantly, changing.

CONCLUSION

Schifter, Lancaster, Carrillo, Prieur, Parker, Gutmann, and many other researchers connected to the field of HIV/AIDS prevention benefited from the ballooning budgets allocated by health governance for HIV prevention after the 1998 UNAIDS report. The alarm sirens that were set off and the deep concern over MSM shifted not only AIDS funding and the anthropological method but also the texture of Latin American sexual cultures. Traditional sexual practices made visible for surveillance soon dwindled under modernization and the spread of modern sexual identities. The field of HIV/AIDS prevention had a revolutionary effect in creating a network of global health development. But, as Ilona Kickbusch claims, the supposed "crisis" of public health was after all simply "a governance crisis" ("Foreword" xv). Under neoliberalism and governmentality, identities are more easily regulated than irregular sexual practices.

The elusive *bugarrón* sexual practice continues to generate concern whose utility becomes apparent in the expanding global health governance. Even when surveillance is one of the key techniques used in fighting an epidemic and MSM unsafe sexual contacts are a legitimate concern for the spread of the virus, the targeting of a particular sexual practice for the boosting of funding pushes the limits of medical ethics. What remains unsaid is the justification of surveillance, neglect, and demonization of a vector that does not conform to clearly delineated identities. At the same time, global health governance used rhetorical advantage strategically to help prevent the spread of the virus even when it exaggerated the risk of infection to the general population.

To think about the *bugarrón* is to think about the conundrum Foucault explained to be "sex" as a "political issue" in the addendum to *The History of*

Sexuality, Vol. 1, entitled "Right of Death and Power over Life" (145). There, as if he were thinking about *bugarrón* sexual practice at the time of AIDS, he writes:

> [Sex] was the pivot of the two axes along which developed the entire political technology of life. On the one hand it was tied to the disciplines of the body: the harnessing, intensification, and distribution of forces, the adjustment and economy of energies. On the other hand, it was applied to the regulation of populations, through all the far-reaching effects of its activity. It fitted in both categories at once, giving rise to infinitesimal surveillances, permanent controls, extremely meticulous orderings of space, indeterminate medical or psychological examinations, to an entire micro-power concerned with the body. But it gave rise as well to comprehensive measures, statistical assessments, and interventions aimed at the entire social body or at groups taken as a whole. (145–46)

At this particular moment in history, the tracking of *bugarrón* sexual practice gives rise to "infinitesimal surveillance" (e.g., by anthropologists, ethnographers), "permanent controls" (e.g., Cuba's isolation camps), "indeterminate medical or psychological examinations" (e.g., Oaxaca care), "comprehensive measures" (e.g., safe sex), "statistical assessments" (e.g., WHO), and "interventions" (e.g., COESIDA) to maintain the health of the "entire social body" (e.g., general population). The construction of this surveillance web was imperfect, convoluted, and a patchwork. Still, it nevertheless proved to be an asset for the accumulation of knowledge and for the organization of mechanisms of control. Deborah Cook reminds us that for Foucault, "Western states seek to manage and regulate the biological life of the population" (*Adorno* 110). For this reason, Foucault encourages reflection on how biopower "has taken hold of our bodies, forces, energies matter, drives, thoughts" (110). Population regulation entails a proliferation of ways and methods whereby the state secures information. Yet along with these developments, it exposed misguided policies in the health surveillance network that had been exploited by those willing to seize changes in the socioeconomic landscape.

The rise of *bugarrón* surveillance coincided with the expanding network of global health governance, with the activist shift in ethnographic knowledge, vast funding for local initiatives for tracking *bugarrón* sexual practice, and the modernization of Latin American societies. The creation of UNAIDS coincides with the incremental strengthening of neoliberal policies in the Americas and the Caribbean. Even after billions of dollars have been invested in its surveillance, *bugarrón* sexual practice remains a paradox. But with the unstoppable spread of neoliberalism, *bugarrón* sexual practice changes into something different. If in neoliberal governmentality identities become useful, this same formula becomes advantageous for those men who will be marketing *bugarrón* sexual practice. Schifter alerted us to this change in *Lila's House*, but he did not understand how far along the transformation had materialized in a neoliberalized Caribbean. In chapter 2, I discuss the transformation when *bugarrón* sexual practice becomes commodified and sold in the tourist marketplace. In these Caribbean sites, *bugarrón* sexual practice no longer lingers concealed in the shadows of a neoliberal state. The opposite is the case; in the sex tourism marketplace, it will shine with the brilliance of a new commodity available for a client's pleasure. Where is the *bugarrón* practitioner? In a website at your tourist destination site.

CHAPTER 2

The *Neobugarrón*

A Lesson in Neoliberalism and Biopolitics

Bugas—the truth is that I don't think they exist anymore.
—Annick Prieur, *Mema's House*

Prieur's claim in the epigraph that a particular sexual practice may have disappeared raises questions about the potential extinction of anomalous sexual practices. What kind of cultural transformation could lead to a sexual practice's extinction or mutation into something different? Whereas the previous chapter explored a theoretical conundrum in which recent anthropological discourses failed to explain the living sexual anomaly named Bolívar in the history of Latin American sexual practices, this chapter studies another wrinkle in *bugarrón* cultural history that so far has passed undetected in cultural criticism. *Bugarrón* refers to a traditional sexual practice of ostensibly heterosexual men who participate in sex with other men but perform only the "active," "penetrative," or "insertive" role.[1] Practitioners of this sexual activity maintain their identity as straight men. At the time of the AIDS crisis, *bugarrón* practice became a target of surveillance by anthropological and medical researchers involved in containing the epidemic. Anthropologists and medical personnel trained in the US and Europe were at the forefront of this effort to ascertain and contain a *bugarrón* practice, as it was considered high-risk. The discourses produced at this time interpret *bugarrón* practitioners as "closeted" men who disavow their true homosexual "identity." The previous chapter covered these

---

1. In "Three Decades of Male Sex Work in Santo Domingo" (1999), E. Antonio de Moya and Rafael García explain the term's possible origin: "This term derives from the French word *bougre* ('bugger' in English), heretics of supposed Bulgarian origin who were said to practice 'sodomy'" (128).

efforts by examining anthropological and medical discourses; this chapter examines the region's economic changes and its effects on *bugarrón* practice. While anthropologists were busily distracted by the traditional specter of the *bugarrón*, a *bugarrón* practice was being transformed into something else.

This chapter investigates the unexpected cultural transformation of the traditional *bugarrón* sexual practice into a *neobugarrón* subject. Notice here the distinction between practice and subject. In neoliberalism, sexual practices mutate into cultural subjectivities. This distinction is thereby marked by the prefix *neo-*. What I am examining may be illustrated in two representative images that frame this chapter's focus (see figures 2.1 and 2.2). The first figure is adjudicated to the *bugarrón* and the second figure to the *neobugarrón*; I use these images to help theorize a transition that takes place in the historic-politico-theoretical space between *bugarrón* and *neobugarrón*.

As punctums, that is, moments of crystallization in the archive, these images work as discursive limits but also as representative figures of a transformation. They tell an occulted story of sexual practices, of the misapprehension of sexual constructs, and of the shifting economies of the Global South. But before we discuss them in detail, it is necessary to prepare the field of comprehension. Their story requires contextualization and explanation of neoliberal practices, sex tourism, and the political dynamics of globalization in Caribbean societies during the twentieth century.

The *bugarrón*'s location has shifted, and his position has suffered an unanticipated revitalization thanks to neoliberalism. Understood as "a socioeconomic philosophy," neoliberalism expresses inordinate confidence in "the unique, self-regulating power of markets as it links the freedom of the individual to markets" (Connolly, *Fragility* 20). In the Latin American and Caribbean contexts, neoliberalism has been the dominant economic model since the 1960s, that is, before expanding to the centers of capital in the US and Europe.[2] Neoliberal market ideology during the Cold War spread widely in the Global South and accelerated its pace in the Caribbean, seeking to contain the regional enthusiasm of an optimistic socialist revolution in Cuba. Referred to as "free market," neoliberal ideology became the preferred tool in a new globalist economic initiative against Fidel Castro's threat of exporting the Cuban experi-

---

2. On the history of neoliberalism in the Americas, David Harvey recounts that after the neoliberal changes pushed by the US in the Caribbean, the Southern Cone nation-states followed: "How was neoliberalization accomplished, and by whom? The answer in countries such as Chile and Argentina in the 1970s was as simple as it was swift, brutal, and sure: a military coup backed by the traditional upper classes (as well as by the US government), followed by the fierce repression of all solidarities created within the labour and urban social movements which had so threatened their power" (*Brief History* 39). Also, see Noam Chomsky's *Profit over People* for a closer look at US-sponsored neoliberal practices in Central America and the Caribbean during the 1960s and 1970s, esp. 19–40.

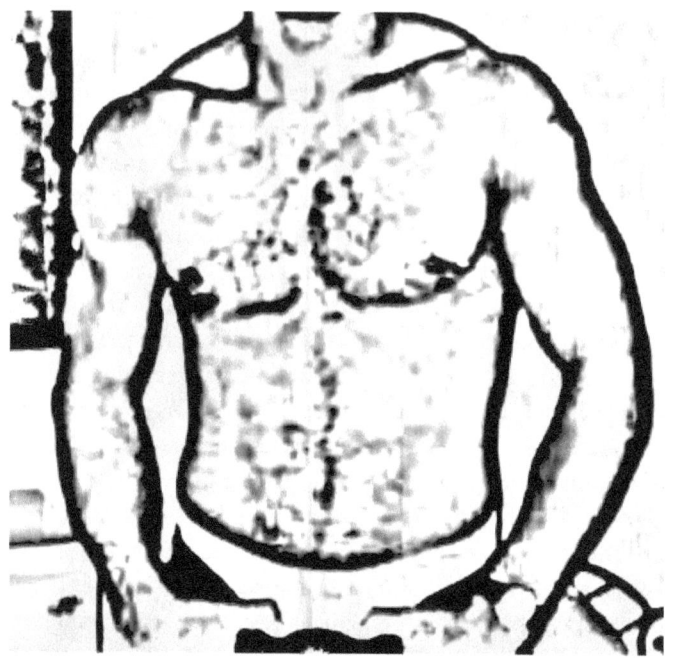

FIGURE 2.1. Drawing of a *bugarrón* ("Josué")

FIGURE 2.2. Typical online representation of *neobugarrón*

ment across the Americas. It is in this context of political containment and unregulated economic liberalization that traditional economies built on plantation agricultural models were meant to crumble and generate new markets.

I begin my analysis by explaining the *neobugarrón*'s emergence in the Caribbean relative to recent theoretical work on neoliberalism and the growing market of sex tourism, and I discuss attempts to capture the *neobugarrón* in sex work's ad media. Also, I analyze his presence via art and other aesthetic forms. Whereas the discourse of anthropology has failed to give visibility to the traditional *bugarrón* subject, and merely reproduced more complicated sexual anomalies, other technologies of visual narration managed to "capture" this newly constituted neoliberal sexual subject. I propose here that the *neobugarrón* achieved the cultural visibility that had been denied to the traditional *bugarrón*. This visibility troubles the understanding of the traditional *bugarrón* in the Americas by blurring the distinction between traditional and neoliberal types.

Furthermore, I elucidate how this visibility challenges our understanding of neoliberalism and of sexual market "identities" as commodity forms. If, as a result of neoliberal interventions, *bugarrón* as a sexual practice has mutated into a market type, this conversion muddles further the idea of neoliberal incorporation by emphasizing a need to conserve anti-identitarian forms of sexual intimacy. Neoliberalism undoes any claims of genuine authenticity as it advertises and profits from the visibility of anomalous sexual types. Whereas anthropology and governmentality sought to capture premodern forms, late twentieth-century neoliberalism incorporates old forms into market commodities. I illustrate how the *neobugarrón* sheds light on the interconnections between capitalism and sexuality. Here I theorize a *neobugarrón* subject who functions as a link, a market simulacrum, in a burgeoning self-regulated sector of the economy, thus making possible the transit of capital and the flow of pleasure and finance. Against the primary understanding of capital as a homogenizing force, I understand the *neobugarrón* as an example of what Vivek Chibber refers to as capital's diversifying effectiveness for "producing new heterogeneity" (*Postcolonial* 244). Therefore, I see the *neobugarrón* as a key component in the relationship between capital and sexuality in the Caribbean and the Global South.

CONSUMING THE NEOLIBERAL *BUGARRÓN*

In chapter 1, I examined the institutionalization of gay "identity" in Latin America as a strategy for containing the spread of HIV. That chapter explored the claim that the spread of gay "identity" in Latin America occurred hand in hand with the expansion of free market economic policies. But, I ask, what other sexual types have become visible thanks to shifts in the flow of capital? Recent anthropological work on globalized sexualities—such as Mark Padilla's *Caribbean Pleasure Industry* (2007), Kamala Kempadoo's *Sexing the Caribbean* (2004), E. Antonio de Moya and Rafael García's "Three Decades of Male Sex Work in Santo Domingo" (1999), and Amalia L. Cabezas's *Economies of Desire* (2009)—adds another layer to the understanding of the relationship between capitalism and sexuality. Whereas most of these anthropological works illustrate the explosion of sex tourism that emerges along with neoliberal policies, Padilla offers a deeper analysis of *bugarrón* sexual practice, explaining how the industry of sex tourism has revived an ostensibly outmoded practice. Emphasizing the transition from a traditional agricultural economy to one based primarily on the tourist industry, Padilla distinguishes a new *bugarrón* sexual practice from previous incarnations and argues that the contemporary *bugarrón* has become a neoliberal commodity type in its own right. The traditional *bugarrón* was considered a sexual practice that did not give rise to an "identity," and, as such, it defeated most attempts at capture in the social field by health organizations. Padilla's ethnographic study of sex work in the Dominican Republic shows that the *bugarrón* practice *does* give rise to a market type via capital. Yet his analysis also raises questions about how to make sense of the sexual subjects he studies; as a result, his book provides a golden opportunity for understanding the difference between sexual practice and sexual "identity" in contemporary culture. This is because Padilla's work conflates sexual "identity" and sexual practices, thereby inadvertently providing a misleading account of variations within heterosexuality. His book reveals the speed and complexity of social changes at historical junctures when shifts in sexual cultures challenge identitarian frameworks.

In *Caribbean Pleasure Industry*, Padilla shows how the traditional Latin American sexual practice of heterosexual males having sex with other males has become commodified. He argues that neoliberal economic practices such as deregulation, privatization, tax breaks to multinational corporations, low-paying jobs for local workers, and the busting of labor unions have dramatically increased male unemployment. In neoliberalism, where markets are determined globally, tourism has become the primary market for developing countries in the Caribbean. As he points out, the development of the tourist industry is based on a high percentage of tax breaks to private corporations and a greater increase in government coverage of corporate externalities.

Among the most vibrant sectors of Caribbean tourism is the so-called pleasure industry, of which gay tourism is a component. In Padilla's view, the process of globalization "commodifies—that is, produces a global demand for the 'production' of—certain expressions of masculinity and male sexuality" (*Pleasure Industry* 77). Global demand creates spaces for the development of a lucrative "marketable fantasy." This "marketable fantasy" is responsible for emergent self-regulated markets in which "a socially constructed desire . . . drives touristic sexual practices and consumption patterns, as well as providing an opening for local entrepreneurs to . . . 'get money out of the tourists'" (77). Padilla's perspective is consistent with Aihwa Ong's theory about spaces of opportunity that become possible once neoliberal market forces are unleashed.

Ong's key contention is that "neoliberal decisions have created new forms of inclusion" (*Neoliberalism* 5). Departing from the claim, belabored in Latin American cultural critique, that neoliberalism crudely exploits developing nations, Ong maintains there is an overlooked side of neoliberalism, in which we find "new spaces that enjoy extraordinary political benefits and economic gain" (5). In her view, neoliberalism's zoning technologies have carved "special spaces" where inducements for "self-animation and self-government" work to optimize efficiency, choices, and competitiveness (6). Where Ong sees neoliberal governmentality having a strategic hand in withdrawing regulation in order to create spaces of innovation, I see Padilla's *neobugarrón* subjects seizing on the displacement of manufacturing and its replacement in the form of tourist markets as a window of opportunity for improving their economic lot. Ong detects neoliberalism's "ethos of self-governing" in its ability to manufacture these spaces of possibility (9). Her "spaces of inclusion" demonstrate a double move: a market's inclusion (incorporation) of new economic spaces and a displaced subject's ability to capitalize on new appropriations and inclusions. Of course, Ong does not believe that all spaces have such optimistic outcomes or that all subjects are able to capitalize; her point, rather, is that there are some who do, and that those instances are worth studying. As sectors of society adopt the neoliberal market logic, they mutate into semiautonomous systems of networks and links designed to facilitate self-regulation. Sex tourism, as Chris Ryan and C. Michael Hall define it, is such an emerging market. The pleasure industry of sex tourism, as they see it, comprises "a series of links that can be conceptualized as one between a legally marginalized form of commodification (sexual services) within a national industry (entertainment), essentially dependent on, but with a dynamic function in an international industry" (*Sex Tourism* x).[3]

---

3. Padilla's approach is also consistent with David Harvey's critique that neoliberal spaces are marked by the deep inequalities that shape them (*Spaces* 18). According to Harvey, neoliberalism creates profoundly uneven growth areas, given that opportunity is entangled with exploitation, and innovation with hardship. The economic reality in those neoliberal economic zones requires subjects to be able to fit or to perish. Sharing Ong's and Harvey's perspectives, Padilla argues, "the political economy of sexuality requires us to view the globalization of sexuality in light of the large-scale inequalities that frame and condition the structures through which globalizing processes unfold" (*Pleasure Industry* 6). Economic inequality is one of the central tenets of Padilla's work, and he examines the connection between neoliberal governmentality and sex work.

Padilla's work intervenes in two academic discussions: the discourse of the commodification of otherness in pleasure industries, and the discourse of capital involvement in the construction of sexual "identities." Like Padilla, several scholars of Caribbean sex tourism have emphasized the economic inequality and history of commodification that give shape to developing areas of the Global South. For instance, Kempadoo points out that the Caribbean is no stranger to the production of commodity forms (*Sexing* 3). In actuality, she argues, its economies originated in centuries of imperial extraction. The depletion of natural resources and the commodification of African and Indigenous populations into an enslaved labor force lie at its origins. For Kempadoo, no text captures the *longue durée* of commodification in the Caribbean better than Mimi Sheller's *Consuming the Caribbean* (2003). There she describes how consumption has been a factor in the history of the region.

> During the period of colonial expansion there was an intensification of consumption within Europe and North America enabled by the wealth generated by the system of slavery. But there was also an attendant extension and proliferation of forms of consumption as Caribbean landscapes, flora and fauna, bodies and labour, images and cultural objects were all being consumed along with particular goods. It is not only "goods" which circulated in the transatlantic world economy, but also people, texts, images, desires, and attachments. (14)

In *Economies of Desire*, Amalia Cabezas concurs with Sheller and Kempadoo that "the global empire of capitalism . . . conflat[ed] emergent opportunities with old forms of oppression" (6). In this sense, for Cabezas there is a remarkable similarity between the inequality found in "sugar cane work" and the one found in "sex work" (11). On the subject, she claims, "the tourism corporate structure of the Caribbean . . . creates similar outcomes to the plantation economies" (5).

The political economy of sexuality is another academic discourse that Padilla's work engages. *Caribbean Pleasure Industry* provides a different twist on a decades-long debate about the relationship between sexual "identity" and the free market. Historians of gay "identity," such as John D'Emilio, trace the emergence of gay "identity" to changes in the mode of capitalist production during the middle decades of the nineteenth century:

> I want to argue that gay men and lesbians have *not* always existed. Instead, they are a product of history, and have come into existence in a specific historical era. Their emergence is associated with the relations of capitalism; it

has been the historical development of capitalism—more specifically, its free labor system—that has allowed large numbers of men and women in the late twentieth century to call themselves gay, to see themselves as part of a community of similar men and women, and to organize politically on the basis of that identity. ("Capitalism" 468; original italics)

D'Emilio delineates how the free labor market consolidates sexual practices into a politicized sexual "identity." By contrast, in *Gay New York* (1994), historian George Chauncey describes a shift in men's sexuality by identifying more strongly heterosexual limits to gender behavior during the onset of the Cold War. Chauncey points to the development of an ideological inflexibility of the boundaries between heterosexuality and homosexual behavior that coincides with mid-twentieth-century American prosperity. He emphasizes a cultural shift in which the rise of the middle class during the postwar era leaves behind the more sexually adventurous decade of the roaring 1920s. Where D'Emilio visualizes capitalism's role in the making of gay community formation, Chauncey adopts a more geopolitical perspective by emphasizing the Cold War effects on policing American male heterosexuality. Thus he points to self-regulation, or self-surveillance, of heterosexuality in a more strictly enforced heteronormativity at a moment of globalizing economic expansion.

Where D'Emilio understands inclusion in the wage labor force as an opportunity for anomalous sexual subjects in urban areas to become self-reliant outside the traditional family unit, Chauncey argues that the emergence of the middle class leads to the reinvigoration of heteronormativity in the Cold War period. The postwar era represents for Chauncey the rise of surveillance and self-regulation of heterosexuality and the taming of the 1920s excesses. These accounts suggest that the relationship between free markets and sexual "identity" formation remains undecided, in the sense that the two historical accounts lead to contradictory findings. On the one hand, D'Emilio finds that economic expansion paves the way for the formation of new sexual "identities"; on the other hand, Chauncey points to geopolitical factors that, in tandem with economic expansion, lead to the re-establishment of middle-class heterosexual "identity" and toward the invisibility of nonexclusive heterosexual sexual practices. If, as D'Emilio explains, there is a connection between the market need for the creation of wage labor and the emergence of gay "identity," then in Padilla's *Caribbean Pleasure Industry* we have a counterexample of a market type that works by remaining politically and socially invisible, precisely because the conditions of neoliberalism have transformed an economy based on formal wage labor to one based on service industries. At the same time, the geopolitical détente policies against the spread of communism, as a regional expression of a global cold war, make possible in the Caribbean a boom in visible *neobugarrón* sex work. In an inversion of Chauncey's account, where geopolitical factors create a recrudescence of heteronormativity and an invisibility of nonexclusive heterosexual subjects, the Global South shows geopolitical concerns leading to a loosening of sexuality and a marketable visibility of heteroflexible sexual practices. Yet in Padilla we encounter a new discursive wrinkle. Economic shifts lead to the "workings" of a sexual practice that resists the language of sexual "identity." His research explains the formation of sexual practices, failed "identities," and market forces pointing to an increasingly complex relationship between sexuality and capitalism.

STYLES OF REASONING AND PADILLA'S "IDENTITY" INDUSTRY

Neoliberalism creates the conditions for the emergence of a new *bugarrón* subject, one that has occluded and exceeded the limits of the traditional *bugarrón*. Padilla critiques those prophets of doom who argue that globalization and the spread of gay "identity" have made the *bugarrón* an "endangered species." It is as if Padilla were to ask, How can anyone claim that the *bugarrón* is extinct when field interviewees offer evidence of his existence? Padilla thus finds fault with Latin American scholars of male sexual cultures discussed in chapter 1, such as Richard Parker and Roger Lancaster, who argued that the spread of globalizing gay identity "entails an implicit assumption that the traditional *activo* is an 'endangered species'—an artifact of local sexual systems that will ultimately be displaced by globalizing notions of sexual identity" (Padilla, *Caribbean* 78; original italics). Padilla disagrees with the view that gay "identity" necessarily means the displacement of local sexual "identities" and practices: "The globalization of *gay* as it unfolds in the Dominican Republic should not be understood as a process that leads to the inevitable erasure of traditional identities and practices, but as one that incorporates, reworks, and commodifies particular constructions of sexuality *vis-à-vis* global capitalism" (103; original italics). Padilla argues that economic processes of globalization have incorporated local sexual practices to the point of modifying their cultural meaning:

> There is no reason to assume that the meanings of *bugarrón* today—incorporated as they are into tourism markets and processes of sexual commodification that extend far beyond the country's borders—have direct or unambiguous connections to the "traditional" Dominican sex/gender sys-

tem, since these meanings are now the products of global discourses and evolving representations of Dominican masculinity, *as well as* local cultural expressions. (102; original italics)

At this point in his argument, Padilla tips his hand to reveal that the *bugarrón*, or *activo* masculinity, that he studies is an "identity." He states: "I avoid analyzing Dominican *activo* identities as reflections of a presumably 'older' or more 'traditional' sex/gender system—an approach that tends to essentialize Dominican sexuality" (78; original italics). With this sentence, Padilla conflates two different perspectives into one. First, that *activo* (*bugarrón*) is a sexual "identity" in its own right, and second, that the contemporary commodified *activo* is not a "reflection" of the old *bugarrón*. Padilla believes that the concept of "traditional types" unavoidably "essentializes" those types. He misses the close connection between the concept of "identity" and that of essence—the latter signifying a retroactively attributed inherent trait to legitimize an "identity." Padilla considers the *bugarrón* not to be at risk of disappearing because this sexual "identity" has shown itself to be opportunistic and resilient. But where he sees a modification of the traditional *bugarrón* that makes its contemporary counterpart somewhat different, he remains bound to the disciplinary discourse of "identity."

In eliding the distinction between sexual practice and sexual "identity," Padilla forgets the biopolitical lessons of Michel Foucault. Sexual practices for Foucault occur outside the orbit of identity-making and "identity" construction. He explains that sexual "identity" construction is the result of the power/knowledge discourse that consolidates itself in the nineteenth century and that continues to shape Western thought to this date. In *History of Sexuality, Vol. 1*, Foucault provocatively argues that "the homosexual" as a psychological or clinical *type* emerges in the discourse of power/knowledge that developed as *scientia sexualis*.[4] In contrast to *ars erotica*, *scientia sexualis* is "the task of producing true discourses concerning sex . . . by adapting . . . the ancient procedures of confession to the rules of scientific discourse" (*History* 67–68). In his view, it is this discourse on human sexuality that constructs the homosexual as a subject that would evolve into an "identity." Once sex was "transform[ed] into discourse," then it could be "managed," that is to say, "inserted into systems of utility" (20, 24).

---

    4. Provocatively stating that the birth of homosexuality took place in 1870, Foucault argues that "homosexuality appeared as one of the forms of sexuality when it was transposed from the practice of sodomy onto a kind of interior androgyny, a hermaphroditism of the soul" (*History, Vol. 1*, 43). By contrast, *ars erotica* represented the experience of pleasure, that is to say, a long tradition of the arts of pleasure.

In terms of the 1990s discursive deployment of the traditional *bugarrón*, no study except Padilla's has claimed the *bugarrón* to be a sexual "identity." Indeed, previous studies struggle to make sense of a sexual practice that takes place under the umbrella of male heterosexuality. Padilla intervenes in this discourse and raises doubts about the authenticity of these subjects' claims. However, his ethnographic prodding shows his subjects' inability to justify logically their beliefs within the frame of his questions. That is because Padilla questions his interviewees in a discourse framed by concepts of "identity": "They very rarely express the desire to voluntarily disclose their sexual *identity*" (*Caribbean* 93; original italics). When subjects answer his specific question about sexual "identity" with the unsatisfying answer that they are "normal men" or simply "men," Padilla cannot help but write, "It was therefore somewhat difficult for some men to interpret questions that framed these identities as fixed personal traits" (92). There is a cleavage here between expert and subject. The latter assumes within Padilla's discourse the position of a subject who is supposed to know his own truth but doesn't. The gap between analyst and subject is profound. The interviewees' inability to comprehend their own sexual practices as "fixed" or as "framed identities" demonstrates less their lack of conceptual understanding than an unwillingness to make their sexual practices intelligible within the identitarian language that frames Padilla's questions. Padilla shows surprise when his interviewees "did not seem to feel that being a *bugarrón* . . . expressed a basic aspect of their identity" (92). In his view, these subjects' "side-stepping" of the importance of sexual "identity" means that they are in "disavow[al]," and in "denial" (94). Within Padilla's framework, those practices resemble a "fixed identity." In fact, the interviewees' refusal to acknowledge their true "fixed identity" makes sense to him only in terms of disavowal. Puzzled by someone who looks like and performs equal to *x* but claims not to be *x*, Padilla cannot help but misinterpret the practice as a disavowed "identity."[5] He does not see that he is misinterpreting them; in his view, they are hopelessly misinterpreting themselves. His queries displace

---

5. In *Three Essays on Sexual Theory* (1905), Freud lists "*contingent* inverts" as one of three types of inversions that fall under the general category of "perversion." He describes how this type practices sexual inversion under special circumstances, one of which could be the "inaccessibility of any normal sexual object" (137). It is striking that, like Padilla's interviewees and like the traditional *bugarrón* practitioner, members of this type "accept their inversion as something in the natural course of things, just as a normal person accepts the direction of *his* libido, and insist energetically that inversion is as legitimate as the normal attitude" (137). Freud attempts to illustrate that what is considered a perversion is in fact not one. In fact, according to Freud, psychoanalysis sets out for the "stretching of the concept of sexuality" to coincide "with the Eros of the divine Plato" (134). Padilla misses Freud's insight and persists in seeking the subject's truth in a supposedly disavowed sexual "identity."

the interviewed subjects' sexual practices onto a zone better described as out of place. Or, as Foucault put it in his *Archaeology of Knowledge*, these subjects' understanding of their sexuality places them in a different constellation of concepts, one where anomalous sexual practices are intelligible.

How can we explain this gulf between Padilla and his interviewees? In *The Emergence of Sexuality* (2001), Arnold I. Davidson argues that discourses are framed by what he calls "styles of reasoning." According to Davidson, thoughts and ideas are shaped by their own "system of concepts" (136). Narratives, arguments, and articulated thoughts cohere as discursive constructs because they are "internally related by a set of rules to form a structured conceptual space" (136). This conceptual "space," Davidson claims, is what Foucault called a "discursive practice" (136). For Davidson, Foucault's insight suggests how the emergence of new concepts requires the creation of a space where a new style of reasoning or thinking happens (137). A case in point would be the emergence of "the homosexual" in the nineteenth-century understanding of personhood. For Davidson, at crucial historical junctures we can find a fundamental incomprehension that keeps two types of discourses apart. Padilla articulates his anthropological insights at the time of dramatic historical changes between a traditional society and a neoliberal economy. The effect of this historical shift is felt on all emerging markets and on traditional gender roles. Readers of Padilla's account of his fieldwork are exposed to two concurrent ways of thinking about sexuality: Padilla's Western understanding of sexuality in terms of sexual identity and the interviewees' understanding of their experience in other terms. Padilla's work reveals the interviewer–interviewee interaction as a space of collision between two styles of sexual reasoning. *Bugarrón* practitioners understand their sex with men as a practice that does not have any bearing on their heterosexuality, and, as a result, Padilla's identitarian reasoning remains unintelligible to them. Instead, he argues that *bugarrones* are inconsistent because "these identities ... change from place to place, situation to situation" (*Caribbean* 92). However, that is not the case, because these subjects have demonstrated fairly consistently that they believe themselves (in their own style of reasoning) to be heterosexual men—what they call "normal" men.

These "normal" men, who have sex with men, continue to view themselves as heterosexual. Their concept of heterosexuality is inclusive of sexual encounters with men. Confronted with these subjects' different style of reasoning, Padilla's discourse exudes an imperial, condescending tone implying that they fail to grasp what they are saying, and, further still, who they are. Insisting that these subjects' "identities" are unstable, Padilla contends, perhaps a bit condescendingly, that they find "difficult" to understand the concept of sexual "identity." From the perspective of Padilla's discourse of power/knowledge, their sexual practices are in reality "repressed" sexual "identities."[6]

My critique here is not intended to condemn Padilla, for his blindness turns out to be, despite his avoidance, quite revealing. After all, Padilla's misconceptions lead us in the right direction by clarifying the distinction between "reality" and "simulation." Unaware of the "epistemic break" he was addressing, and sure of his sexual "identity" framework, Padilla claims: "I avoid analyzing Dominican *activo* identities as reflections" of the traditional *bugarrón* (78). Padilla remains unaware that it is precisely the neoliberal *bugarrón* as "reflection" of the traditional *bugarrón* that is of importance. His tunnel vision of "identity" has led him to a crucial discovery that he fails to grasp. I venture past Padilla's avoidance by arguing that, in fact, the neoliberal *bugarrón* is not simply a reflection but, rather, a simulation. Although emerging market types of sex work should not be confused with "traditional" types, it is also important to recognize that new market types increase their *salability* by tapping into the alluring legacy of an exotic *activo* masculinity. Where Padilla sees the resignification of a sexual "identity" provoked by a growing pleasure industry, I see the emergence of a simulated market type. This new *bugarrón* is the product of a recombined global assemblage that gives "vital life" to an old form. Here I refer to the emerging market that provides gay consumers with an exoticized traditional sexual practice that, in order to market itself, mirrors the language of "identity." The transformation that anthropological research corroborates is one in which an economically driven *neobugarrón* succeeds the traditional practitioner of *bugarrón* sex.

In other words, the discourses of power/knowledge (anthropology, health discourses) have conjured a *bugarrón* subject out of a practitioner of traditional *bugarrón* sex in the process of tracking and surveillance. Once *bugarrón* subjectivity has been created, it becomes fair game for use and abuse by the discourses of power/knowledge or by cultural strategies of survival. The newly constructed subject resists political identification but uses his practices *as if they were* a sexual "identity." *Neobugarrón* marks a shift from a culture regulated by the practice of lust to a society governed by the marketing of economic "identities."

The neoliberal *bugarrón*, or *neobugarrón*, is a different construct altogether from the traditional *bugarrón*. Neoliberalism in Latin America marks

---

6. Padilla adjudicates a disjuncture between reality and fiction in his interviewed subjects. He claims that they are unable to distinguish wish from reality. They conceive mutually exclusive concepts, concepts that narrate a difference, as inclusive. In his view, their logic inverts the purpose of categorization by unmaking distinctions that are at stake in the process of knowledge formation.

this rupture in the history of the *bugarrón*, where the social apparatuses that gave vitality to the traditional *bugarrón* have become obsolete. If, for the most part, studies of Latin American neoliberalism have focused on issues of class inequality and the deleterious effects of free market practices, the impact on sexual cultures has been filtered through the study of "identities." The discourse of power/knowledge that saw its birth during nineteenth-century imperial Europe has spread globally. The marketing of "identities" is successful because it not only categorizes but also provides classifications for easily filtered searches. Marketable "identities" make it easier for consumers (or interested parties) to fulfill a want.

However, the emergence of the *neobugarrón* in the marketplace signals the disappearance of traditional *bugarrón* sexual practice. At stake here is not an evolutionary account of *bugarrón* "identity" but rather a rupture in the cultural history of *bugarrón* sexual practice. This is a rupture in which one type superimposes itself on another. The story of transformation ends up occluding a geopolitically induced break, manifested in the *neobugarrón*'s veering from eros to capital. In other words, a lethal shift has taken place: from a sexual practice seeking pleasure—considered to be under the umbrella of heterosexuality—to commercialized sex work. Now sexual "identities" sell the mystique of an authentic "anomalous" pleasure. The marketing of this sexual "identity," and the utilitarian logic that this conveys, dismisses the nonutilitarian, nonproductive character of the traditional *bugarrón* practice. Unlike a highly politicized gay "identity," the *neobugarrón* is a *market* "identity" simulating a sexual "identity" construct that never existed as such, and one that attains visibility only as a commodity. To repeat: *neobugarrón* is a market "identity" that simulates a sexual "identity." Accordingly, the *neobugarrón* achieves visibility by means of the "invisible hand," in the market of trading pleasures. The lure of traditional exoticism grants this sexual "identity" a quality beyond itself that is key to the system of commodity exchange. Tradition as a cultural resource vests sexual "identity" with a new dose of market value. However, outside the mirror of production, this simulation remains invisible as if it were but a reflection in a mirror.

For nonexperts, it would be easy to confuse the simulacrum of a market "identity" with the "real" thing. By overlooking the epistemic break triggered by neoliberal economic practices, an untrained eye may fail to appreciate its impact on the making of simulated "identities." Jean Baudrillard proposes that the logic and effect of the market have been so influential in contemporary times that "identities" are produced in a world of simulations or market differences. He defines simulation as that which "threatens the difference" between the "'true' and the 'false,'" the "'real' and the 'imaginary'" (*Simulacra* 3). For

Baudrillard, contemporary capitalist developments assure that "never again will the real have the chance to produce itself" (2).[7] Like commodities, "identities" function by demarcating their differences. The *neobugarrón* has marketed this difference by selling himself as an "identity" while claiming not to be one, thus heightening his mystique and salability.

Of course, when in *Das Capital* (1885) Marx characterizes the commodity as a "very queer thing," he did not have in mind the *neobugarrón* subject (vol. 1, 76). Instead, he refers to that change that takes place when, for instance, a wooden table becomes a commodity and suddenly becomes linked to a commodity chain where "it is changed into something transcendent" (76). Describing this newly acquired characteristic as the "mystical character of commodities," Marx clarifies that this supplement does not originate from commodities' use value or nature (76). Having "absolutely no connexion with their physical properties and with the material relations arising therefrom," the acquired characteristic transforms the commodity into a "mysterious thing" (77). Marx ends his explanation of commodity by pondering, What would commodities say if they could speak? He answers his own query: "In

---

[7]. Baudrillard uses the example of a patient who, in faking his illness, develops the symptoms associated with the real disease. He asks, "Is the simulation sick or not, given that he produces 'true' symptoms?" (*Simulacra* 3). I find interesting the link between simulation and psychosomatic symptoms because it provides a connection with Foucault's sense of the origins of psychiatric power and the creation of an identity, the hysteric, during the last decades of the nineteenth century. Investigating a capillary form of disciplinary power that developed during that period, Foucault studies the emerging institutions of psychiatry as vectors of power that crossed Western societies diagonally. For instance, institutions such as asylums and hospitals instituted policies of permanent visibility ("methods of observation") regarding their patients. If psychiatric power developed as the institutionalization of "mastery" over illness, then it is not surprising that the construction of the hysteric crisis emerges in the late nineteenth century with its "magnificent symptoms" as a resistance strategy (*Psychiatric* 174, 254). The hysteric creates a niche in the spaces opened by the state's retreat and the rise of disciplines of mental health. "Identity" and "resistance" are terms entrenched in hysterical constructions of modern subjectivity. Psychosomatic symptoms, or simulations, characterized the exacerbation of symptomatic clusters. Bodily attacks such as seizures and spasms represented moments of resistance to psychiatric power. That is to say, as Foucault, puts it, "you want this trauma, well, you will get all my life, and you won't be able to avoid hearing me recount my life and, at the same time, seeing me mime my life anew and endlessly reactualize it in my attacks" (*Psychiatric* 322). The emergence of this type of simulation represented a problem not only for psychiatric knowledge but also for the economic side of medicine. As Foucault explains, "the problem at this time, still in terms of profit, is whether they should be considered as patients, and so covered by insurance, or as malingerers (*simulateurs*)" (*Psychiatric* 314; original italics). The hysteric nonorganic illness, by emphasizing posttraumatic psychological disorders, placed pressure on an emerging economy of health and on the study of sexuality in order to understand the trauma behind the visible seizures of a "hysteric's victory cry" (322). In this way, the hysteric becomes not only a new medical subject and a new insured subject. Its emergence brings together the study of a new subjectivity with studies of simulation and the economy.

the eyes of each other we are nothing but exchange-values" (87). Having transcended their exchangeable value in the marketplace, commodities are no longer anchored in "true essence" or "inherent value," as these have also become selling points. To Padilla and others, the *neobugarrón* says precisely what he is selling: sex with a hetero man who is "not gay."[8] Padilla refuses to hear the "not gay" packaging of a marketable sexual commodity. After all, Padilla is not a consumer advocate looking for fraud (although readers may sense this inclination); he is an "identity" surveillance officer wanting subjects to reattach themselves to something akin to the truth of "identity." As a politicized anthropologist, Padilla becomes an "identity" consciousness-raiser at best, or an "identity" propagator at worst. During the height of neoliberalism in Latin America, the *neobugarrón* transcended the *bugarrón*. The market has made sexual practices of the "not gay" male subject a visible product. Padilla's monster of disavowal has become a commodified pleasure in the "mystical" marketplace of consumer culture.

---

8. The "not gay" of *neobugarrón* commodity resonates with Jane Ward's concept of "not gay," a practice by young white straight men that is found in greater concentration in US frat house culture. Sexually themed hazing and other fraternity pranks of a sexual nature are understood in terms of a new male heteroflexibility. Heteroflexibility, according to Ward, is composed of a set of uniquely white heteromasculine styles of reasoning such as "sex with men is often necessary, patriotic, character-building, masculinity-enhancing" (*Not Gay* 25). Heteroflexibility also understands sex with men as "paradoxically, a means of inoculating oneself against authentic gayness" (25). As a result, homosexual contact appears to be part of a "basic fabric of human sexuality, and central even to the social organization of heterosexuality" (26). The difference between white heteroflexibility, the "not gay" found in the US, and the one discovered by Padilla centers on the economic necessity that drives the *neobugarrón* subject to market this sexual practice in the neoliberal marketplace. Similar to the traditional *bugarrón*, the heteroflexibility of white men seems to be connected to pleasure via rite of passage rituals. Ward's "not gay" is a rationalized form of bonding, fun, and pleasure, and ultimately, it serves a purpose: a way to keep gayness at bay. In terms of what is suspected of the traditional *bugarrón* practice, he seems always already inoculated from devolving into gayness despite his pleasure in having sex with men. Unlike the traditional *bugarrón*, the heteroflexible "not gay" man posits his heterosexuality in contrast to a more or less accepted gay "identity." The claim "not gay" is a negative confirmation indicating that what one does should not be understood as a "sexual identity" (9, 30). As Ward explains, the newness of this practice is not really new, as sexuality according to Sigmund Freud and others such as Alfred Kinsey has always been understood as fluid or as a spectrum of sexual possibilities. Ward has explained the difficulty of understanding heteroflexible males as "not gay" in the era of gay acceptance. As she argues, the pressure seems to be at the level of politics. How can a sexual "identity" (hetero) perform what another sexual "identity" (homo) has struggled to make acceptable to society? Heteroflexibility happens, but it is not an identitarian movement. *Neobugarrón* subjects share this characteristic. What makes this newly emergent market type paradoxical is the fact that it seeks neither a minoritarian sexual identity nor a political agency.

THE SOCIAL PHOTO

This Is Not a *Bugarrón*: The Simulacrum

Adopting some of Padilla's insights but also going beyond them, I would like to exemplify *neobugarrón* subjectivity by examining closely an instance where the *bugarrón* seems to have been captured as an image (see figure 2.1 on page 48).

This is the case of Josué Pérez, a.k.a. "El Martillo" or, in English, "the Hammer." Born in the Dominican Republic on November 1, 1970 (and about thirty years old at the time the web page describing him was live), Josué is the son of Carmen Guzman and José Pérez.[9] We know these details about Josué because of his occupation, which was listed, on a now-defunct web page, as *bugarrón*. The web page, which in 2002 was the only component of the website bugarron.com, translated *bugarrón* as "homosexual prostitute."[10] The web page listed Josué's date of birth, his identification number ("008-12418345-7"), and the name of his father and mother and promised visitors that pictures of his brothers and sisters were forthcoming. If an essential component of *neobugarrón* practice is a double life where the immediate family remains unaware of the sexual activity that their ostensibly heterosexual father, husband, or brother practices with other males, then this web page transgressed that limit and invited a public gaze into a very intimate space in the *neobugarrón*'s life. Exposed were not only the *bugarrón* but also his familial network. Anthropology tells us that essential to this compartmentalization is a code of silence: the family does not ask and the *neobugarrón* does not tell what takes place outside the home. This web page directly violated those unwritten norms and thus sought to expose the *neobugarrón* and his relatives to public shame.

---

9. All biographical data have been changed; in some cases, drawings have been used instead of photos, and heads have been cropped to protect the identity of social subjects in this chapter.

10. De Moya and García define *sanky-pankies* as *gigolos* or *activo* masculine "young men who sell sex to both male and female tourists in beach towns" ("Three Decades" 128). They are part of a wide *bugarrón* mythology in the Dominican Republic because, during the first decades of the twenty-first century, *bugarrón* becomes the preferred term in the pleasure industry, as it conveys a more desirable masculine connotation. The antonym of the *bugarrón* and *sanky-panky* in the Caribbean is the anally receptive man derogatorily called *pájaro* (bird, queer) or *maricón* (fag).

In 2002, bugarron.com was a web page that served as a warning to potential customers of Josué.[11] Its function as a cyber signpost for crime prevention lent it a type of law enforcement "WANTED" flavor. But in this case, it was a warning *against* wanting Josué. The page was designed not to help capture the delinquent "Hammer" but to dissuade wanting / desiring / looking for him. The site basically told you that the Hammer was a very bad boy and that one should not want bad boys. Yet the photograph at the center (figure 2.1) was in tension with the page's overall intention, since it did not resemble a typical mug shot on a wanted sign, where the menacing gaze of a violent suspect sends shivers down our spines. We get a different sensation from the colored photograph of a copper-skinned, muscular, fit, clean-cut, and shirtless Dominican man. Not only do we have a sense of the culprit's great arms and body; we also can appreciate the symmetry of his face: his great jaw, thick lips, and perfect light-brown skin. This very intimate photo of an evil being was perhaps taken by one of Josué's customers, or even by one of his victims; it might also have been taken by one of Josué's friends to help him advertise his business—although it was used on the page for a different purpose. Its origin is uncertain. Below the picture, the web page promised more photos, but the link was dead.

Today, as noted, the web page has been removed. The fact that at some point visitors were able to view a photo album of Josué sheds some light on the relationship between Josué and the person who made the web page, but we remain unsure whether it is the work of a victim, a spurned lover, or a concerned citizen.

The web page's text was written in Spanish and in English, which points to Josué's potential customer base in both the Dominican Republic and the US. The English text told readers that Josué was "dangerous":

> He is a dangerous homosexual prostitute (**Bugarron**) who works in the capital of the Dominican Republic taking advantage of unaware tourists. Until the end of May 2003, he was using Aire Club, a homosexual bar in the Colonial sector of Santo Domingo, as his operation center. "El Martillo" has already defrauded two American Tourists, one in excess of $20,000 by using credit cards to purchase commodities, which landed him in jail for a few days. **BE VERY CAREFUL WITH THIS MAN, HE IS A WOLF IN SHEEP'S CLOTHING AND HAS NO QUALMS ABOUT TAKING**

---

11. Today's website, bugarron.outpersonals.com, is nothing like the single web page where the warning about Josué appeared. Not unexpectedly, over the years, bugarron.com has morphed from a web page in 2002 to a blog in 2005 to a dating site with a blog as of 2022.

ANYONE WHO GETS INVOLVED WITH HIM TO THE CLEANERS. BEWARE!!! (bugarron.com; bold in original)

The Spanish text provided further clarification on "why Josué [was] so dangerous" by mentioning that he carried a gun. It also told us that his modus operandi was to play nice guy and that after gaining your trust, he robbed you. The language used, "espaldarazo mortal," meaning "mortal betrayal," indicates a personal connection between the writer of the text and Josué. Furthermore, readers were told that when a robbery took place, Josué did not act alone but that members of his immediate family helped him. This conflates identity theft with armed robbery and, possibly, gang robbery by the Pérez family. The web page captures Josué for us in a manner that anthropological research fails to.

However, the idea that we have finally captured the *bugarrón* in image form or that Josué is a real *bugarrón* may be misleading. We need only be reminded here of Roland Barthes's reflection, in *Camera Lucida,* that "a photograph is always invisible: it is not it that we see" (6). When posing for a photograph, Barthes says, "I instantaneously make another body for myself, I transform myself in advance into an image" (10). Josué's pose in the photo approximates the standard pose found in the marketing of the *bugarrón* to gay consumers in the US via internet sites such as LatinMenSociety.com (see figure 2.2 on page 48).

The idea of an original *bugarrón* fades in the uncertainty about which is the referent and which is the copy. Is Josué mimicking the dudes of LatinMenSociety.com, or are they copying a Josué-idea of a traditional *bugarrón* masculine pose? At the same time, we find ourselves perplexed by the proliferation of meanings for the *bugarrón*—from sex worker to "homosexual prostitute." *Bugarrón* (referring to a straight guy) seems opposed to "homosexual prostitute" (meaning a homo guy) by definition. What are the limits of *neobugarrón* sexual practice? Although in general, websites use the term *bugarrón,* Josué is in fact a *neobugarrón,* that is, the simulation of a traditional *bugarrón,* now selling these practices of sexuality for profit. Neoliberalism has freed the term *bugarrón* of its original singular signification. It has been transformed into a marker for the free-floating signifier of a commodity exchange.

In the neoliberal marketability of Caribbean sexuality, questions of referent or origin become muddled, since both Josué and the men of LatinMenSociety.com are *neobugarrones,* that is to say, images of images of a questionably authentic practice. As market images of trade types, they have eroded distinctions between traditional and new. The impact of this collapse of difference raises doubts concerning traditional *bugarrón* existence. If a traditional *bugarrón* was never captured in writing or in image, how can his existence be attested? Josué's photograph puts us in the position of the viewer/consumer/capturer/stranger who desires and judges him. His photograph deploys a double invisibility. Josué's gaze stares at we who are invisible to him, as we are in the space outside the frame, in the field of invisibility.[12] Yet, as Barthes points out, Josué remains invisible to us, since by posing as a commodity he invents a different body and a different kind of *bugarrón*. As a commodity-image, Josué is not what we see.

A Land of Cops and Robbers

By 2005, bugarron.com had transformed into a blog. On Saturday, November 12, an entry was posted with the simple heading "Beware." As with Josué's case, the post warns clients about Ismael, a *neobugarrón* in the Dominican Republic. The post begins by telling us a sad story: "Ismael used to be one of the nicest guys you could meet. He had a car, and an arrogance that was mildly appealing. Unfortunately, drugs have gotten the best of him." Ismael has begun robbing clients and tourists to satisfy his need for illegal substances; the post warns that he represents a danger to sex tourists. As evidence, the blog narrates a recent incident that shows Ismael's dangerous new behavior: "Very late

---

12. In *The Order of Things* (1966), Foucault conveys the centrality of invisibility in the seventeenth-century aesthetics of Velazquez's painting *Las Meninas, or Maids of Honor* (1656). Providing one of the most sophisticated readings of this complex work of art, Foucault reveals the foundational void at the heart of Velazquez's composition. That is to say, the painting portrays the "necessary disappearance of that which is its foundation" (16). According to Foucault, this painting marks the rupture with the Renaissance world of resemblance and the shift toward the classical world of representation. Taking us first through an analysis of the focal point in the painting and looking very closely at the orthogonal lines, Foucault traces for us an entire picture that is "looking out at a scene for which it is itself a scene" (14). In the same way, Josué looks at a scene that is outside the frame and that is, after all, a scene of a john or a friend taking his picture. This scene outside the spectator's scene leads Foucault to argue that in *Las Meninas* we find a center that is of necessity "doubly invisible" (8). Foucault states: "The profound invisibility of what one sees is inseparable from the invisibility of the person seeing—despite all mirrors, reflections, imitations, and portraits" (16). The viewer is "force[d]" to enter the picture and is assigned a place that is "at once privileged and inescapable" (5). For Foucault, it is precisely this gesture of controlling the viewer's relationship to the work that permits invisibility to dominate the field of vision. The viewer, Foucault argues, "sees his invisibility made visible to the painter and transposed into an image forever invisible to himself" (5). Of course, there is a double invisibility at play here: the sovereign authority outside the painting whose trace is invisible yet reproduced as a mirrored image. In our case, with Josué we are spared the looking-glass reflection. As such, our viewpoint resides in the domain of pure invisibility, that is to say, in a spot where we can see his image but remain outside the realm of what his eyes can see. The invisible spectacle outside the frame is the viewer's gaze. On Foucault's reading of *Las Meninas*, see Tanke, *Foucault's Philosophy* 27–28.

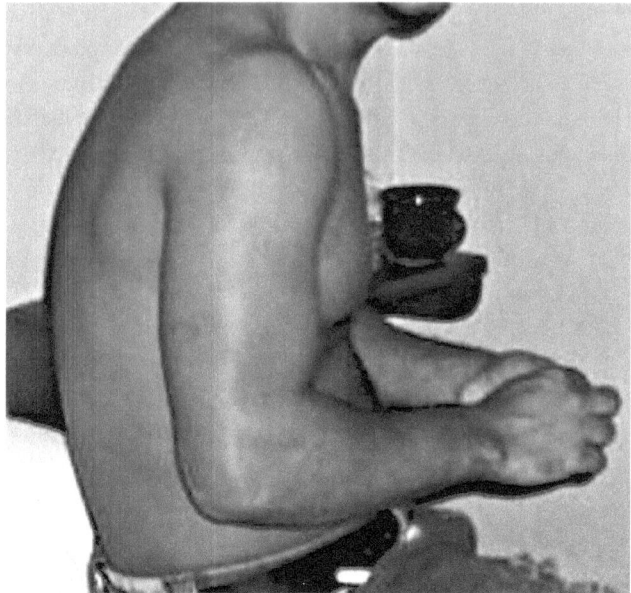

FIGURE 2.3. *Bugarrón* social photo ("Ismael")

Thursday night he followed a tourist walking back to his hotel and snatched his watch from his arm. The watch was a Rolex and very expensive." Nothing else is said about the episode, and there is no mention of reporting the incident to the police.

The photograph that accompanies the blog post (see figure 2.3) shows Ismael seated on what appears to be a bed. We see a white pillow behind him and, at the top left corner, a white reading lamp. Ismael is shirtless, his body positioned at the picture's center. The camera angle, which shows him in a flattering partial profile, draws the gaze to the left eye and eyebrow. Ismael's dark-brown eyes and dark eyebrows are complemented by well-trimmed, dark-brown curly hair, a faded goatee, and copper tanned skin. We glimpse Ismael's white teeth through his semi-open lips. He looks pleased, semi-asleep with what we intuit is a relaxed afterglow. His well-defined left arm and broad shoulder frame his chest and stomach, and we have a partial view of his solid pectoral muscles. He is wearing blue jeans, and his black belt is visible just below the abdominal area. His arms are in front of him, and he is doing something with them. Counting money? Opening something? The camera does not show us what he is doing, yet the look on his face signals that he is pleased. Unlike Josué's picture, Ismael's photo takes us to a new level of intimacy. The photo of a *bugarrón* in the bedroom, seated on a bed, triggers the imagination.

Bugarrón photos are interesting to think with, and Ismael's photo fits quite well Merleau-Ponty's idea of how to approach images. For Merleau-Ponty, the challenge is not simply to plainly see an image but to "see according to it, or with it" ("Eye and Mind" 126).

The bedroom background evokes the reversal of a scene in John Rechy's *City of Night* (1963). Rechy's novel is composed of a series of vignettes in which a male sex worker listens to his clients' life stories. In *City of Night,* each chapter voices a different storyteller, that is, a different client. If, in Rechy's novel, the sex worker listens to his clients' stories, in this post we listen to Ismael's client telling his story. This reversal, where the client speaks not about himself but about the sex worker, flips the convention of the sympathetic sex worker who provides comfort to his or her clients. The blog post narrates Ismael's downward spiral into a world of drug addiction and crime. In this context, we may consider the Ismael of the photo, half-naked, vulnerable, and pleased. Is this the precriminal Ismael before his fall from *neobugarrón* grace? When we see the social photo of a *neobugarrón,* we notice his likeness, but this visibility emphasizes the fact that in the process Ismael's image remains muted.

The post provides tips for what visitors should wear in public when touring the area where Ismael works. The site also provides advice for how tourists can protect themselves. The most important tip appears at the end of the post: "If you see Ismael, RUN!" The blogger's warning spurred other clients to provide anecdotes of their encounters with Ismael. One claimed that Ismael had been a "bugarron since he was young" and provided information about Ismael's online profile: "He is very famous in the internet, his alias is Chiquito ('Lil one'), go to www.panterboys.com or www.amazonaboy.com to see him in his full glory." Those sites no longer exist; the links are dead. Another client shared a story of how Ismael stole his Unica underwear after having sexual intercourse with him. According to him, Ismael could not find anything else to steal, given that the client had placed all his valuables in the hotel's security safe. So, unable to steal a watch, money, or jewelry, Ismael engaged in what could be considered the last trade of the evening: "He stole my new Unico underwear and left his dirty underwear behind in my drawer. His underwear was SOOOOO dirty that I was pissed that they were even in the drawer with my underwear."

This conversation goes on to reveal another vital component in the neoliberal biopolitics of a Global South city. According to another respondent, a handsome local policeman is known to have been using his charm as a *bugarrón* to entrap gay men into coming on to him. The comment reads: "There is one particular policemen named Martinez who is an expert at extorting money from the gay tourists. . . . He is very handsome and uses that to get the extortion started." In *Simulacra and Simulations,* Baudrillard warns us that the law is unforgiving of those who impersonate law enforcement or a criminal activity: "Simulate a robbery . . . how do you persuade security that it is a simulated robbery?" (20). But, what if you have a guard, a policeman, simulating a *bugarrón*? And what if this takes place at the heart of a *neobugarrón* marketplace? Simulation is here turned on its head as the cop, simulating a *bugarrón,* extorts money from those prospective *neobugarrón* clients. In this paradoxical setup, the *neobugarrón* marketplace ends up lending authenticity to Martinez as a real *bugarrón.* Where other *bugarrones* are playing the *bugarrón* game for money, Martinez is not selling sex but rather presents himself as willing to engage in *bugarrón* sexual practice, thus embodying the "real" *bugarrón* modus operandi. That is the fantasy, until the moment when extortion is revealed as the true aim. In this case, the law of simulations finds reversibility by a simulation making a fake look authentic. At the same time, the logic of the law is turned upside down by a representative of law enforcement participating in criminal tactics. A supposedly straightforward post about a potential *bugarrón* criminal (Ismael) has exposed another layer in the world of *neobugarrón* simulations: the tactic of a simulated *bugarrón* as bait for police entrapment. This is a case of a double simulation, as *bugarrón* and as legitimate enforcer of the law.

To *Bugarrón,* Take Route C

Another blog post on bugarron.com, "Mis [*sic*] Bugarron," introduces us to a *bugarrón* on-site in the municipality of San Pedro de Macoris in the Dominican Republic. This town is located in a high-transit area between the capital, Santo Domingo, and the tourist area named La Romana. Macoris is well known because two major highways intersect there, one leading to the northern part of the Dominican Republic and the other to the eastern tourist area of the island. Along this route, the blogger exposes an individual whom he names "Mis [*sic*] Bugarron." The description is brief, but the post includes a picture (see figure 2.4).

The entry, dated March 7, 2007, names the *neobugarrón* as Javier. Unlike Josué's example, the post doesn't include surnames, parental names, or the names of his brothers and sisters. It only has a specific location: Route C. The picture accompanying the post is of a young Afro-Caribbean man wearing black underwear and covering his bulge with his hands. Wearing a hat, sunglasses, and a silver military dog tag around his neck, Javier stares at the

FIGURE 2.4. *Buqarrón* social photo ("Javier")

camera, assuming a pose. Unlike Josué's, Javier's body is not what we would normally call a gym body; he comes across as slender by today's standards.

We learn that Javier's line of work is "Cobrador de la Ruta C," that is, he works as a "highway toll collector in Route C." The post informs us that his "hobbie" is to "fuck every gay man at the Universidad Central del Este for money." Also, it explicitly tells readers that he makes "gay men pay for him to fuck them." It is not clear whether he is an actual "toll collector" or whether this term serves as a euphemism to signal his sex "trade." Javier is referred to as "Mis" because in the eyes of the blogger he is now a "pajaro escondido," that is, "a closeted gay man." The blogger seems to adhere to a particular rationality about *bugarrón* sexual practice and sexual "identity" similar to the one found in Padilla. Adopting a gossip column style, the blogger warns Javier about the open secret of his behavior, telling us, "He thinks nobody knows what he is up to." The blogger believes that a "gay man wants to keep him as a kept man" ["un maricon lo quiere mudar"]. The post ends with a warning: "May God protect him from any gay man who would like to fuck him in return." This warning positions gay versatility against *bugarrón* sexual practice by raising the possibility that one of his clients may seek to reverse Javier's role during sex.

Given that tourists search the internet for information about their travel destinations, it is unsurprising that *neobugarrón* warnings appear online. The internet has become the primary marketplace for *neobugarrones* in the twenty-first century. Over the years, bugarron.com has evolved into a website with a blog that intervenes in the *neobugarrón* marketplace and seeks an effect by alerting future clients to hidden dangers. To be more effective, sites of this kind usually post pictures, which become what Nathan Jurgenson defines as social photos, not mug shots. As "media objects," they function as units of communication because "they transmit a general alertness" (*Social* 15). From this perspective, the aesthetic value typical of the work of art (photography) is subordinated to the image's "circulation as communication" (15). Jurgenson explains that social images are "a kind of visual speaking," that is to say, "forms of sociality" (16). This attribute of social images becomes useful in making sense of the photos accompanying the warning posts of *bugarrón* subjects. As a form of "visual communication," Josué's and Ismael's images are communicated as social warnings. "There is a pleasant contradiction in a photograph," Jurgenson argues, because "at once it traps life and sets it free" (35). On the one hand, he understands photographs as technologies where the "ephemerality of lived experience is captured and made docile for later viewing" (35). The photograph documents, that is, serves as "proof" of, an ephemeral "lived experience" (35). Jurgenson's argument resonates with works on the evidentiary use of images by Susan Sontag and Jennifer Mnookin.

For instance, in *On Photography* (1977), Sontag states that photographs "furnish evidence. Something we hear about, but doubt, seems proven when we're shown a photograph of it" (5). Likewise, in her seminal essay on photography, "The Image of Truth" (1998), Mnookin expands on Sontag's viewpoint by asserting that "seeing a photograph almost functions as a substitute for seeing the real thing" (2). For Mnookin, the photograph serves as "demonstrative evidence" (5). Javier's photograph serves the purpose of "*making the criminal visible*" (Finn, *Capturing* viii; original italics). However, in this particular case, Javier's violation refers not only to breaking local laws but to transgressing the morals of his community.

Whereas the other examples of *bugarrón* blog posts communicate with past, future, and present clients of Josué and Ismael, in the case of Javier the blog post is a warning to the *bugarrón* himself. The post raises the specter of Javier's falling into trouble at the hands of his clients ("May God protect him from any gay man who would like to fuck him in return"). It alerts Javier to the fact that members of his local community are aware of his antics. They know his behavior and, as a result, his reputation is at stake. This is an unequivocal warning to Javier. In *Discipline and Punish* (1977), Foucault argues that the disappearance of the practice of punishment as a spectacle coincided with the emergence of a different practice of justice. One practice disappeared and another emerged: "The disappearance of punishment as a spectacle . . . survived only as a new legal or administrative practice" (8). As Finn argues in *Capturing the Criminal Image* (2009), for Foucault the new disciplinary regime is visibility (4).

A community member is exposing Javier, stating openly what everyone has learned about his behavior. Making his behavior visible is a form of public shaming. More important for this project is that the community interprets Javier's antics in the discourse of *scientia sexualis*. For this tourist zone community near the country's capital, *bugarrón* sexual practice signifies something different. It does not signify the heterosexual flexibility of foregone years but rather the behavior of a modern gay man. This blog unveils that another constellation of interpretive values has emerged to describe the local meaning of *bugarrón* sexual practice in a new way. Javier's case reveals how a social photo becomes a nodal point of contradictions, signifying at the same time *bugarrón*, closeted gay man, kept man, target of community ostracism, and subject of potential anal penetration.

Jurgenson argues that a photograph "captures the ephemerality of life" and as such serves as "proof" of a lived experience. At the same time, he points out that there is another side to a photograph. In his view, the ephemeral living experience that the photograph captures "is also enlivened by this trapping" (*Social* 35). The photograph used to expose and corroborate Javier's antics gives the *bugarrón*'s seductive image a particular power; it lends Javier's transient experience a seductive permanence. For those attracted to Javier, his photo gives the "toll collector" a "power to live on, even if it must be wrestled into the confines of a static frame" (35). The photo signals to blog readers that there is a *neobugarrón* ready to collect his payment in an easy stop and in a convenient location. If there has been a particular "joy" associated with the transferring of the real "Mis [sic] bugarron" image into a lasting visual document of social shame and condemnation, this is not clear on the blog. Could the blogger's intention, of keeping Javier in check, have led to an increase in demand for Javier's services? Is he collecting a bounty? The post may make us wonder: How many other eager travelers would quickly change their driving route so that they can pay Javier his "toll"?

Buggaron [sic] Alert!

In the comment section of the blog post "Buggaron [sic] Alert!," "Nena" [approx. translation "Giiirl!"] writes, "When I was a kid, a buggaron [sic] was a straight male who had sex with gays on the sneak but again that is what Ricans called them." Nena's comment reveals a moment of reflection whereby Nena thinks through the transformation that has taken place in Caribbean sexual cultures from the traditional *bugarrón* to a *neobugarrón* subject. Being observant, Nena points to this shift marking the distinction between the "sneak bugarron" and the neoliberal sex worker.

Nena's comment was in response to an April 4, 2006, blog post by the anonymous gay blogger "battle-hardened" under the catchy headline "Bugarron Alert!" Despite the obvious misspelling of *bugarrón* as *buggaron*, the post uses a warning code to draw attention to the problem. Written by a self-described tourist, the post is meant to warn other US citizens visiting the Dominican Republic. The blogger writes with a hint of exasperation: "When you are dealing with buggarones [sic] you have to treat them like buggarones [sic]. . . . They are prostitutes . . . they will steal anything they can from you." "Battled-hardened" continues his explanation with sarcasm: "You would think all buggarones [sic] are potential 'magicians,' with special powers for making things disappear." He explains further, "I don't want to paint all buggarones [sic] with the same brush, but there is a very high percentage that will steal anything they can from you. This is even after you have given them money, let them take the extra pair of sneakers you had, along with cologne, hats, t-shirts, underwear, or anything else they can beg you out of." Scarred by a *bugarrón* interaction gone wrong, he warns others of a *bugarrón*'s spellbinding effect on the client: "He is sleeping with you because of the money you are going to pay him. This is, for lack of a better term, a business transaction. No more, no less. Whatever you are lacking in your life, a good buggarone [sic] will sense it and play off it. His job is to get you to 'trust him.'" Other comments on the blog concur that sex with *bugarrones* is just a business transaction: "No money, no fuckie no suckie." After a series of advice statements—such as "Don't tell strangers when you are leaving the country," "EVERYTHING that you value should go into your safe," and "I know you want to cuddle but . . ."—the blogger informs us that he is originally from New York City and that he moved to the Dominican Republic in January 2004. "Battled-hardened" shares with blog visitors that he is "following [his] dream of being his 'own boss'" and "looking forward to the journey where life takes [him] next."

The "Buggaron Alert!" blog post and comments contain five insightful observations regarding the *neobugarrón* world, calling attention to a thriving market, transformation, extinction, commodification, and misspelling. The first insight tells readers that there is, in fact, a thriving *bugarrón* market, and some of the feedback "Battled-hardened" received indicates the unbelievably high demand for *bugarrones*. For instance, frequent traveler Kevin H. confesses, "The sex is great and the men are hot, lord knows you can have any man for a few dollars. I have traveled there three times and I had a great time." Some feedback tries to understand the *neobugarrones*' economic condition by stating that "they are very poor and need to hustle to live." At some point in the thread, someone uses the "bugarrones/trade" combination to refer to these sexual performances. Numerous posts ask about prices, availability, and where to gain access to "bugarron dick." "Anonymous" argues that "Some buggarons [sic] make more money then [sic] the Police" and provides a price scale of how much "buggarons" [sic] earn per evening:

> 7:00 pm first customer 1500 peso's [sic]
> 9:00 pm second customer 1000 peso's [sic]
> 11:00 pm third customer 1000 peso's [sic]
> 01:00 am forth [sic] customer 800 peso's [sic] "last sale of the night" and the customers [sic] cell phone is stolen.

This outline of prices and income led some to argue that 1,500 pesos (47 dollars) was too much money for some "DICK." In a rant, one visitor states: "HE'S LUCKY IF HE GETS 500 PESOS, DAMN YOU GUYS PAY THAT MUCH TO HAVE SEX WITH A PROSTITUTE." Some commentators thought the price was right for what they enjoyed because, as another poster put it, his *bugarrón* was a "spectacular specimen of Dominican manhood." Other commentators excoriate the sex tourists who complained about prices: "There is nothing worse than an old queen on a bar stool . . . except an old cheap queen on a bar stool." At a point in the thread, "Battle-hardened" intervenes in this exchange: "LOL. Now that's an angry queen." And, again, he states, "Whenever I write about buggarones [sic] it always gets some people riled up."

The second and most important observation is Nena's comment about the transformation of the traditional *bugarrón* into the *neobugarrón* (cited at the beginning of this section). Most visitors were skeptical that these men were really straight: "Most of the buggarones [sic] you meet are not STRAIGHT!!! I'm not saying they're gay, but for me there is no way you can be 'straight' and do what you do so well." Nena was the most insightful when she highlighted that a transformation has happened—the traditional *bugarrón* has disappeared, and in his place has emerged a *neobugarrón* market "identity."

The third insightful observation from the post is Rafael's claim that "bugarrones/trade," like the ones found in the Dominican Republic by Nena, are extinct in Puerto Rico: "Sadly they are all extinct here." This raises many questions about the existence of the *bugarrón* in San Juan, Puerto Rico, and in chapter 4, I address the inconsistencies of the *bugarrón*'s transformation and extinction in Puerto Rico while discussing the figure of the *bugarrón* in Caribbean literature. The fourth observation from the blog is the confirmation of sex tourism as commodification: "Tricks are a commodity. It's like going to a restaurant. You can choose the meat loaf or the steak and you pay accordingly." Another visitor chimed in with his own version of this profound insight: "Sex is sex. a ho is a ho. money is money. money buys hoes. more money, more hoes."

The fifth worthwhile observation drawn from the blog concerns the creative ways *bugarrón* is misspelled. In *Tacit Subjects* (2011), Carlos Ulises Decena speculates on the misspelling of *bugarrón* by arguing that "BUGGARON is an Anglicism of the Spanish word *bugarrón*" (239). Like me, Decena is attentive to *bugarrón* word use. But he goes further: "I began to hear the sound modulations, the disappearing rolling of the *r*, and the doubling of the *g*" (239). Decena finds that this misspelling adds historicity to the term *bugarrón*, that it emphasizes the term's global scope, and that it exposes its veiled anti-imperialism: "For a word that traveled from the French *bougre*, through the English *bugger* (bugger on?!), to the Spanish *bugarrón*, going back to the Anglicized pronunciation may be the completion of a cycle, one that returns the word to travel and to U.S. empire" (239). "Buggaron Alert!" does not have just one misspelling but rather thrives on variety. Beyond the one Decena mentions, there is an abundance of "BURGGARONES" (27), "burrarones" (28), and, my favorite, "buggis" (29). It is not clear, then, what kind of anti-imperial critique a *bugarrón* misspelling provides or what type of traveling cycle it ends up closing.

A *Neobugarrón* Blogosphere and Post-Padilla Ethnography

In her post-Padilla ethnographic work on Dominican *bugarrones*, Lauren M. Pérez-Bonilla discovers that social media and other web-based platforms are the preferred venue for *bugarrones* because they grant them privacy, control of their image, and an easier way to select their clients ("Dominican" 44). As she points out, "online communication allowed them to protect (or hide) their identity and create a new one by using a nickname or username allegorical to either their sexual organs/physical attributes, or their sexual preferences or role(s)" (44). For instance, "John First-Grade Sausage" ("John Salchichón") is one of her subjects, and Pérez-Bonilla was able to contact him via social media. "A retired bugarrón," First-Grade Sausage has been working at a health clinic that administers tests, distributes condoms, and provides health-related services primarily to sex workers (44). Through him she was able to contact other subjects. Let me clarify that for Pérez-Bonilla, *bugarrones* are sex workers, what I call *neobugarrones*. In her work there is no mention of a traditional *bugarrón* sexual practice. The traditional *bugarrón* is, plain and straightforward, nonexistent. In this post-Padilla ethnographic work, the idea of a subject's sexual truth has been displaced by concerns over sex workers' rights and their perceived exclusion from visibility in the body politic. In this context, when First-Grade Sausage says he is a retired *bugarrón*, it means he is a retired sex worker.

Pérez-Bonilla's work emphasizes that *neobugarrones* prefer the visibility provided by social media; it was not hard to find posts on Josué, Javier, and Miss Bugarron while looking for more instances of *bugarrón* represented in image form online. Pérez-Bonilla explains that her first attempt at interviewing *bugarrones* was unsuccessful because she attempted to spot them face-to-face on the street; subsequently, she discovered a series of web pages, blogs, and sites that assisted in her research. Beyond her discovery of a cyberworld of *neobugarrones* online, Pérez-Bonilla's account highlights the language of *bugarrón* sexual practice that remains as a trace tied to the *neobugarrón* subject. If Padilla delved into a moment of cultural transformation, Pérez-Bonilla has moved beyond that moment. By the time Pérez-Bonilla begins her research, *neobugarrón* subjectivity has sublated *bugarrón* sexual practice and has enacted a market "identity" *as if* a "real" thing. In this context, we find juicy insights about the sublated traditional *bugarrón* sexual practice in *neobugarrón* sex work. Like echoes of a lost language, we hear between sentences remnants of the "style of reasoning" of traditional *bugarrón* sexual practice. For instance, we encounter in Pérez-Bonilla's interviews *bugarrón* practitioners voicing the following statements:

> They also referred to themselves as "normal," "100 percent man," and heterosexual, because they only offered penetrative services to their clients. ("Dominican" 50)
>
> They have never allowed another man to penetrate them. (50)
>
> A real bugarrón hits from behind. (39)
>
> I do feel like a man because, until today, thank God, I haven't given my ass [to other men] understand? And sorry for my language, but I haven't sucked a penis nor will I ever do it. (51)

Pérez-Bonilla argues that these men "are doing something they do not enjoy" (45). She also contends that they "continued to perform the activo role in the relationship" (53). Furthermore, she claims that "their economic precarity is necessary but not sufficient to make these men offer their bodies to foreigners" (45, 54).

A new meaning has taken over the term *bugarrón*; only traces of its former meaning remain. If precarity is an important component in Pérez-Bonilla's investigation, this is due to her impulse to find out why those men have become involved in sex work: "It is the ability of making money at a fast rate that makes this profession popular among low-income groups or those with immediate economic needs" ("Dominican" 45). Concerned about processes of "invisibilization," that is, "processes of exclusion [the] sex workers face in the Dominican Republic," Pérez-Bonilla is invested in creating a network of institutions to secure their safety (48). Stripped of the traditions of a forgotten *bugarrón* practitioner's life of pleasure, *neobugarrones* mainly "see their bodies as commodities" (49). Their play of visibility and invisibility takes place as commodities in the virtual marketplace of the *neobugarrón* sphere. In Pérez-Bonilla's work, we encounter the fully neoliberalized *bugarrón* subject. It is only by transforming himself into a commodity, as sex worker, that the *neobugarrón* could gain future access to some political rights. Yet Pérez-Bonilla's goal continues to be an ideal, and it is not clear how *neobugarrones* would balance their entrepreneurial individualism, guaranteeing their craved invisibility, with the compromises that come with a political pressure group.

NEOBUGARRÓN ART

Commodifying *Neobugarrón* Paintings

If, in the domain of social image, Josué's and Javier's images and Nena's consternation highlight the commodification of *neobugarrón* sexuality in Latin America, then it is not surprising that *neobugarrón* marketability has led contemporary artists to "play" with the *neobugarrón* figure in their visual representations. Yet for these artists, just as for anthropologists before them, the *neobugarrón* becomes a slippery subjectivity. The difficulty of capturing the *neobugarrón* can be seen in Cuban artist Elio Rodríguez's artwork.

In *Tropical, 2,* Rodríguez paints a scene reminiscent of Padilla's anthropological work (see figure 2.5). Highly allusive, Rodríguez's art reminds us of Cuba's vintage travel posters. The painting illustrates a typical moment in the pleasure industry where a white tourist admires the rear end and legs of the

FIGURE 2.5. Elio Rodríguez's *Tropical, 2* (2010)

indigenous male stripper. The stripper's silhouette reminds us of the history of exotic dancers that have made the Americas' visual history so distinct. The dancer resembles figures such as Josephine Baker and Carmen Miranda. We are reminded of Baker's exotic display of her breasts in a banana costume and Miranda's use of headpieces with a range of bananas (see figures 2.6–2.8).

The US Cold War military officer represented in Carmen Miranda's figure has been displaced in Rodríguez's poster by a Western tourist wanting to grab

FIGURE 2.6. Josephine Baker in a banana skirt from the Folies Bergère production *Un Vent de Folie* (1927)

Cuba's latest tropical morsel (see figure 2.7). However, note that the male stripper bears a striking resemblance to Che Guevara. The traditional *bugarrón* seems to be lurking behind the scene at the top of the image. Or is it the real Che Guevara, showing his displeasure at the sight of an "American" tourist's interest in a spectacle of a queen performing Che?

Guevara's piercing look resonates with famous poster art that displays his image (see figure 2.9). For instance, compare Rodríguez's staring Che with the one found in Suitberto Goire's *La Fuerza de Tu Mirada Nos Guía* [*Your Piercing Gaze Guide Us*] (2002), where Che's forward-looking gape leads the nation from capitalism to socialism and the promise of a new man (see figure 2.10).

Note also that Goire's Che wears his red beret with a Cuban flag stamped on it. We can find the same iconography in Rodríguez's poster where the famous beret with the star completes the Cuban flag that covers the stripper's

FIGURE 2.7. Carmen Miranda and a US officer (played by Don Ameche) in *That Night in Rio* (1941)

FIGURE 2.8. Carmen Miranda

body. Opposing the invisible hand that characterizes the neoliberal space of laissez-faire is the visible hand of governmental communist intrusion at the right edge of the word *Tropical*. We could speculate further on the meaning of Che's presence here performed not by a communist youth attempting to imitate the revolutionary leader but by a dancer performing a communist leader for the pleasure of neoliberal entertainment. Wouldn't that be the best outcome of the Cold War? What is better than a transformation of communist icons into erotic fetishes? Beyond Baudrillard's idea that Cuba has become a world communist theme park, we encounter the notion that communist icons could be profitable for neoliberal consumers. Where dictators failed to be sexy (who would be excited by a male exotic performance of Pinochet or Trujillo?), revolutionary icons like Che retain their erotic appeal. As Rene Wanner points out: "It is through posters that Che's known portrait after a photograph by Alberto Korda became a global symbol of romanticized rebellion" (1).

David Kunzle explains that political posters have been at the "forefront of commercialization" in Cuba, where they have become "a million dollar" industry (*Che Guevara* 21). In the context of a postrevolutionary Cuba, this is

FIGURE 2.9. Alberto Korda's *Guerrillero Heroico* (1960)

a significant part of the tourist industry's contribution to the country. Before the revolution, Kunzle affirms, there was no such thing as a Cuban poster. It is only after 1969, with Che's death, that the photographic simplification of Che's image in graphic art provides the immediate "visual impact and symbolization" that led to this "commercial commodity" (22). Influenced by Cuban critic Edmundo Desnoes's work on Che's imagery, Kunzle clarifies what drives this Che commodity form: "The continuing vitality of this iconography flows from the vitality of the legend itself and shares the vitality of all Cuban poster art, of which it is a central component" (22). It is therefore no coincidence that Rodríguez has chosen to combine the hypercommercialized commodity of Che with the commodification of *neobugarrón* sexual practice.

The sentence at the top of the poster leaves no doubt as to the sexual nature of the exchange taking place here. It reads, "in the darkness of the night he waits for you," which openly suggests the sexual culmination of the trade in question and the powers of seduction involved. In Rodríguez's poster, which mimics the commodification of Che's posters plus the *neobugarrón* commodified practice, exchange is depicted as a transaction taking place in the dark.

FIGURE 2.10. Suitberto Goire's *La Fuerza de Tu Mirada Nos Guía* [Your Piercing Gaze Guide Us] (2002)

Yet Rodríguez's painting is misleading. Even when we encounter the relationship of the sex tourist with the local sex worker, here we have a non-*bugarrón* scene. As I mentioned before, the *bugarrón* modus operandi is to be on top in a nonreciprocal relationship, whereas the Che Guevara look-alike is tempting the tourist by shaking and showing his ass. On first sight, two different readings are possible: first, that this is a gay tourist and gay stripper relationship. Second, that Rodríguez, as a local artist, is challenging *bugarrón* mythology by demystifying the precept that the old *bugarrón* rules of nonreciprocity have been deregulated in the *neobugarrón,* where everything is for sale. At the heart of this critique, we find the idea that the *bugarrón* is after all a closeted gay man who has over the years conveniently managed not to lose the advantages that accompany his privileged heterosexual position in straight society. The word *Tropical* divides the two local figures in the picture and recalls the famous Tropicana club in pre-Castro capitalist Cuba. The layers of ambiguous symbolism in Rodríguez's art are significant, but I find more significant that at every turn, the image of the *bugarrón* is partly if not com-

FIGURE 2.11. Elio Rodríguez's *La Leyenda del Macho* (ca. 1996)

pletely invisible. A partial or invisible *bugarrón* image is to be expected since visibility lies in the realm of *neobugarrones*. Neoliberalism has unleashed the *neobugarrón* as the latest weapon in the Cold War containment of Cuba's communist revolution by *bugarronizing* Che as its sexy poster boy.

In *La Leyenda del Macho,* there is something like an aesthetic "push back" against foreign entertainment's encroachment into Cuban society (see figure 2.11). Rodríguez's *La Leyenda* portrays a possible Sinbad look-alike grabbing and massaging Elvis Presley's big banana. The Sinbad look-alike is grinning behind Presley, and "the King" seems defenseless against this forced fondling. We are drawn to Elvis's reddish banana sac, where the size of his white endowment corroborates the anatomy expected of male members of a notoriously licentious, poor white class. The poster's cowboy motif is reminiscent of the Wild West as a lawless zone of US westward expansion. It brings to mind the

US doctrine of Manifest Destiny and its consequences in the late nineteenth-century US expansion overseas into Cuba, Puerto Rico, and the Philippines after the Spanish–American War. But with *La Leyenda,* we also witness the *bugarrón* disappearing into a foreign *neobugarrón. Bugarronizing* Hollywood and US celebrity male icons may be the perfect culmination of an unanchored market sexual type. Once the national referent is lost, once the origin disappears, the *neobugarrón* becomes an aleatory practice; one that is mobile and widely applicable because it had been commodified.

CONCLUSION

In sum, the *neobugarrón* brings vitality to that which is inauthentic and unoriginal: we will never know the original *bugarrón.* It makes that which it succeeds eventful, colorful, and new. We witness the emergence of a marketable "identity" form that is visible in neoliberal economies but invisible as of yet in minoritarian politics. The *neobugarrón* is a market type that, in his paradoxical position, opposes and complements the visual field of progressive liberalism. In this context, *neobugarrón* art and *neobugarrón* social photos mark a rupture in tracking local sexual practices at a time when there is more at stake than ever in conjuring his image. In these examples we observe the emergence of *neobugarrón* in the field of neoliberal visible "identities." The rise of the *neobugarrón* seals the fate of an always already elusive *bugarrón* practice now further receding from the cultural horizon of a post–Cold War neoliberalized Caribbean. Rodríguez's demystification of macho "identity" is not just a political subversion. His work brings to the fore examples of visual representation that show aesthetic strategies of a disappearing *bugarrón* subject. The social photos point to a new frontier in "visibilization" where the commodity exchange-values have displaced the "truth" of sexual "identity" in a *bugarrón*'s virtual marketplace. In the next chapter, I explore the challenge of representing something that views itself as belonging to invisibility, a complexity key to *bugarrón* cinema.

CHAPTER 3

Bugarrón Cinema

A Disturbance in the Field of Vision

> A confusion at the level of sexuality brings with
> it a disturbance of the visual field.
> —Jacqueline Rose, *Sexuality in the Field of Vision*

In Argentinian director Marco Berger's film *Young Hunter* (2020), the protagonist, Ezequiel, is seduced by Mono, a straight young man who uses his sexual appeal to engage other young men in sexual intercourse. Mono has sex with young men, but his goal is to film them surreptitiously while having sex, since he works for Chino, a pornographer who sells his products on the dark web. Chino pays Mono for supplying this type of illicit pornography. The film's title refers to Mono, who has sex with men to entrap them even though he has a girlfriend; his heteroflexibility is part of the job description. The film represents this complexity in a particular scene where, via a technique of "double exposure," Mono's and Ezequiel's facial reflections merge to form a composite image on the windowpane. Forming a layered image, both faces reflected in the glass produce a "disalignment" in the field of vision. The images' contours shift, slightly overlapping each other, thus creating an unstable shape that preserves and cancels the original facial contours in its dynamic form. Reminiscent of Jacqueline Rose's insight that "a confusion at the level of sexuality brings with it a disturbance of the visual field," Berger's use of the technique of "double exposure" introduces visual confusion at the precise moment when viewers learn of each character's sexuality (Rose, *Sexuality* 226). The resulting layered reflection illustrates the complexity of representing sexuality via images, and it evokes Rose's claim that a disturbed image often indicates a "type of murking of sexual properties" where "something hidden but not forgotten can only come into focus . . . by blurring the field of representation" (228–29).[1] Via "double exposure," Berger's *bugarrón* heteroflexibility becomes visible.

One of the quagmires of *bugarrón* sexual practice concerns the limit of visibility and invisibility. Having in previous chapters explored the anthropological works of Jacobo Shifter, Mark Padilla, and Carlos Ulises Decena, who studied Latin American sexual cultures, I examine in this chapter a conundrum in understanding visual representations of *bugarrón* practice. I focus on films such as Ricardo de Montreuil's *La mujer de mi hermano* (2005), Marco Berger's *Plan B* (2009), *Absent* (2011), *Hawaii* (2013), and *The Blonde One* (2019), Javier Fuentes-León's *Undertow* (2009), Lorenzo Vigas's *Por Allá* [*From Afar*] (2015), and José Campusano's *Men of Hard Skin* (2019), which represent "heteroflexibility" in a way that does not signify *maricones* (or new fags) but rather cinematic *bugarrones*.[2] These films disturb the field of vision by representing *bugarrón* sexual practice in cinema. *Bugarrón* cinema portrays a heterosexuality that exceeds the cultural ideal of exclusive sexual identities.

SITUATING LATIN AMERICAN *BUGARRÓN* CINEMA: NEITHER *MARICÓN* NOR QUEER

Scholarship on Latin American cinema has grasped the existence of this recent boom in film production, but it has failed to account for *bugarrón* sexual practice. Instead, its interpretive lens continues to apprehend predominantly gay, *maricón*, queer subjectivities and "identities." Scholarly works—such as Paul Julian Smith's *Vision Machines* (1996), Sergio de la Mora's *Cinemachismo* (2006), Gustavo Subero's *Queer Masculinities in Latin American Cinema* (2014), Andrés Lema-Hincapié and Debra Castillo's *Despite All Adversities* (2015), Vinodh Venkatesh's *New Maricón Cinema* (2016), and Benedict Hoff's *Reprojecting the City* (2016)—tend to interpret these films as gay or queer. Yet

---

1. Indeed, in *Sexuality*, the source of this chapter's epigraph, Rose refers to Freud's misguided reading of Leonardo da Vinci's drawings, where the master painter attempted to capture sexual intercourse in visual form. Freud reads the drawing as a monstrous hermaphroditic shape lacking limbs and mixing genital traits. Through Freud's reading, Rose gets a clear sense of the difficulty in representing sexuality via images. Freud's interpretation heightens the potential of failure as a key factor in understanding the workings of the unconscious processes via visual representations. For her, Freud had "found its aptest analogy for the problem of our identity as human subjects in failures of vision" (*Sexuality* 227).

2. I use "cinematic *bugarrón*" given that the representation of a celluloid *bugarrón* is a fairly recent paradoxical development in Latin American cultural history. As a cinematic image, the *bugarrón* practitioner becomes a celluloid subject, that is to say, a visual representation of a type or image of a sexual practice.

those works that refer to anti-identitarian queer do not mention or acknowledge *bugarrón* sexual practice, thus raising the question of specificity. When interpreting films as queer, these scholarly works exclude local terminology (*bugarrón*) and specific subaltern thinking. Ignored are those categories south of the border produced to make sense of male sexual practices. For instance, when, in Argentine director Marco Berger's *The Blonde One* (2019), Juan tells Gabriel that he wants to live a normal life (meaning with wife and kids), his definition includes a flexible meaning of normal. His request to continue seeing Gabriel on the sly—"I want to keep seeing you"—is consistent with being a normal man. If, as Sharon Marcus argues, queerness refers in part to how sexual practice, sexual fantasy, and sexual identity fail to line up consistently with each other, then *bugarrón* sexual practice exemplifies those instances where subaltern thinking exceeds an agreeable alignment with either heterosexual norms or with queer.[3]

Yet this perplexing subaltern category, *bugarrón* sexual practice, is often absent in interpretations of cinematic representations of Latin American male sexuality. Take, for instance, Venkatesh's *New Maricón Cinema,* a work that describes the genealogical development of cinematic production in Latin America. Venkatesh identifies a "divergence" in Latin American cinema between what he calls a traditional *maricón* and a new *maricón* cinema. To clarify, in the Latin American context, *maricón* is a term close to the pejorative English slang "fag." There is no other equivalent to the English term "gay" in Spanish, so Venkatesh finds *maricón* (fag) a term fitting for categorizing the latest developments in Latin American cinema. For Venkatesh, *maricón* would be the closest word in Spanish to encapsulate what he calls "homosexual-themed" cinema (*New Maricón* 24). In his view, we are "on the cusp of an aesthetic renovation and uncharted circulation of non-normative representations in the cinema" (14). New "fag" cinema for Venkatesh is nonnormative. Like Venkatesh's book, other works in this body of cinema criticism also share the inclination to disregard *bugarrón* sexual practice and perpetuate gay or new fag identities and queer sexualities. Of these, Venkatesh's project is the only one that establishes a historical shift from *maricón* to a new *maricón* cinema in Latin American filmmaking. *New Maricón Cinema* historicizes three stages of development: *ficheras* films (Mexican sex comedies) produced during the 1970s; late twentieth-century films, such as Cuba's *Fresa y Chocolate* (1993);

---

3. See Marcus, *Between Women,* esp. 4–5. Sedgwick's broad claim of queer as an "open mesh of possibilities, gaps, overlaps, dissonances and resonances, lapses and excesses of meaning" is also at issue here since it is so ambiguous that it encompasses anything known and yet to be known (*Tendencies* 8). It decontextualizes that which falls into the mesh from local specificity and cultural complexity.

and twenty-first-century films exemplified by *Contracorriente* (2009) and *Plan B* (2009). By studying these cinematic developments, Venkatesh draws our attention to an epistemic break in his genealogy of new *maricón* cinema. This epistemic break becomes useful when thinking through local paradigms of sexual classification.

Unfortunately, missing from Venkatesh and other studies is the recognition and analysis of *bugarrón* sexual practice. Also missing is the inspection of the murky images that point to heteroflexibility. Critics either take for granted or fail to scrutinize particular instances of rack focusing, erasures of pictorial representations, and scenes of mental disorientation (disturbance triggered by enigmatic mnemonic traces). These scenes typical of cinematic conventions for representing *bugarrón* sexual practice remain underexamined points of reflection. More precisely, the scenes point to cinematic techniques that represent intervals of heteroflexible *bugarrón* sexual practice in film. At the heart of my study lies the contention that these films' selective focusing, mnemonic artifacts, and other traits open a different understanding, an undercurrent, of a *bugarrón* sexual practice.

Consider an example of this complexity in Berger's film *The Blonde One*, where we find two men in their late twenties, Gabriel and Juan, attempting to cope with persistent sexual tension. The film blurs Gabriel's bare buttocks at a crucial moment when Gabriel is undressing and his roommate Juan is present. The commonplace technique of rack focusing exemplifies an intention by the director "to shift the [viewers'] attention from one subject to another" (Monaco, *How to Read* 86). But in this case, only the buttocks are blurred; Gabriel's back and legs and the furniture around him are evident. Structured in an over-the-shoulder shot, the scene shows only the back of Juan's head as Juan stares at Gabriel's naked ass. Because of his location, we presume that Juan can see what film viewers can't. The camera's manipulation lets viewers only imagine what Gabriel's rear looks like. The idea that Berger may be censoring nudity is immediately dispelled when, not long after this shot, we are confronted with many scenes in which both men are represented in rear and frontal nudity. If the film shows plenty of scenes where viewers can see Gabriel's genitals, then why was the shot of his behind distorted in that initial scene? Is this disturbance of the image a strategy for alerting viewers to a sexual confusion? Rose's connection between confusion at the sexual level and a resulting disturbance in the visual field seems to be at work here. This is not the first time Berger has used rack focusing and other film techniques (such as double exposure) to make us think through what we see. Instead of the usual interpretation of censorship, it becomes apparent that Berger makes the audience think through a complex visual and sexual relationship. Neither censorship nor capriciousness, the instances of rack focusing in Berger's films function as visual *punctums* for thinking through the complicated connection between sexuality and its visual representation.

The disturbance in Latin American cinema reveals the hidden presence of a nonexclusive heterosexual practice between men. This chapter examines scenes in films that do not fit perfectly or that exceed the categories of *maricón* or queer. The eight films I address here—de Montreuil's *La mujer de mi hermano*, Berger's *Plan B*, *Absent*, *Hawaii*, and *The Blonde One*, Fuentes-León's *Undertow*, Vigas's *From Afar*, and Campusano's *Men of Hard Skin*—depart from previous generations of Latin American visual representation of male–male sexuality. These films challenge traditional expectations of heterosexuality from the position of exclusive heterosexual experiences rather than from the perspective of a self-conscious gay "identity." They problematize the viewer's expectation of heterosexuality by contesting the ideal of exclusive heterosexuality from within. In a Latin American region where, as Sergio de la Mora writes, "virility is a metonym for Mexicanness," machismo and heterosexuality have been mostly interchangeable concepts (*Cinemachismo* xiii). In this cultural context, a cinematic shift challenging the boundaries of heterosexuality is significant.

Accordingly, these films show the limits of a homosocial–homosexual continuum, such as Eve Sedgwick argues in *Between Men* (1985), where homosociality is understood as a structure of desire between men mediated through women. I argue that these films disturb the sexual continuum, revealing a gradation of male heterosexuality that includes the sexual flexibility to engage in nongay, nonexclusive heterosexual desire between men. Sedgwick's homosociality is altered in *bugarrón* cinema because in love triangles desire between men is transmitted through the *bugarrón* practitioner, that is, the heteroflexible male who engages sexually with both his wife and a male lover. In these cases, *bugarrón* sexual practice mediates nongay-identified heterosexual sex between men. But it is not only in love triangles that characters show their nonexclusive heterosexuality. In fact, heteroflexibility represents a series of separate and distinct gradations along the sexual continuum. These graded sexualities ("mostly straight," "primordially straight") show degrees of heteroflexibility that set them apart from ideal categories such as exclusive heterosexuality, exclusive homosexuality, and bisexuality. Thus, cinematic images of *bugarrón* sexual practice complicate the conventional understanding of a male sexual continuum.

My study of these films' disturbance of heterosexuality in the visual field uses insights from the works of Freud, Laplanche, Merleau-Ponty, Rancière, and Rose. In Rose, I find compelling insights on the role of sexuality's disturbance of the visual field and her critique of Freud's interpretation of sexuality and the image. At the same time, I find Freud's observations on the "Mystic Pad" useful for clarifying the role of visual apparatuses in reproducing "mnemonic traces." Along with Freud, Rancière's understanding of the "intervals of cinema" helps explain the discursive dynamic between literature and cinematic works. And, last, I have found Merleau-Ponty's philosophical observations on visibility insightful about the role of invisibility in *bugarrón* cinema. It is Merleau-Ponty who explains that to see is an invitation to observe not only the surface of visibility but also the horizon of its farthest point.

I begin my analysis with an examination of Berger's films *Plan B, Hawaii,* and *Absent* because they provide representations of *bugarrón* practitioners in the context of enigmatic sexual practices and mnemonic traces. I then proceed to study Fuentes-León's *Undertow,* de Montreuil's *La mujer de mi hermano,* and Vigas's *From Afar* because they combine the filmmaking techniques of rack focusing and the close display of pictorial objects (such as paintings and photographs). These cinematic techniques provide an interpretive space for theorizing a *bugarrón* cinematic ecology composed of film effects and specular objects. As Jocelyn Dunphy-Blomfield explains, ecology is "the science of relations," and films create a visual narrative where relations come to view ("Harmony" 217). In the realm of ocular objects and images, a cinematic *bugarrón* ecosystem takes form.

BAD BROMANCE: MARCO BERGER'S *PLAN B*

Marco Berger's *Plan B* (2009) is the story of Pablo and Bruno, two young Argentine men trapped in a love triangle with a young woman, Laura. Bruno, believing the gossip that Pablo once had sexual relations with a male friend, decides to seduce Pablo away from Laura. Presumably an exclusive heterosexual man, Bruno establishes this scheme to make Laura fall in love with him again, but his plan fails, and, instead, we see an unexpected development where the two male characters enter into an awkwardly close relationship. After several attempts to resolve their feelings, Bruno confesses to Pablo that he has fallen in love with him, a confession that triggers the beginning of a raucous intimate relationship. The narrative stops at the point when Pablo and Bruno accept their mutual love for each other while refraining from embracing a gay identity.

The film's title, *Plan B,* refers to the management of erotic possibilities and, accordingly, to the working-through of emotions that are not immediately verbalized but condition the actions these characters take. The title is directly related to the scheme that Bruno puts in place to reconquer Laura and the counterscheme that Pablo enacts to undermine Bruno's plans, perhaps even seduce him. The possibility of this seduction strategy is disclosed at the film's end when Pablo reveals to Bruno a picture he has taken of him at the park. This event took place during the film's opening scene. He also tells Bruno that he had seen his framed picture in Laura's bedroom. In light of this uncertainty, viewers can't be sure whether Bruno's plot is the main one or yet another counterplot. In other words, which plan is secondary or primary remains uncertain. This visual narrative could be described as evoking the romantic dramas of a Jane Austen à la *bugarrón* cinema in this conundrum of plots, counterplots, twists, and turns. But the unpredictability of their plans and the manipulation of emotions and expectations assures that both male characters fall in love with each other while pursuing their individual seduction plots.

Their new relationship does not solve the puzzle of sexual "identity," since the film is silent on this score. During a crucial scene, Pablo states clearly, "I don't like guys," thus making us aware of the limits of categorizing his sexuality. It is not a question of bisexuality, gayness, or queerness; neither is the pejorative *maricón* embraced here. The film does not provide further clarification or confession of their sexual preferences. Their newfound intimacy is refreshing precisely because it leads us into uncharted territory beyond expected categories of gay or even queer. The film takes us in a different direction, not expecting any clear sexual identification. What is certain is that the film leaves open the possibility that male–male desire could be a manifestation of heterosexuality. If, for decades in Latin America, male homosexuality has been understood as equivalent to effeminacy, it is not surprising that these characters might hesitate to come out as gay even when, as the film shows, they share a commitment to not adhering to society's prejudices. However, there is also the possibility that these two men have developed a degree of intimacy that does not alter their heterosexual self-identification.

Plan B challenges the viewer to believe that two heterosexual men can fall in love with each other and establish a sexual relationship without affirming an exclusive homosexual or bisexual "identity." Unlike Jack, one of the characters in Ang Lee's *Brokeback Mountain* (2005), Pablo and Bruno are not closeted gay men who hide their "real" desires. Rather, these characters discover a strong physical attraction for each other slowly and much before achieving sexual intimacy. In *Brokeback,* Jack seems to enjoy sex with other men, while Ennis seems to follow a trajectory of not liking men in general but loving only one man. Pablo and Bruno seem to belong to Ennis's camp. Moreover, the specter of violence against gay men that prevails in *Brokeback* dissipates in *Plan B*'s Argentine context. In *Brokeback,* the mountain represents a spatial retreat from the civilized world and society's cultural trappings. *Plan B* does not show a retreat to the wilderness. Instead, the film shows an urban space of visibility for a heteroflexible form of male–male intimacy located outside the parameters of gay "identity." Whereas in *Brokeback* an escape into nature seems necessary for the manifestation of same-sex relations, in *Plan B* civilized society secures this evolution of intimacy without the need for escape from urban life. What makes the film even more interesting is the geopolitical space from which it emerges—Argentina, one of the few Latin American countries where gay marriage and, therefore, gay relationships have been legalized in all provinces and localities.[4] It seems as if the legitimizing of gay identity and gay marriage may have conjured new ways for heterosexual males to be sexually intimate.

Plan B may be seen as depicting a trajectory in the Americas for reconfiguring male–male expressions of intimacy in nonidentitarian forms. Nevertheless, it develops a perspective on sexual subjectivity that at first sight may seem similar to the one expressed in the US by critic Jack Malebranche in his contemporary *Androphilia* (2006) manifesto. Recognizing that being gay has a cultural visibility generally associated with effeminate stereotypes, Malebranche proposes a noneffeminate, nongay category, *andro,* that could understand relationships between men differently from contemporary stereotypes: "While separating masculine-identified homos from those who embrace gay culture and the gay identity, *androphilia* brings together all men who love men by describing their shared desire, but does not create a complete, confining identity" (28). His manifesto exposes a minoritarian viewpoint in conversation with a dominant assimilationist gay culture that he sees as retaining the baggage of a prescriptive behavior.

Although some similarities may be intuited between Malebranche's manifesto and Berger's film, the differences are meaningful. Whereas Malebranche's idea of a nongay, nonheterosexual masculinity may be perceived as writing into prose what *Plan B* represents in cinematic form, this is not the case. While Malebranche excludes gay and straight cultures equally, *Plan B* points to heteroflexibility. Thus, whereas Malebranche's narrative reads like a self-conscious political manifesto, *Plan B* resembles a journey in the evolution of

---

4. In Buenos Aires and other provinces, gay civil unions had been legal since 2002. By 2008 same-sex couples that had been in relationships for a two-year period or longer were allowed to share rights before granted only to married couples. This measure was instituted in advance of the same-sex marriage law that was to take into effect in 2010. Berger's *Plan B,* released in 2009, could be seen as a product of this remarkable trajectory in same-sex marriage rights in Argentina. Argentina was the first Latin American country and the second country in the Americas to legalized same-sex marriage.

a structure of desire. In *Plan B*, Sedgwick's heterosexual–homosexual continuum is turned upside down by understanding desire between men taking place within the structure of male nonexclusive heterosexuality. While Malebranche's book raises questions about his tolerance for effeminate gays and for gay culture itself, *Plan B* describes a plausible development of affection between two hetero men. *Plan B* represents a bad bromance, that is, a nonheterosexually exclusive, not-gay attraction between men leading to intimacy. Accordingly, the film shows their relationship as a singular experience rather than as a general sexual proclivity for members of the same sex. That is to say, their attraction is not to other men but to each other. This seemingly organic development of intimacy surprises everyone, including them.

If viewers were to approach *Plan B* as a visual space where heterosexual subjects show their evolving journey into heteroflexibility, then they would understand that these men's newfound intimacy would cut through any sense of logical contradiction such as the one found in the anthropological *cachero* sexual practice in chapter 1. There, we saw how a lack of thinking about the consequences of their sexual practice led *cachero* practitioners to actions that come across as contradicting their own views on sex, identity, and gender. Instead, *Plan B* portrays an intimacy that short-circuits all sense of exclusive identitarianism. For these two men, sexual categories have bent organically and are reasonably in tune with their newly developed not-gay sexual desires. *Plan B* represents a space where a flexible heterosexuality between men includes an assortment of affects. Gayness is neither desired nor embraced in a space where heterosexuality has spread beyond its traditional limits.

The cosmopolitan urban setting of Buenos Aires gives the characters in *Plan B* the flexibility needed to explore new modes of being together. The idea of the closet, which has been so important for gay identity, is irrelevant to these men's experience as they move from exclusive heterosexuality to an active sexual relationship between hetero men. *Bugarrón* cinema functions as an undercurrent that disturbs the field of vision because it alters the flow of the heterosexual–homosexual continuum. Sedgwick contends that Western culture has "radically disrupted" the continuum between male homosociality and male homosexual desire (*Between* 2). In doing so, it has understood male homosociality as a structure of desire between men transmitted by women. Whereas Sedgwick seeks to re-establish the disrupted continuum between male homosociality and homosexual desire, *bugarrón* sexual practice adds an unexpected complexity to the mix. Whereas in homosociality, heterosexual men do not fuck each other, in heteroflexibility they do. The highly mediated and often platonic homosocial relationship turns raunchy in *bugarrón* sexual practice.

The cinematic *bugarrón* sexual practice disturbs the male heterosexual–homosexual continuum by rerouting a libidinal current to a structure of desire that is altered here by heteroflexibility to include a nonidentitarian relation and a particular sexual practice between men. In *Plan B*, heteroflexibility mediates the desire between men. Bruno and Pablo's nonexclusive affects mediate their relationship. This trend in Latin American cinema can be traced back to Alfonso Cuarón's film *Y tu mamá también* (2001), where the film exposes the limits of homosociality. Whereas in Cuarón's film the relationship between the two teenage male protagonists Tenoch and Julio changes from homosociality to sex between men, this mishap destroys their friendship. *Bugarrón* cinema represents the transition from exclusive heterosexuality to sex-between-heterosexual-men.

Whereas in *Y tu mamá también,* the one-night stand between male protagonists leads to the immediate dissolution of their friendship, *Plan B* revels in the characters' consternation at their personal situation. Many of the shots consist of close-ups showing the worried looks on Bruno's and Pablo's faces as they grapple with this upheaval in their lives and ponder the unexpected direction their futures might take. Often they verbalize their angst by confessing that they feel their heads might explode from thinking about this situation too much. The idea of exploding heads could have many meanings, but in this case it is a sign of deep introspection and confusion. Rational goals become thwarted in *Plan B,* and their shortcomings are digested slowly. Confusion dominates the characters' inability to make sense of their feelings in the context of gayness. At the level of sexuality, this lack of clarity disturbs our ability to make sense of this film. Confronted with this problem, some scholars of Latin American cinema have claimed, "it is problematic to label *Plan B* as an LGBT or Q film; it is almost disingenuous to call it a New Maricón film" (Venkatesh, *New Maricón* 154). This is an illuminating moment in a work that advances the theory that *Plan B* is key for developing a new *maricón* cinema. More eyebrow-raising is the contention that *Plan B* shows "no crises of identity, affirmations of sexuality, or broader politics of desire" (154). At this moment, something reveals itself in Venkatesh's approach. *New Maricón Cinema* prioritizes films that only disseminate a specific type of identification; one that consistently aligns with queer or gay structures of desire. It seems that the angst of heteroflexible characters is seen as less "productive" and not exactly the "positive" identitarian feelings expected of an "LGBT or Q film" (154).[5] Accordingly, heteroflexibility as mediation in *Plan B* is neither considered nor expounded.

---

5. Although advancing a contagious sense of identification through feelings, *New Maricón Cinema*'s narrow approach risks perpetuating precisely what Eugenie Brinkema finds to be a prevalent problem in some affect-oriented scholarship today. "So celebrated for its resistance to systematicity," she argues, affect theory "becomes not only what does not resist, but in fact what confirms every time the same model of vague shuddering intensity" (*Forms* xv).

Not surprisingly, advancing the idea that there is a new *maricón* "Latin American cinematic ecosystem," Venkatesh's work misses other parts of this ecosystem that are not immediately perceived (18). This may be due to the structural limits stemming from his theoretical framework. By contrast, considering Foucault's idea of the rules of discursive regimes can shed light on the presumed blind spots of this cinematic ecosystem in order to "reexamine the original distribution of the visible and invisible" in Latin American cinema (Foucault, *Birth of the Clinic* xi).

Depicting an anomalous relationship between heterosexual men in a cosmopolitan city, *Plan B* takes viewers in a new direction—it shifts the story from exclusive heterosexuality to a nongay intimacy between men. But even when it succeeds in making us think seriously about the complexity of an "identity"-driven classification of male sexual desire, it nevertheless lacks the inner depth and symbolic complexity of Berger's two other films to be discussed: *Hawaii* (2013) and *Absent* (2011).

TOWARD A CINEMATIC *BUGARRÓN*

"If you were a toy, what would you be?" asks Bruno in *Plan B*. Whereas Pablo's answer to the question is endearing—a beach bucket and shovel—Bruno's answer is more complex: a view-master. Invented in the 1930s, the view-master is a stereoscope, a device for viewing images set in round reels. For Bruno, the view-master represents a sequence of constantly changing images. The selection of a view-master in *Plan B* is enigmatic. The act of capturing images could be associated with other technological gadgets visible in the film. For instance, Pablo as a photographer had captured Bruno's image at the park in the film's opening scenes, an act that is revealed much later. The reference to a view-master is significant beyond its mechanical practicality of viewing images illuminated on reels. The enigma of the view-master as the object of Bruno's imaginary becoming is not found in *Plan B*. Its significance is outside *Plan B*'s filmic frame and in another cinematic visual narrative. For an explanation of the view-master's function, we need to analyze its presence in a later film by Berger: *Hawaii*.

Much remains unknown about the life of Martin (a.k.a. "El Ruso") and Eugenio in Berger's *Hawaii*. Set in Argentina, in a suburb an hour outside Buenos Aires, this charming film tells the story of a re-encounter between two childhood friends. Exploring the topic of forgotten emotional connections, *Hawaii* portrays the rediscovery of latent memories between Martin and Eugenio. Martin re-emerges in Eugenio's life after losing his grandmother and ending up homeless. Looking for a job and a place to stay, Martin stumbles upon Eugenio, who welcomes him into his home. At first Eugenio remembers little about Martin but feels a strong physical attraction to him. Only after Eugenio rebuffs Martin's advances for closer intimacy does he remember that Martin recently mentioned "two pineapples." Reminiscent of *Plan B*, Eugenio retrieves from the attic a particular optical gadget, a view-master. Finding a way to make the old gadget work, Eugenio begins looking at the images of a specific reel labeled "Honolulu, Hawaii." As he looks into the view-master, the slides come alive. It is when he stumbles upon an illuminated image of two pineapples in a lush Hawaiian field that Eugenio's memory becomes, as Freud says, "'reproduced'" once again in consciousness ("Mystic" 227).

In "A Note Upon the 'Mystic Writing Pad'" (1925), Freud uses the term "memory trace" to refer to the latent image of a memory that is forgotten and that can be used to recall lost memories (227). The "'Mystic Writing Pad,'" Freud argues, is a "small contrivance"; "if it is examined more closely," he claims, "it will be found that its construction shows a remarkable agreement with my hypothetical structure of our perceptual apparatus and that it can in fact provide both an ever-ready receptive surface and permanent traces" (228). Like the mystic writing pad, the view-master gadget has the ability to reproduce memory traces of particular moments in childhood. "Reproduce" here means reawakening, reactivating, or making alive once again. The memory triggered by the view-master image is that of Eugenio and Martin resembling two pineapples while lying in an open field. Earlier in the film, Martin had spoken of this moment of childhood after remembering the "two pineapples," but Eugenio did not want to hear. The medium-range close-up shot shows Martin's mouth moving while telling a story, but viewers cannot discern his voice. Sound and image are out of joint. The audience's visual perspective can see Martin speaking and Eugenio lost in thought. Viewers are suddenly aware that Eugenio is not listening to Martin. They begin to share Eugenio's shutting down of his auditory faculties. They hear only the last phrase in Martin's discourse: "two pineapples."

The image of the pineapples in the view-master reel opens a floodgate of emotion and recognition. For Eugenio the innocuous image of a Hawaiian field with two fruits provokes an overwhelming and disruptive feeling of longing. Suddenly, a foundational loss becomes comprehensible, revealing Martin as a missing part of Eugenio's emotional life. Functioning as an enigma, the image of the pineapples reawakens in Eugenio a web of emotional connections. Loss becomes intelligible as a missing bond that Eugenio has buried but that Martin seems to have remembered and cherished over the years. Martin, in his role as a memory keeper, is the one who vividly recalls those childhood scenes Eugenio had forgotten. He even remembers when Eugenio's father gave him an old winter sweater with the name "Eugenio" woven into it. Martin tells Eugenio how he walked around town with the name Eugenio on his chest, as if it were a tattoo branding his body. Eugenio cannot read Martin or, more importantly, hear him talk. For Eugenio, Martin is an enigma.

In Berger's *bugarrón* cinema, the view-master becomes not simply an inanimate object but a portal, a passageway to a set of connections and modes of relationality that remain mostly latent memories in the adult male subject. With its changing images, the view-master, as a stand-in for memory traces, disturbs the boundaries of male heterosexuality in *Plan B* and in *Hawaii*. The silent, yet still moving, images in a view-master reel unlock a different path to knowledge, feeling, and belonging. As a portal, the image takes the subject to a zone between past and present. In this zone where memories are lost and recovered, the view-master represents the moment of still pictures and emotional change. The image of two pineapples reproduces those feelings that complete Eugenio's shattered psyche. Eugenio sees not just an image but what it relates to. In other words, he sees "two pineapples" and those relations that outline and exceed their image. In *Signs* (1960), Merleau-Ponty writes, "To see is as a matter of principle to see farther than one sees, to reach a latent existence. The invisible is the outline and the depth of the visible" (20–21). The pineapples are important as signs of an invisible depth and of those emotions and actions that exceed the frame. In *Hawaii,* the image of the "two pineapples" outlines a not-yet-visible horizon.

For critic Mauro Carbone, Merleau-Ponty's visibility is an idea that should not be misunderstood as "an ensemble of visible things"; instead, it should be understood as inclusive of those "lines of force and the dimensions suggested by visible things" (*Flesh* 1). Explaining that visibility as a spectrum includes what is not necessarily visible but suggested by the image, Merleau-Ponty brings together the specular and the psyche, the eye and the mind. From his perspective, that which is an ocular image in the narrow sense is part of a web of connections suggested by the image. These include related or evoked mental images. Merleau-Ponty refers to this when he states that one sees "farther than one sees" (*Signs* 20). Berger's use of a view-master, as a rotating series of still images, illuminates the invisible connections of the image's outline, depth, and contour. The view-master introduces an optic retrieval of what lies outside the visible image. The latency of the shadows retrieves the mnemonic traces imperceptibly linked to the visible form.

Not all of Berger's films share this narrative ruse of showing the contours of invisible connections with the help of gadgets. This is the case in films where depth remains invisible. If Berger's cinema is known for expanding the limits of heterosexuality, his 2017 film *Taekwondo* pursues once again this particular proclivity. Set in a dilapidated mansion on the outskirts of Buenos Aires, the film takes us to the world of a group of young men at a spa-like retreat. Unlike *Plan B*, with its angst-inducing plot, *Taekwondo* can be characterized as a type of gay fantasy.

Taekwondo tells a loose story of two friends, heterosexual Fer (Fernando) and gay Germán, who end up spending a short vacation at Fer's country house. Accompanied by six other straight male friends, Fer and Germán find their interest in each other growing more each day. *Taekwondo* explores the relationship of these men as they hang around, sometimes naked, and have sexual relations with their female friends. In *Taekwondo* we enter a hybrid space reminiscent of a bachelor's pad, a *Bel Ami* reality show, and a frat house party. As with *Plan B*, heteroflexibility is present in Fer's case, and the central plotline is the main protagonist's growing affection for his friend. Although no one knows that Germán is gay, viewers are aware of his sexual orientation because they can overhear his conversations on the phone with a gay friend. For all practical purposes, Fer thinks he is falling in love with another straight man. Whereas *Plan B* feels like the story of two heterosexual men, *Taekwondo* modifies this storyline to satisfy the tastes of gay audiences. *Taekwondo* showcases flexible heterosexuality, but the film lacks the neutrality and suspense of *Plan B*; neither does it have the impulse to explore deeply the complexity triggered when crossing the limits of exclusive heterosexuality. *Taekwondo* does point to Fer as a heterosexual variant, that is to say, as a cinematic *bugarrón*, in that his attraction seems to be directed at Germán only. Unlike Pablo and Bruno in *Plan B* and Martin and Eugenio in *Hawaii*, Fer is a type of cinematic *bugarrón* who develops a non-angst relationship with an out gay man. As that of a non-angst type, Fer's heteroflexibility takes place without any apparent emotional struggle. Lack of prejudice opens Fer to an undramatic intimate relationship, the slow recognition of a unique gradation of flexible heterosexuality. Has the cinematic *bugarrón* reached the point where he disappears into visible homosexual representation altogether? The film plays with this uncertainty by having Fer and Germán kiss only after all other guests have departed.

There are no enigmatic signifiers in *Taekwondo,* and the film lacks the invisibility within the visible field that structures *Plan B* and *Hawaii*. The film produces a non-angst *bugarrón* subject, a cinematic type in the minority. The development of Fer's sexual "identity" is not pursued at the film's end, and what is left for the spectator to ponder is whether Fer sees inside himself more than what we see in him. Despite this enigmatic conundrum, there is a level of unsatisfying self-containment in *Taekwondo* that points to the lack of a connection with an ecology of optical retrieval. By contrast, the invisible outline of the visible in *Plan B* and *Hawaii* gives Berger's films the sense of an ecological relationality between them. That is to say, these films resonate with each other, thus introducing their more explicit relatedness. *Plan B* and *Hawaii* portray a world where a collection of objects triggers unconscious connections between the cinematic *bugarrón* and his intimate partner. The ecological connections between things, beings, and films begin to display a network of relatedness where the cinematic *bugarrón* comes to light.[6]

THE DEPTH OF VISIBLE SKIN; OR, ON *BUGARRÓN* RELATEDNESS

Bestowed with a Teddy Award for best picture at the 2011 Berlin Film Festival, *Absent* is Berger's most successful film but also his most haunting. Set in Versalles, a suburb of Buenos Aires, *Absent* tells the relatively short history of an encounter between a sixteen-year-old high school student, Martin Blanco, and his thirty-year-old professor, Sebastian Armas. The drama centers on Martin's scheme to get closer to Sebastian by pretending to have a health-related emergency and no place to stay after school. Following several attempts to take Martin from the hospital to his grandmother's home, Sebastian allows Martin to sleep overnight in his apartment. After taking a shower and cleaning himself up, Martin falls asleep on the living room couch. In the middle of the night he approaches Sebastian in bed and slides his hand under his sleeping shorts. He gets to touch the inner skin of Sebastian's upper right leg, and as a result Sebastian wakes up, only to find the room empty. When Sebastian checks the other room, Martin shows no sign of having been awake.

---

6. Berger's most recent film, *Horseplay* (2022) [*Los Agitadores*], combines elements from *Taekwondo* (2017)—a team of sportsmen on a weekend getaway hanging out and partying naked—and the repetition of objects from the *bugarrón* habitat, such as the view-master gadget. Like *Taekwondo*, *Horseplay* includes visual representation of sportsmen sleeping together naked and performing college "not-gay" homosexual pranks with each other. The mischievous feeling at the film's beginning turns serious after Poli, one of the athletes, receives a view-master as a Christmas gift from the group. Poli does not show angst about his sexuality. Instead, Nico seems deeply unsettled when discovering that Andy occasionally has sex with Poli. In an earlier scene, Andy confessed to Poli that while he enjoys penetrating him, he always prefers women over men. "If, for example, we go to the mountains and there is a woman present, I would always go with her. It is my natural inclination. I like shagging and getting my cock sucked," he explains to Poli. Nico feels disgusted when he discovers Andy's indiscriminate sexual appetite ("You are sick"). When Andy confronts Nico by accusing him of being a "closeted homo," Nico kills him. Unlike Berger's previous films, the view-master is given here to Poli, not Nico, who seems haunted not only by an unresolved understanding of his sexuality but also by Andy's heteroflexible *bugarrón* sexual practice. The optical ecology of *bugarrón* objects has been extended to *Horseplay*, thus resonating with earlier films such as Berger's *Plan B*.

This sleepover leads to a series of events that exacerbate the film's suspense. Martin's accidental death triggers in Sebastian a deep longing. Overwhelmed by an unexpected feeling of loss and grief, Sebastian is unable to concentrate at work. He also struggles to keep his feelings from his longtime girlfriend. Martin played a trick on Sebastian that could have cost Sebastian his job. Why does Martin's absence suddenly unleash such a profound longing?

From the first to the last scene, the film focuses on Martin's persistence in inching physically and emotionally closer to Sebastian. This increasing intimacy is also anticipated by the film's opening scenes where the camera looks closely at Martin's skin. Viewers are subjected to an inch-by-inch inspection of Martin's body. An extreme close-up shot sequence exposes the viewers to close-ups of Martin's heels, inner thighs, hands, shoulders, eyes, feet, lips and nose, abdomen, buttocks, knees, ears, chest, and right nipple. Martin's body is inspected slowly, one extreme close-up at a time.[7] As a fragmented body, a body in parts, Martin's corpus introduces us to the erotic optics of the film's beginning. The skin takes center stage as the camera lens focuses closely. But although the viewer is presented with images of classical beauty in the form of a male body in fragments, the film's music uses the auditory faculty to warn viewers of the dangers associated with admiring a young male body. Berger alludes here to a sense of the male body's aesthetics reminiscent of Thomas Mann's admiration for beautiful young males in *Death in Venice*. The viewers' specular inspection of male skin and seductive body parts is revealed to be not from an aesthetic perspective but from a medical one. The close inspection of Martin's skin is actually the filming of a medical exam for a case of fungal infection that the school is urgently addressing. This confluence of perspectives, between the spectator's leisurely and medical gaze, is revealed when the film shifts from still shots to action movement. As Martin spreads his toes, fingers, armpits, and mouth for the camera, we overhear the physician asking him to show one part of his body and then another. The clinic's medical gaze displaces the aesthetic spell of the film's beginning scenes. This is especially the case when the physician's white robe moves in front of the camera from left to right as if a curtain has taken us into another room where the body is subjected to the rigors of functionality and where the ideas of a classical scene crumble under the reality of a basic public physician's office. The young male body clashes with the bare-bones, lackluster setting.

The fact that discourses of knowledge, education, medicine, and sexuality converge in these initial scenes alerts us to the film's many layers. The young

---

7. In *The Filmmaker's Eye* (2017), Gustavo Mercado explains that the "extreme close up" shot establishes a sense of "closeness and intimacy" with the character (35). It establishes a "powerful visual statement" within the image system of cinema (29).

male body becomes visible not in a single discourse but through a confluence of discourses. However, the film is less about what is seen than what the visible image connects to in other registers. It points to those invisible connections outlining that which is visible, consistent with Merleau-Ponty's claim that the invisible functions as the outline and depth of the visible. That is to say, for Merleau-Ponty, the invisible "renders present to us what is absent" ("Eye and Mind" 132). Berger's *Absent* reveals the outlines of the visible but does not make visible the complete picture. Viewers can see beyond the visual image by connecting with the film's profound sense of loss. The absence of visible images makes palpable the loss of a solid emotional connection between a middle-aged heterosexual man and his adolescent student. Viewers can witness the outlines of the visible, the disturbance in Sebastian's psyche, the dislocations of his desire, and the uncertainty over the unsettling intimacy toward a new love object.

Two scenes are emblematic of Merleau-Ponty's insight about images that serve as venues in allowing us to see farther than one sees. One occurs early in the film when Sebastian is looking at the young boys preparing for their swimming lesson. Sebastian concentrates on Martin and follows him with his gaze as he walks to the restroom. This scene is repeated at the end of the film but in altered form. Supplemental scenes dramatize a sequence of events that makes visible more than the initial image. Sebastian decides to return to the swimming pool by breaking into the gym. In the process, he cuts his arm on a windowpane. There, confused about his own feelings over Martin's death, he reinvokes the image of Martin socializing with his friends by the pool, getting ready for their swimming lesson. At this moment, that which had been omitted, that is to say, the invisible outlines of the initial image, becomes visible via the reproduction of mental images that were out of sight in the original shot. Making the occluded connections visible enriches the shot sequence's impoverished character. Now awakened, the world beyond the outline provides scenes showing Sebastian following Martin into the locker room. Sebastian is happy and comfortable in these shots and asks Martin to wait for him in one of the scenes.

The space where this sequence takes place is a locker room that acquires a labyrinthine dimension. Here we get a classic sense of Perseus lost in a labyrinth; but instead of a Minotaur pursuing him, Perseus pursues the image of his beloved. Or should we understand Sebastian as the Minotaur that pursues young Martin through the labyrinth? This vast maze of vibrant objects—especially illuminated lockers, steam, towels, and jockstraps—could be construed as a gay man's fantasy but also as a *bugarrón*'s heaven. The endless passageways and rows of tall, old-fashioned lockers made of mahogany, floor-to-ceiling mirrors, numerous benches with half-used towels thrown on them, and the ambiance caused by the steam reveal the outlines of an image that, until this moment, was hidden from view. These details of a world outlining the initial shot represent not only a version of an inner world of mental images but also a system of objects that give shape to a peculiar *bugarrón* ecology. This doubling, of an externalized inner world and a mirroring ecology, becomes key in supplementing a world not immediately visible to the naked eye.

Via this invisible world of mental images that has suddenly acquired visibility on the screen, viewers increase their capacity to see farther than before. Not only do we see the transfer of those mental images onto film; we also become spectators transported to a world beyond life and death. In this ecology of loss, we find a different Sebastian, confident in his own skin.[8] Sebastian's bleeding flesh opens the visual narrative to a particular scene sequence. In the outlined world of vibrant images, Martin tells him, "You are bleeding too much." The opening of the body where the inside seeps outward transports the viewer to a different horizon of visibility. From a place that is dingily lit, the film shifts to a dazzling quality of light that intensifies all colors and makes the surroundings vibrant. The glaring sequence of images connects us to the inner world of mental images but also to the other world. The world of images here takes us to the brilliant images of a posthuman existence. There, the clarity of images is exceptional and shining. It is in this space of vibrant images of loss that Sebastian asks Martin to forgive him.

The scene introduces a world of spectral vitality where sudden energy is felt in the images of an afterlife but not in the world of death and living. Whereas the film has been haunted by silence and hesitancy, in this space of vibrant images Sebastian can communicate clearly with Martin. The film shifts from a dearth of communication where language fails to be uttered to a world where language becomes fluid. Sebastian is temporarily detached from the world and finds fluidity of expression in the mourning process. For Freud, mourning is "the reaction to the loss of a loved person, or to the loss of some abstraction which has taken the place of one" ("Mourning" 243). During this process, "it is the world which has become poor and empty" (246). A rich world of mental images assists Sebastian in the work of mourning by allowing

---

8. My analysis here has been informed by the work of Merleau-Ponty but also by Jane Bennett's work on vibrancy in the nonhuman world, which she defines as a "vitality intrinsic to materiality" and as an "active, earthy, not-quite-human capaciousness" (*Vibrant* 3). Her term *vibrant matter* attempts to undo a binary understanding of human and nonhuman worlds. She posits that the typically divided split between dull matter and vibrant life is a misguided construction, so she coins the term *vibrant matter*. Her concept challenges the matter/life binary by alerting us to ways in which humans and nonhumans are vital members of our understanding of ecology.

him to come to terms with the absent, and unconsciously loved, object. However, the sequence shows that something marvelous occurs at this moment in the film. Sebastian's mourning process does not impoverish the world but instead makes the world visible for the first time. It is as if the veil that had made the world bleak and impoverished has been suddenly lifted. Sebastian's opened veins show him a new visible reality. Mourning has unveiled the world lurking at the outlines of everyday images. If bleakness was associated with Sebastian's negation of his relationship with Martin, at this moment his exclusive heterosexual spell breaks. The spotlight falls on the gradation of a nonexclusive heterosexual experience. *Bugarrón* sexual practice has awoken a constellation of relationships hidden in plain sight. As we will see in the next section, this set of relationships takes us not only to the beyond but also to occluded undercurrents of *bugarrón* practice.

SCREENED IN

Fuentes-León's *Undertow* (2009) explores the depths of visible limits in the sexual relation between heteroflexible men. *Undertow* narrates the story of Miguel's relationship with Santiago. Miguel, a fisherman in Peru's coastal region, engages in an intimate relationship with Santiago, an openly gay painter who travels to the impoverished fishermen's village from Lima, the country's capital. Miguel lives in a humble fisherman's house with his wife, Mariela, and his newborn son. Santiago perishes at sea, drowning in an ocean undercurrent that traps his body underwater. His spirit visits Miguel and requests that his body be properly buried. The film culminates with Miguel's eulogy at Santiago's funeral. Structured in a series of binaries, the film explores the complications of Miguel's sexuality in a traditional town where everyday life is organized around work, church, and family. The simplicity of life stands in sharp contrast to Santiago's sexual openness, metropolitan background, and cosmopolitan upbringing. Santiago's sexual orientation is unquestionably gay. By contrast, Miguel's sexuality is undetermined. He declares that he is not gay and emphasizes that he is not "like that." Miguel claims not to be bisexual, either; he sees himself as heterosexual. Miguel's flexible heterosexuality includes his same-sex relations with Santiago, thus placing him in the orbit of a cinematic *bugarrón*.

Santiago's wealthy background and his potential "Americanized" lifestyle introduce a counterweight to Miguel's apparent limiting provincialism. Miguel's darker physical complexion, brown eyes, and suntanned skin are easily distinguished from Santiago's relatively fair physical traits. This binary logic is present in the film from its beginning, where it alternates between two main subjects, a close-up of Mariela's pregnant belly, and its opposite, the dead body of Carlos (Miguel's cousin), during the burial of his body at sea. Two competing forces, life and death, frame the film. The binary schema also structures the landscape where the blue-green waters of the Pacific Ocean sharply contrast with the arid barrenness of the coastal shores. Complicating this logic is how each side of the binary contains a space for its opposite. This is best appreciated because the ocean is understood as a traditional burial site and the barren shore as the land where ghosts roam in penance.

Framed between two offerings to the dead, Carlos's funeral at the beginning and Santiago's funeral at its end, the film focuses on Miguel, a *bugarrón* practitioner. It depicts Miguel's tribulations, complicated relationship with an openly gay man (Santiago), and new role as a father. Miguel confesses that he loves Santiago and rejects any adjudication of a gay "identity." We may think that Miguel is posing as a heterosexual man, but he tells us "Yo no se posar" ["I do not know how to pose"]. This sentence is clearly ambiguous, as Miguel's "Yo no se posar" could also be translated as "I do not know how to fake or dissemble." Even the most sympathetic viewer would be hard-pressed to square this claim with his life experience as a person living a double life. When the film tries to pin down this meaning of *posar* as "posing for a painting," it still reveals his statement as problematic given that Santiago painted him in a collection of still drawings. Yet, incredible as it may seem, Miguel is accurate in his statement. He has not posed for Santiago's paintings, but that did not stop Santiago from drawing his likeness while he slept during one of their romantic encounters. Miguel is also correct; he does not fake, but neither does he gratuitously reveal. He compartmentalizes his truths. It is in the context of his doings and undoings that Miguel's heteroflexibility disturbs the film's binaries and blurs the limits of what is or could be heterosexual intimacy between men. In *Undertow*, this constantly refocused intimacy is portrayed as an invisibility that has become visible via art.

In Santiago's clandestine collection of portraits of Miguel, we find the fisherman in many poses. One painting shows Miguel asleep on the beach, lying on his back, with the cloudy sky on the horizon. Miguel's profile exudes peacefulness, and his copper-skinned, shirtless torso alludes to a lazy Sunday morning on a nearby beach while on holiday. A second painting shows Miguel fully naked, lying on his chest. We do not see his face, only the top of his head and hair. His arms are folded and his forehead rests on his forearms. His body is resting on a sandy beach, and the light-colored sand makes his buttocks look more tanned. Another painting shows Miguel standing on the beach, among the waves, with a blue sky above. Miguel is depicted looking sideways, away from the viewer's gaze. He is in movement; his arms move back and forth, and his curly hair seems free in the ocean breeze. All the paintings show Miguel looking elsewhere, in all sorts of directions, inward in sleep, or outward to the horizon and the ocean wind. These are luminous paintings of Miguel in a state of nature, free from human constraints and "identity" trappings. These aesthetic representations are thematically idealistic but are also reminders of a human balance with nature that makes the environment resonate with a primordial sense of an Edenic order. The ecology these paintings depict is that of humans in tune with their surroundings, not attempting to subdue or subjugate nature but in a harmonious relationship with it—that is, in a state of supporting and being supported by it. This state of balance with nature is combined with an ecology of human sexual expression that challenges artificial constraints such as "identity" categories. In these paintings, sexual "identity" vanishes in the sand, sky, and flow of ocean waves. The film's slow-motion movement from painting to painting reminds us of Merleau-Ponty's explanation of cinema: a "slow motion shows a body being carried along, floating among objects like seaweed, but not *moving itself*" ("Eye and Mind" 145; original italics).

The collection of portraits embedded in a series of slow-moving shots in the film brings to mind an early scene at the beach where Santiago had teased Miguel about acting serious while offering Carlos's dead body to the sea. Miguel responded that his seriousness was required as part of this ultimate offering. In local culture, seriousness at burial is crucial for the soul to rest in peace. Unbeknownst to Miguel, Santiago had captured his seriousness in one of his paintings where he portrays the funeral procession. Miguel is in the foreground carrying his cousin's body. Santiago had admired Miguel's role at the funeral, and his painting of the burial scene emphasizes Miguel's seriousness.

Later in the film, Miguel smudges his likeness from the burial painting in order to conceal his "identity." He refuses to be captured in image form even when the context seems far from erotic themes.[9] The smudging of his likeness is none other than the act of placing under erasure the *bugarrón* subject's image. Not surprisingly, Miguel's decision to place his face under erasure adds another layer of representational meaning to an already rich painting. The film portrays the *bugarrón* subject and his reflected image on a canvas. The scene shows where the *bugarrón* subject erases his likeness from the painting. The gesture in fact points to the shot of a layered *bugarrón* subject's visibility.

---

9. Kaja Silverman explains this reaction from the subject to their self-image thus: "The subject can only successfully misrecognize him- or herself within the image or cluster of images through which he or she is culturally apprehended" (*Threshold* 18). This sense of an "unlocalized" gaze creating meaning makes the *bugarrón* erase images of himself that he cannot control.

If we were to peel off the layers hidden at this moment, we would discover the following. The first layer shows the *bugarrón* subject placing his painted image under erasure. A second layer, underneath, shows a painting where the *bugarrón* subject is literally under erasure. The third layer depicts the *bugarrón* subject's image before being placed under erasure. A fourth layer reveals Miguel's image captured in the painting by his male lover, thus situating him as a *bugarrón* practitioner. The final layer shows an empty canvas where the *bugarrón* practitioner will be painted. The scene, which captures the movement of the *bugarrón* subject erasing his likeness, introduces an unexpected layering of visual depth at the surface of the canvas.

Jacqueline Rose, whose work frames this chapter, underscored that for Freud modern painting is the "image of the unconscious" (*Sexuality* 229). Rose explained the connections between images found in visual art and those stemming from the inner world by elucidating that "images require a reading which neither coheres them into a unity, nor struggles to get behind them into a realm of truth" (230). Placing truth and unifying coherence under erasure and within brackets, the images of the *bugarrón* in film and the images that make up his habitat bring to light a literal ambiguity. *Bugarrón* sexual practice becomes visible in images attesting to the invisibility of the subject's truth, which projects outward ever more sexual gradations.

Like Rose, Leo Bersani and Ulysse Dutoit argue that "a major virtue of the visual arts is their capacity to make the invisible visible" (*Forms* 1). Bersani and Dutoit use Caravaggio's paintings to point to techniques the painter uses to direct "our look to spaces outside the painting itself, spaces designated as the necessary but unpainted extensions of certain formal elements within the work" (1). Similarly, Latin American critic Sylvia Molloy argues that posing is the "representation of invisibility" ("Politics" 145). Unlike gay men, *bugarrón* practitioners crave not representation but invisibility. Cinema seeks to undo the *bugarrón* practitioner's insistence on remaining at the edges of the visible field. *Bugarrón* cinema has unleashed this disturbance.

Miguel's claim that "I do not know how to pose" is truthful in that he has not posed for Santiago's paintings and has not posed or faked his heterosexuality. Miguel crossed sexual boundaries when he elected to be a different type of heterosexual. This posing is not political in the sense of activism, but his struggle against the community takes a political form that borders on a politics of principle and thus is easily politicized. There are echoes of Sophocles's Antigone in his struggle, that is, of an ethical subject burying a loved one while risking an assured social death. In the film, society takes the place of the state in Sophocles's play. At the same time, there are signs of hope, for as the funeral procession (the modern version of the choir in Sophocles's Greek tragedy) walks on foot through town, the younger generation joins the funeral party at the point where older folks stopped marching. Unlike classical Greek tragedy, the chorus in *Undertow* divides itself into two parts: a younger and an older generation. Unlike *Plan B*, *Undertow* captures a strategy of power that makes a subject tell the truth of his sexuality. As Foucault explains in *History of Sexuality, Vol. 1*, at a historical moment "an imperative was established: not only will you confess to acts contravening the law, but you will seek to transform your desire, your every desire, into discourse" (21). This "objectification of sex" into discourse is not for oneself but "for another" (confession) (33). Foucault also refers to this technique as "the singular imperialism" because it "compels everyone to transform their sexuality into a perpetual discourse" (33). Ever since then, Foucault argues, sex has been "driven out of hiding and constrained to lead a discursive existence" (33). This technique of publicly telling the "truth" of sex takes place at the connecting point of several discursive practices in the film, where religious, sexual, economic, societal, cultural, and familial disciplinary forms coalesce around the character of Miguel.

Complicating matters further is the fact that in *Undertow* the gay subject is visible but dies. There are echoes here of *Kiss of the Spider Woman*. The couple, Miguel–Santiago, evoke a similar binary logic that has structured the representation of homosexuality/heterosexuality in Latin American films ever since Héctor Babenco's *Kiss*. In *Kiss of the Spider Woman*, the main couple, Valentín–Molina, set its dramatic parameters from the beginning. The plot is already known by virtually everyone: Molina, a window dresser, has been imprisoned on charges of molesting a minor, and Valentín, a political prisoner, has been arrested for revolutionary practices against the state. The warden places them in the same prison cell, hoping that Molina will serve as an informer. But Molina falls in love with Valentín and convinces him to have sex before his imminent release from prison. At the end of the film, Molina is killed by the secret police while serving as an informer for Valentín's revolutionary movement. The homosexual dies tragically in *Kiss* as a result of his complicity in crimes against the state. By comparison, in *Undertow* the gay character dies, only to return in spectral form seeking assistance to reach his final repose. In *Kiss*, Valentín's delirium transforms Molina into a hybrid entity, half-woman/half-spider, thus creating a composite image that merges human with nonhuman; Valentín expands the horizon of what is human by crossing into nonhuman territory. But whereas Puig, in the novel that inspired the film, takes us to the border where human and animal come together in a new hybrid form (spider-woman), *Undertow* takes us in a different direction, to the borders of human and nonhuman. In *Undertow*, Miguel's inner world expands and opens a connection to the spiritual world. But it is the undertow, the unexpected current of water, and the rocks that trap Santiago's body that connect to an underlying flow of emotions of a nonexclusive and heterogeneous sense of heterosexuality. When Miguel finds but leaves Santiago's body underwater, hidden among the ocean rocks, he wants these nonexclusive connections to remain buried at sea. The spiritual realm is part of this posthuman ecology that began with *Kiss*; in *Undertow* it has morphed from the figure of a spider-woman to the spiritual image of a gay painter. Sebastian's presence as spirit, invisible to everyone but to Miguel, inverts the traditional *Kiss* narrative. The *bugarrón* subject is invisible to others as long as the gay lover is absent.

Smudging the *bugarrón* subject's image is analogous to blurring the limits of heterosexuality by including within it nonexclusive heterosexual relationships between men.[10] The smudged image in the painting, the distorted image of Santiago's body underwater, and the luminous landscape all contribute to this erosion of limits. This flexibility reawakens relations connecting sexual practitioners with landscapes and objects. To this ecology of material objects—such as a dead body or a rock—we can add other *things*, such as a counterflow of water and a spirit that is no longer invisible. Santiago's paintings capture more than a *bugarrón* subject's likeness in images: they become part of a cinematic ecology of a flexible and visible sexual practice.

THE INTERVALS OF CINEMATIC FICTION

"I will never leave you. I wouldn't leave you for anyone else. But if we are going to be together I need to know that if I feel like being with a man, you won't say no," states Ignacio during a conversation with his wife, Zoe, in an attempt to find a way to reconcile their marriage. Until this moment in Ricardo de Montreuil's film *La mujer de mi hermano* [*My Brother's Wife*] (2005), there were only hints of Ignacio's sexual orientation. In an earlier scene, Ignacio's brother, Gonzalo, had accused him of being a "fag," basing this accusation on

---

10. In *The Four Fundamental Concepts of Psychoanalysis* (1973), Lacan answers the question "How can we try to apprehend that which seems to elude us in this way in the optical structuring of space?" (93). By arguing that "if you wish to see a star . . . do not look straight at it," Lacan signals that by looking at the edge of our field of vision, we could successfully apprehend the reflective image that triggers the confusion in the visual field (102). In other words, the slight sideways glance, the "mere shift of our gaze" or strategic murking, separates the disturbance in the field of vision from the confusion that generates it. Shifting the gaze alters that which creates confusion in the visual field. What is left is an image which, for Lacan, does not necessarily equal an authentic appearance.

an incident during his childhood when he recalled Ignacio sexually molesting him. Ignacio replied to his brother's accusation: "You are sick, Gonzalo." At this point in the film the audience cannot be sure whose version of events to believe.

The film, an adaptation of Peruvian writer Jaime Bayly's best-selling novel *La mujer de mi hermano* (2002), is one of the first Latin American visual narratives to explore a modern *bugarrón* practitioner's situation. The plot is as follows: Ignacio and his wife, Zoe, are going through a rough patch in their marriage due to their inability to conceive a child. Ignacio is sterile and Zoe does not want to adopt children. Zoe and her brother-in-law, Gonzalo, begin a torrid love affair that ends abruptly when Zoe becomes pregnant. Ignacio and Zoe decide to reconcile and to raise Zoe and Gonzalo's child as their own. The film ends with the conversation cited above and the couple's reconciliation.

De Montreuil provides a stylish, modern background central to the novel's aesthetics. The film is shot mostly in a new mid-century glass-style house with hypermodern architecture in a suburb of Mexico City. This type of setting situates the drama in a generic environment not rooted in Latin America; local flavor has been diminished to convey a more cosmopolitan look. As a result, the only remnant of local culture is the Mexican Spanish used by the actors. The setting alternates between Ignacio's house, a downtown studio apartment where Gonzalo lives and paints, and the hotel where Zoe stays at the end of the film (where she and Ignacio work out the details of their new marriage arrangement). If, for the most part, the film is an accurate rendition of the novel, it does take some poetic license with the character of Ignacio and his sexuality.

In the novel, a particular scene reveals Ignacio's male–male desire. In the bathroom, as Ignacio masturbates, the narrator describes what he is thinking:

> Se deleita pensando en algo que no hará, que no se atreverá hacer: besar a un hombre, poseerlo con violencia. . . . Piensa en ese hombre, un hombre cualquiera que no conoce, y goza en secreto. (193)

> He delights himself thinking about something he would never do, that he would never dare to do: to kiss a man, to violently possess a man. . . . He thinks about this man, a generic man that he does not know or care to know, and pleases himself in secret. (my translation)

In the film, this masturbation scene is missing. Instead, de Montreuil combines it with another scene in the novel where Ignacio is supposedly out of town and telephones Zoe. Whereas in the novel Ignacio masturbates after the phone call, in the film we see the modern hotel room where Ignacio is staying and notice that he is not alone. From within the shadowy background, an image forms behind what seems to be a modern walk-in shower area with steamed glass walls. We become aware of an unidentified figure drying his or her body with a towel. Viewers struggle to get a clear view, as the image never comes into full focus. Via the technique of rack focusing, the figure's blurry image confirms Ignacio's infidelity while disorienting viewers' assumptions about his sexuality. The murky image disturbs the field of vision by making an out-of-focus background our primary focal point. As a result, the usual importance of the foreground recedes. The narrative sequence confuses the viewer, as Ignacio's image and voice reiterate his love for Zoe at the same time that spectators attempt to decipher the gender of the blurred figure. De Montreuil's shot is a classic reversed perspective where the background action acquires greater attention than the foreground. Yet this technique complicates the reversed perspective by emphasizing the nebulous image. Typically, an accentuated background highlights a scene taking place behind a character who is understood to be unaware of it. The viewer sees both foreground and background, and thus the character's limited vision and obliviousness. In de Montreuil's scene, the background setting is perfectly clear while containing within itself a blurred image behind the steamed shower walls. This act of complicating a reversal, of lending visibility to an unclear image, disturbs and heightens curiosity. At this moment, the film focuses on what Merleau-Ponty refers to as "the horizon of its farthest point," manifested here as a moving blurry spot. By focusing on a wholly unclear background image, the shot displaces Ignacio's clear image from the foreground to the frontal periphery of our field of vision. As a result, Ignacio's image, that is, the *bugarrón* practitioner's image, is displayed at the edge of the screen. This process where the mystery of a nebulous image seduces viewers intensifies the spectatorial desire to know the "truth" of Ignacio's sexuality. The cinematic reversal heightens viewers' inclination toward an already culturalized rationality of *scientia sexualis* (our wanting to know Ignacio's sexual orientation).

Scenes like this one suggest a fruitful dynamic between literature and film. In *The Intervals of Cinema* (2014), Jacques Rancière argues that cinema as an aesthetic form has historically struggled to remove itself from the influence of literature. The novel's mastery in storytelling (with its structural conventions of the primacy of plot and ordering of actions) was influential in shaping the telling of an imaginative story, but as filmmaking improved its techniques of mobility and editing, it began to see itself in a different light. As Rancière puts it, "Cinema . . . arose *after* literature" (43; original italics). By which he means that in terms of the arts, cinema gave sound to the written word and a faster-paced movement to the literary scenes where cause and effect drove the narrative forward (44). In this way, Rancière understands cinema as a "multitude of things" that emerge from in between silent words (novel) and "the spectacle of shadows" (film) (5). Between film and novel, Rancière identifies "a play of encounters and distances" that defines cinema (1). Therefore, cinema is "a set of irreducible gaps between things (novel and film) that have the same name without being members of a single body" (5). The irreducible differences between the written text or script and its visual narrative (film) create cinema.[11] Cinema is the creative visual narrative that takes shape in the encounter and distances of the gap between novel and film. In *Jacques Rancière* (2011), Joseph Tanke explains that for Rancière, "cinema is a mixed art in that it continually negotiates between these two" (112). Following Rancière, I see the relationship between Bayly's novel and de Montreuil's film as one where de Montreuil expands on a nonidentitarian principle hidden behind an anomalous sexual practice truncated prematurely by Bayly in his novel. It is from this space of playfulness between film and literary representations that an encounter with *bugarrón* sexual practice becomes possible. *Bugarrón* sexual practice emerges from the hidden gaps of Bayly's novel. These narrative gaps have been purposely widened in the film.

Instances of these encounters and distances, between the literary work and the film, are as follows. Whereas in the film Ignacio informs Zoe that he wants to see men on the side, in the novel Ignacio never confesses to Zoe that he is "attracted to men." The novel ends with the re-establishment of the exclusively heterosexual nuclear family. Ignacio has accepted Zoe's child with Gonzalo as his own son, just like in the film. But the theme of Ignacio's desire for men is dropped entirely, as if it were a symptom of his inability to be a father. Never again in the novel does he demonstrate any interest other than love for his unfaithful wife and an illegitimate son.

More importantly, a second instance where the film widens a gap in Bayly's novel occurs during the confrontation between Ignacio and Gonzalo. In this scene, viewers are presented with a painting hidden behind another canvas in the studio. The medium-sized painting depicts a diminutive individual dwarfed by an enormous military tank. It evokes the iconic image of the notorious Tiananmen Square Tank Man that has come to represent globally the 1989 massacre of students. For Gonzalo, the painting depicts childhood trauma. For Ignacio, the image lacks meaning. The film adds a painting that is absent from the original text, and by doing so it pictorially materializes Gonzalo's memory of trauma. Gonzalo's painting widens a sexual gap in the text.

---

11. Rancière refers to this theoretical perspective as a "universe without hierarchy," that is, a perspectival approach from which "the films recomposed by perceptions, feelings and words count for as much as the ones printed" (*Intervals* 8).

In the novel, Gonzalo's description of his memory is only verbal, not pictorial, and it is enough to tap into Ignacio's repressed memory of the event. Suddenly, this forgotten memory emerges. Ignacio confesses to himself that he had completely forgotten this incident and that even now when he thinks of it, it strikes him as innocent play by two boys coming to terms with a growing curiosity about sex. Gonzalo's conscious memory awakens in Ignacio a corresponding repressed memory. But in the text, Gonzalo's conscious memory does not displace Ignacio's unconscious memory. In the film, the painting, as a pictorial object of Gonzalo's memory, does not replace Ignacio's awakened repressed memory either. A difference of opinion and value is presented on the "traumatic" event, but neither displacement nor revision takes place. However, the widening gap allows the inclusion of *bugarrón* sexual practice in the visual narrative. In the film, the painting provides an indexical sign, that is, a clue that links meanings, as another instance corroborating Ignacio's history of engaging in *bugarrón* sexual practice. In the novel, lacking the painting, Gonzalo points to having been penetrated by his brother "in the anus" ("me la metiste por el culo cuando eramos chicos" [268]). In between the film and the literary narrative, de Montreuil inserts the pictorial depiction of a penetrator (Ignacio) and a penetrated (Gonzalo). The duality, not the commensurability, of conscious memory and awakened unconscious memory finds representation in cinema's ability to play with encounters and distances in the spectacle of *bugarrón* practice brought into the limelight from the literary shadows. The number of scenes where *bugarrón* sexual practice emerges in the film gives credence to the creation of a specifically cinematic *bugarrón*. The visual field augments the limitations of the written word.

Cinema opens a space for including other options (variants) not verbalized in literary fiction. As it happens, de Montreuil's opening of Bayly's novel for the encounter with *bugarrón* practice is not the first instance of one of Bayly's fictional works being adapted for the inclusion of a sexual practice not present in the text. In "The Construction of the Bisexual Subject in *No se lo digas a nadie*" (2015), Alfredo J. Sosa-Velasco argues that Peruvian film director Francisco Lombardi's movie adaptation of Bayly's novel *No se lo digas a nadie* (1994) inserts a bisexual subject absent in the text. Bayly's novel is about a gay man who cannot fit in with Peruvian society because of his sexual orientation. Sosa-Velasco's point is that critics such as Stephen Hart have claimed that Lombardi's film adaptation "heterosexualizes" the novel by granting the novel's gay protagonist a bisexual "identity" (186).[12] Instead, Sosa-Velasco agrees with Subero, who argues that bisexuality in Lombardi's film is

---

12. Bisexuality is here understood as sexual versatility, that is, as men who like to penetrate and be penetrated during sex. This is counter to *bugarrón* sexual practice, where the role as penetrator during sex remains consistent (with the exception of sex-working *neobugarrones*).

a "queering," not a heterosexualizing, of a gay "identity." By contrast, I see de Montreuil *bugarronizing* a story that Bayly himself heterosexualizes and thus being consistent with the trend toward sexual variations that Sosa-Velasco and Subero attribute to Lombardi's film adaptation. In *La mujer,* Bayly, not the filmmaker, closes the door on heteroflexibility, and de Montreuil forces it open. In de Montreuil's *La mujer,* Zoe concedes to Ignacio's sexual escapades with other males, while Ignacio agrees to be the father of Zoe and Gonzalo's son. The heterosexual family unit is perceived as reinstated at the end of the film, but in reality it has been *bugarronized* by the flexible heterosexuality of a hidden Latin American sexual practice. De Montreuil conjures the cinematic *bugarrón* from within the shadows of Peruvian fiction.

De Montreuil's *La mujer* is different from more recent films that develop the theme of conscious memory, such as, for the sake of contrast, Argentine director Papu Curotto's film *Esteros* (2016). *Esteros* is the name of a place, a country home, where Jerónimo and Matias had a sexual awakening as children. After many years of estrangement, openly gay Jerónimo and Matias reacquaint. Matias and his fiancée, Rochi, are visiting town from Brazil, where they reside. His re-encounter with Jerónimo leads to a dramatic change of heart. During a day trip at Esteros, Jerónimo reminds Matias of their special moments together as children, and this leads to Matias's accepting his feelings for Jerónimo. For Matias, memories of Jerónimo were conscious but had been relegated to childhood. In *Esteros,* Matias ends up embracing a relationship with a gay man and hints that he could be coming out as well. By contrast, in *La mujer,* Ignacio understands his attraction to men as a dimension of his heterosexuality. For him, heterosexuality is inclusive of homoerotic desires. Following something akin to Alfred Kinsey's scale, in Bayly's novel, Ignacio understands his teenage sexual encounter with Gonzalo as part of adolescent experimentation in which heterosexuality includes incidental same-sex acts.

In Kinsey, male sexuality is understood as a series of degrees between polar opposites, exclusive homosexuality and exclusive heterosexuality. Closer to the polar opposites of exclusive heterosexuality, Kinsey places two other subcategories that may be relatively similar to *bugarrón* sexual practice: "predominantly heterosexual, only incidentally homosexual" and "predominantly heterosexual, but more than incidentally homosexual" (qtd. in Robinson, *Modernization* 74). These subcategories marking degrees of difference in sexual practice are useful in making sense of the sexual anomaly. The subcategory "heterosexual, but more than incidentally homosexual" may describe a similar degree of variation in male sexuality akin to *bugarrón* sexual practice. For Kinsey this gradation in the sexual continuum is different from bisexuality.

De Montreuil's *bugarronizing* introduces a flexible heterosexuality inclusive of incidental acts of sex between heterosexual men. The inclusion of occasional sexual relations with men is at the heart of a *bugarrón* practice, and it is consistent with nonexclusive heterosexual gradations.

NARROWING THE DISTANCE

In Latin American cinema, heteroflexibility becomes visible in *bugarrón* practice. Where the anthropological works of traditional *bugarrón* practitioners chronicle detailed accounts of sex acts in distinct places and across borders, *bugarrón* cinema's representation of a celluloid *bugarrón* practice deepens the representation of desire between men and diversifies accounts of explicit sex. If, in the traditional *bugarrón* sexual practice and the neoliberal *bugarrón*, sex is primary, in *bugarrón* cinema heteroflexible desire for same sex is supreme. These visual narratives augment ethnographic accounts of same-sex practices. In *bugarrón* cinema, scenes of sex acts take place off-camera. For instance, in *Plan B* a growing intimacy between Pablo and Bruno leads to sexual relations, but the film stops just when this is about to happen. Yet distance had been at work in *Plan B* as Pablo and Bruno keep narrowing the gulf of intimacy between them until the end of the film. In *La mujer de mi hermano*, we witness steamy sex scenes between Gonzalo and his sister-in-law Zoe, but Ignacio's sexual encounters with men take place either outside the frame or out of focus. In *Hawaii* an introspective look into childhood memories displaces the sexual relationship between men, and in *Undertow* the visible sex acts take place between Miguel and his wife. In this thematic trajectory, the unintended consequence of *bugarrón* cinema has been the removal of acts from its narratives. Where the anthropological accounts prioritize lust over intimacy, this logic is reversed in *bugarrón* cinema, which prioritizes intimacy over lust. Distance is recreated and widened between the *bugarrón* practitioner and his male partners.

Along with narrowing the distance between heterosexuality and male-male desire, these films depict a widened distance between *bugarrón* sexual practice's visibility on screen and depictions of the sex act. It is as if the curse of Freud's misreading of Leonardo's drawings has reverberated over time, making the visual depictions of *bugarrón* practice too confusing. There is no question that the visibility of the cinematic *bugarrón* creates enough of a disturbance; the play on distance deepens this effect in *bugarrón* sexual practice's visual narratives. Where previously lust narrowed the physical distance but maintained an emotional gulf between men, in *bugarrón* cinema this relationship is inverted, and the visual narrative depicts the gradual narrowing of a previous emotional distance. As a result, a vital sexual tension is created.

Berger pursues this line of thinking about distance and nearness in *Sexual Tension Volatile* (2012), a feature film composed of short vignettes, or short visual narratives, that explore the situations between heterosexual men at different places in the city: a tattoo parlor, a sleepover at a friend's house, and a doctor's office. All the stories depict the distance between men and their inability to cross into a sexual relationship. In the sleepover story, Berger captures the tension between the protagonist and a friend's cousin, who share a room. The two keep stealing glances at each other, and their bodies touch slightly while watching television. As tension rises from this seconds-long interaction, the friend's cousin abruptly leaves the premises and does not return. The film displays how the narrowing to a slight touch triggers a widening distance.

In *Screened Out* (2002), Jean Baudrillard addresses a cultural trend in modernized societies where a collision of polar opposites blurs the distance that has traditionally kept things apart. The dissolution of distance leads to the clash of opposites, and when this takes place, explains Baudrillard, "vital tension is discharged" (176). It is not a coincidence that the latest additions to *bugarrón* cinema depict the existence and dissolution of this distance. Whereas *Sexual Tension Volatile* provides visual narratives of this tension and the misadventures of distance in *bugarrón* practitioner's desire, Lorenzo Vigas's *Por Allá [From Afar]* (2015) revels in this play of distance between intimacy and the sex act.

From Afar is a recent addition to *bugarrón* cinema, and one of the most enigmatic. Vigas's film tells the story of the relationship between Armando, a middle-aged Latin American professional man, and Élder, a street punk, in the city of Caracas, Venezuela. *From Afar*'s visual narrative is shrouded in secrets that cover themes of an unexplained sexual practice and of patricide. Armando pays young punks for sexual release, but viewers soon realize that his sexual relations with young adults are not so simple. His method is always the same. After cruising for his target, he pulls out a wad of cash as bait to lure the youngster to his home. We would expect something like steamy scenes of sexual intercourse to follow, but that is not what happens. Given its complicated narrative, *From Afar* demands a closer look.

The film opens with Armando, the protagonist, looking down from the top of a bridge to the highly trafficked double-lane highway of the Venezuelan capital city of Caracas. From its beginning, *From Afar* plays with the cinematic techniques for manufacturing distance; using the rack focusing method, the director shifts the focus of viewers' attention. At a distance, in a blur, is the bus stop where indistinguishable figures are standing at the street corner. Armando walks toward the bus stop, and his image now blurs with his surroundings. The next scene shows Armando cruising for "sex" at the bus stop. There is a shift in focus, and the face of a young man appears in the screen's foreground. We see Armando moving forward, looming behind the young man and getting closer. The perspective changes again, and we are behind Armando, getting extremely close to the youngster, pressing his body onto his. Once on the bus, we follow Armando from behind as he walks toward his seat next to the young man. No words are exchanged, and the next scene occurs in Armando's apartment. Significantly, these initial scenes are framed in terms of nearness and distance as well as the clarity and blurriness of the cinematic image. Rack focusing becomes in this film a key cinematic technique for portraying a relation between males. In this specific case, unfocusing functions as a tool for alluding to heteroflexibility in *bugarrón* cinema.

The film's first speech act—"Take off your shirt"—is a command given by Armando to the young man. The next is another command: "Lower your pants." The young man is being looked at from afar, and the screen is blurry. This initial sequence ends with a three-quarter close-up of the young man's face. His lips, nose, and chin are accentuated on the screen's foreground, but his eyes have been kept outside the frame. The camera lens is too close to the young man's body to show his full face. Via rack focusing, Armando's image continues to blur in the background, and viewers only hear the clinking sounds of a belt buckle being undone and, subsequently, the sound generated by a hand in rapid movement. Because it is structured as an over-the-shoulder shot, the young man in the foreground does not see, only hears, what's happening behind him.

Armando never touches the young man; no exchange of fluids takes place. Instead, the sex is mediated by a distancing from the erotic object. The over-the-shoulder shot produces a longitudinal plane that increases our perception of greater distance. A distant gaze becomes Armando's way of channeling his desire. He sits on the sofa, orders the punk to stand with his back toward him at a distance, and then asks the young man to take off his shirt. He then orders the punk to lower his pants to the point where they hang at the end of his buttocks. Armando is precise about how low the pants should be lowered. If the pants are pushed below the end of his buttocks, he asks the youth to raise them higher. Only then is some enigmatic signifier triggered in Armando's erotic psyche, as if a recollection becomes alive.[13] He proceeds to masturbate while seated as he gazes at the youth's backside. Armando's erotic object is portrayed in the shape of this young man in front of him posing as if he were a statue, a painting, or a picture. The youth does not bend over, nor is he allowed to perform any lewd gestures. After Armando achieves release, the youth leaves. This setup changes with Élder, who refuses to lower his pants. Instead, he beats Armando by hitting him in the face, and, while Armando is on the floor unconscious, he robs him.

Armando never confesses the truth of his sexuality and, when pressed, retorts with the interrogative: "Who is to say that I am really gay?" Armando is very convincing in (expressing to) Élder that he is not an "old faggot." The fact that Armando's release happens while admiring the archetypal pose of a male body with an exposed butt raises questions of classical beauty and psychological trauma. After Élder is injured in a street fight, Armando attends to his recovery at home. Élder has been beaten because he physically assaulted the brother of his pregnant girlfriend. As they converse at dinnertime, a few crucial details of their lives come to light. Élder confesses that his father beat him as a child, and Armando tells him that he wasn't struck as a child but that he wishes his father were dead. No more is said on the matter until Élder kills Armando's father. The night of the murder, Armando does not reject Élder's advances. Armando penetrates Élder, and for the first time, sexual distance is abolished. Hours later, Armando places an anonymous phone call to the police, which leads to the young man's arrest. The film never clarifies the sexual "identity" of either protagonist, nor does it clarify the question of physical abuse openly. We are put in the position of extracting via pure conjecture some meaning from the unconventional sexual practice that we witness. In this film, sexual-identity claims are missing. The many silences affecting the drama coalesce around the blurred images of a *bugarrón* subject. The unfocused images are matched by many narrative lacunae that create distance between knowledge and certainty in the visual narrative.

If viewers are at a loss to understand Élder's feelings toward Armando, they also find numerous gaps in Armando's story. There is a total absence of information on Armando's relationship with his father, but it would be reasonable to believe that his father was abusive. When Armando rides with his

---

13. In the context of cinema and art, Bersani and Dutoit elaborate on Laplanche's concept of the enigmatic signifier: "Adult sexuality is implanted in the child in the form of what Laplanche calls an enigmatic signifier—that is, a message by which the child is seduced but which he or she cannot read" (*Secrets* 39). In Laplanche and Pontalis, and in Bersani, an enigmatic signifier is a relationality that is renewed in fantasy yet inactive (Laplanche and Pontalis, "Fantasy" 9, 26).

father in the elevator, his father shows no sign of recognizing him. In this context, both Élder and Armando are haunted by undisclosed pasts. Film viewers have only partial accounts of their life narratives and their silences. If their pasts are consistently blurred, this condition seems in tune with a compartmentalized *bugarrón* practice. In a situation where Armando and Élder seem unable to read each other well, many questions remain unanswered: Was Armando searching for the right punk to eliminate his father? Did Armando have a grand plan/fantasy that a punk could kill his father and then have him do the prison time associated with the crime? Is this film a darker version of *Plan B*, where scheming is primordial?

In a world where very little is said, images become fundamental objects of connections across narrative intervals. In narratives where information fails to be disclosed, landscape and objects assume greater significance. They are not simply gratuitous images but rather essential components of relations between human and nonhuman forms. *From Afar* shows a more pronounced representation of those ecological dimensions than is present in other examples of *bugarrón* cinema. The view-master, paintings, photographs, books, and otherworldly forms give shape to a *bugarrón* ecology of objects. Multiplicity increases visibility. These films, which lend themselves to be interpreted as credible examples of heteroflexibility, bring a menagerie of objects to the fore.

In *From Afar*, the viewer witnesses a crucial scene showing Armando's obsessive-compulsive disorder as he reorganizes his collection of books and magazines in the living room. The scene evokes Armando's relationship with an ecology of things and objects and occurs after Élder has returned a second time and taken Armando's money without obliging his demands. We have a sequence of shots in which the only human subjects visible are in framed pictures next to vases, a glass ashtray, magazines, and books. Three framed photographs of someone we intuit to be Armando's dead mother are visible: in one, we see her in a swimsuit resting in the sand at the beach; in another, we see a close-up of her face in the form of a head shot; and in a third, we see a quarter shot from the top of her tanned face and shoulders as she smiles into the camera. In the background, viewers notice beautiful ocean waves and the blueness of the sea. In the next shot are three more framed pictures. Two are of a younger woman who we presume is his mother at a young age. In one of them, she is wearing her wedding gown and looking sideways, holding the bridal bouquet in her hands. In the other picture, she is holding a baby in her arms. She is wearing what appears to be a red wool sweater. In the third picture, we find an older woman apparently holding the same baby in her hands. Vases and a green houseplant surround the last three pictures. As still shots, they illuminate for us a habitat of nonhuman objects. The next shot is of an empty chair and wall paintings. No living human has appeared in these shots that last approximately half a minute each.

In *Undertow,* paintings attempted to capture the *bugarrón* in still images, yet the artwork also had a double purpose. Painting, the capturing of a *bugarrón* practitioner's likeness, provided a pictorial representation of the ecological habitat of a *bugarrón* in the wild. In the ecology of objects characteristic of *From Afar,* pictures replace paintings. Both films, *Undertow* and *From Afar,* show the *bugarrón* within an ecology of images in the form of pictures, paintings, or other aesthetic art objects. In this world of images within images, evocative of Berger's locker room labyrinth of scenes in *Absent,* the *bugarrón* betrays his relatedness to a world he prefers to keep off-screen. It is as if visual objects were a component of the *bugarrón* practitioner's proclivity toward the margins.

In *Camera Lucida,* Roland Barthes expands on the paradox that "a photograph is always invisible: it is not it that we see" (6). By this, he means that when we look at a photograph, we see the rendered image, faces, and figures but not the photograph in itself. When we look at a photographed face, for example, the elements of the face dominate (eyes, wrinkles, nose), and for that moment the photograph disappears into the image. With its play of focused and unfocused images, *bugarrón* cinema uses the "invisibility" of photographs to outline the *bugarrón* practitioner's past. The displayed photographs in *From Afar* provide us with a horizon of what Armando's past might have been. In contrast, the photographs *as mere photographs* disappear in our attempt to find details of Armando's history. This "community of images" that a *bugarrón* practitioner inhabits outlines a past but occludes the question of sexual origins by rendering it invisible (*Camera* 3). The photographs define the cinematic *bugarrón,* but the photographs' own outlines are kept out of focus. For Merleau-Ponty, we don't have things of the world; rather, he argues, "the things have us" (*Visible* 194). The perceptual world enfolds the cinematic *bugarrón.*

The final shot shows Armando from afar; the rack focusing technique blurs his image. He is moving books from one shelf to another, presumably according to size and topic. The framed photographs are filmed up close and are crystal clear. Armando's image is not. He remains out of focus, at a distance. Similar to the scene at the beginning of the film, he is shot from behind. In this milieu, surrounded by objects, we find a disturbing cohabitation of human images and nonhuman entities. Jacqueline Rose pointed out this development when she stated, "Piles of cultural artifacts bring back something we recognize but in a form which refuses any logic of the same" (*Sexuality* 230). Heteroflexibility defies any logic of the same, be it gay identity or exclusive heterosexuality. Yet representations bring to light an ecology of relations to pictorial artifacts (painting, photographs, view-master) that show us more of the cinematic *bugarrón* habitat than has ever been known of a traditional *bugarrón* practitioner. These artifacts mark a break between the celluloid *bugarrón* and the invisibility of traditional *bugarrón* sexual practice.

HARDENING THE SKIN

If, for decades, a disturbance in the field of vision was associated with *bugarrón* practice's representation in Latin American cinema, this may no longer be the case. Gay Latino American cinema, the production of LGBTQ films targeting a minority sexual audience, has made possible the greater visibility of *bugarrón* sexual practice. This chapter has traced the development from *bugarrón* practitioner as a murky disturbance to a *bugarrón* practitioner as erotic image. A shift has taken place in Latin American cinema where greater erotic visibility has displaced the techniques of disorientation that were part and parcel of the representation of *bugarrón* practice in cinema.

A case in point is Argentine director José Campusano's recent film *Men of Hard Skin* (2019), a visual narrative that challenges some of the cinematic conventions of *bugarrón* sexual practice's filmmaking. This film explicitly shows sex between a *bugarrón* practitioner, Julio, and Ariel, the gay protagonist. The fact that the image of the *bugarrón* was used to market this film is an interesting twist, given his supporting role. The film's primary focus is the life of a young gay teen, Ariel, and his search for a romantic relationship. Living in Argentina's countryside where his father owns a farm, Ariel becomes attracted to one of his father's employees, Julio. A married young man with a wife and baby, Julio is younger than the other seasonal farm workers. Without hesitation, Julio shows great receptivity to Ariel's advances. Relatively early in the film, viewers are given a close-up of Julio's penis. After Ariel voices his admiration for Julio's physique, Julio asks him point-blank: "You wanna see what I got?" Ariel indicates his eagerness to see, and Julio's semi-erect penis aligns perfectly in the middle of the cinematic frame. Without shame, he tells Ariel, "Caress it, come." The scene shifts rapidly to Ariel, who quickly grabs the *bugarrón* practitioner's penis and caresses it. We see Ariel's hand skillfully feeling, touching, moving, and prodding Julio's genitals. After a few seconds, Julio says, "Finish what you started." There is no rack focusing in this scene; the camera does not immediately move away, but it stops filming when a pointedly crude pornographic shot would begin. The camera swiftly moves to a sequence of scenes of Ariel performing oral sex on Julio. These are shots taken from behind Ariel's back, and we only have a visual of Julio's upper body. But these shots are also taken from below, and they work to aggrandize Julio's presence and importance psychologically. The film ventures into softcore territory with a sequence illustrating Julio and Ariel having sex. The next scenes follow this sex theme where Julio is seen sexually ravaging the gay protagonist in several rural locations: in the fields, in the barn, and anywhere he can penetrate Ariel with gusto. Often we see them having sex while workers are unaware of what they are doing because the crops hide them. At other times, workers stare at Julio pounding Ariel without saying anything about it. The film shows Julio's sexual exploits with Ariel and other men and women. As the film follows Ariel's life drama, Julio's presence diminishes. This is the typical fate of supporting characters, no matter how profound their impact has been. Without Julio, the softcore component disappears. Although brief, the *bugarrón* subject's presence meaningfully affected the film's categorization in a subgenre as well as Ariel's sexual experiences.

The fading presence of the *bugarrón* subject in the film begins right after Julio introduces Ariel to the spot in the countryside where *bugarrón* practitioners go to satisfy their need for sexual encounters with other men. At this moment in the film, attention shifts from Julio to the other men who congregate in an abandoned old house. We see *bugarrón* practitioners (old and young heterosexual men) cruising gay youngsters like Ariel for sex. Julio had arranged for Ariel not to become attached to him exclusively because he did not want to bring this part of his life home to his wife and children. In this film, sexual flexibility has replaced exclusivity.

Julio remains a lasting image in the film. No other *bugarrón* subject matches his sex appeal and ever-ready disposition for sexual release. Once when Ariel visits him at his home, Julio's wife refers to her husband as "a perv," less in terms of homosexuality than as judgment about his indiscriminate lust. Even to his wife, Julio is a known "lecher" who would screw anything. However, in *Men of Hard Skin*, the *bugarrón* subject is labeled "a perv" because of his heteroflexibility; his promiscuous embrace of sexual experiences is what perverts the category of exclusive heterosexuality. The techniques of the observer may be changing in *bugarrón* cinema. Still, this new openness to more explicit sex scenes seems intended to please a small but growing market of gay viewers driven by their fantasies of *bugarrón* sexual practice.

NEW IMAGES IN OLD CONTINUUMS

No one thought that the disappearance of a traditional *bugarrón* sexual practice would lead to the formation of a neo-economic subject. Even less predictable was the transition of this sexual practice into a cinematic *bugarrón* image. Cinema has become fertile terrain for the proliferation of representations of male heteroflexibility. A disturbance in the field of vision troubles the representation of heterosexuality in places where heterosexuality has included within itself sex practices that counter its exclusivity. From rack focusing to vibrant illuminations, and from mnemonic objects to a play with nearness and distance, these techniques make the invisible visible, but they also leave a remainder effect in the visual field. Their murkiness, over-brightness, and unexpected play with distance are formal elements but also the excess complexity of representing atypical sexual practices.

Given that *bugarrón* cinema does not seek to interpret the origins of sexual identification or attempt to construct a uniform type of experience, it disturbs the visual field and exceeds anthropological frameworks. At the same time, these films differ from previous methods used for understanding the nongay dynamics of male–male relationships such as men-who-have-sex-with-men or homosociality. These films chart new territory in Latin American representations of sexual variance, intimacy, and desire. As such, *Plan B, Absent, Hawaii, Undertow, La mujer de mi hermano, From Afar,* and *Men of Hard Skin* complicate the theoretical frameworks that normally analyze homosexuality, queer, and exclusive heterosexuality.

Over decades, *bugarrón* sexual practice has stymied representation by anthropologists, health management experts, painters, and film directors. This book examines all those efforts to portray *bugarrón* sexual practice via multiple texts, discourses, and aesthetic representations. What remains consistently true is that *bugarrón* practice has, without doubt, mutated in multiple discourses and visual narratives attesting to the *bugarrón*'s existence. In cinema, as in other technologies making sense of *bugarrón* practice, this effort to represent sexual practice leads to modifications in filmmaking. From rack focusing blurriness and intervals to clear images of *bugarrón* sex, *bugarrón* cinema reproduces an ecology of relations. These relations between practices and things lead to a new horizon of visibility where gradations are displayed for us to progressively see.

CHAPTER 4

Mundo Cruel

The Neobugarrón *in Literature*

When one of the characters in Luis Negrón's short story "Botella" ["Bottle"] acquires his nickname thanks to a small bottle of bleach he uses to disinfect his genitals from any HIV he might have acquired via unprotected sex, we know we are entering a strange world of literary representations of sexuality.[1] Negrón's tale, which appeared in his 2010 book of short stories *Mundo Cruel* [Cruel World], is a notable recent example of fiction that accounts for *bugarrón* sexual practice. In previous works of literature, *bugarrón* practice finds manifestation only in minor or supporting characters.[2] However, in Negrón's work the *bugarrón* practitioner takes center stage as a sexual type that complicates the representation of traditional *bugarrón* practice. Negrón's story crosses a significant threshold and thus raises the stakes for literary critics

---

1. I discuss Negrón in terms of material covered in previous chapters, where I explain how *bugarrón* referred to a traditional sexual practice in which a mostly heterosexual man had sex with men for pleasure and did not compromise his heterosexual identification. The term *bugarrón* did not refer to the man's true sexual "identity" but rather to a sexual activity he performed when engaging in an unorthodox sexual practice, that of a heterosexual man who fucks men. I also use material from chapter 2, where I discuss how, in recent decades, *bugarrón* has become synonymous with male hustler, or sex worker, and as such has acquired the market "identity" of a profession. I refer to this newly acquired dimension as a neoliberal transformation from *bugarrón* to *neobugarrón*. This chapter delves into a world of bizarre *bugarrón* sexual-practice representations in literature.

2. In *The One vs. the Many* (2003), Alex Woloch explains that "minor characters" are those "figures who jostle for, and within, the limited space that remains" (2).

to trace the steps leading to the representation of this irregular type in literature. *Mundo Cruel* invites critics to consider: What might a literary study of an anomalous sexual practice look like? How might something akin to a literary history of an in-between, nonexclusive heterosexual practice be written? How does the representation of *bugarrón* sexual practice challenge social realist narratives? By analyzing tropes of *bugarrón* practice in Caribbean and Latin American literature, this chapter sketches a preliminary thread of *bugarrón* literary representation in Latin America, the Caribbean, and its diaspora. It traces a phenomenon coming into representation. Consistent with genealogies, this chapter selects examples in fictional works that illustrate the complex and diverse uses of *bugarrón* tropes, focusing on the works of David Caleb Acevedo, Reinaldo Arenas, Abniel Marat, Luis Negrón, Patricia Powell, Manuel Ramos Otero, and Hugo Villalobos. Although in many instances *bugarrón* sexual practice is interpreted as signifying a closeted gay man, my analyses question those cases that interpret *bugarrón* practice as a closeted gay identity. Rather than imposing a metaphor of the closet, I elucidate how dualisms, binaries, dyads, and other dialectical forms in these works gesture toward *bugarrón* sexual practice.

Following Fredric Jameson, dialectics is here understood as a dynamic narrative composed of antinomies, dyads, and binaries in a forward movement not in need of resolution (*Antinomies* 6). Jameson points to a vein critical to understanding realism dialectically by studying the antinomies, binaries, dyads, paradoxes, and anomalies in which every "contradiction or aporia" promises thinking; he insists that antinomies and binaries are, in fact, dialectical structures (6). This chapter brings to bear consideration of an anomalous sexual practice on dialectical, binary, or dyadic thinking. Focusing on a series of literary examples, I lay out a sequence of *bugarrón* sexual practice in fiction. My study traces a genealogy from the structural antinomy of a character dyad present in the work of Patricia Powell to the dichotomy of Hugo Villalobos and Acevedo's fictional and nonfictional diaries; and from the complexity of Negrón's *bugarrón* sexual practice located at center stage in Puerto Rican literature to the problem of translating a *bugarrón-superbugarrón* dialectic in the work of Reinaldo Arenas. This sequence of dichotomies, dyads, and dialectics illustrates a selective literary thread, a genealogical thread, of *bugarrón* representation in Caribbean and Latin American literature. I close this chapter by connecting the representation of *bugarrón* to Adorno's account of a dialectics of nonidentity and Emily Apter's rendition of untranslatable terms as constructs that are "insufficiently built" into literary history (*Against* 3). As there is no equivalent in the English language for *bugarrón* practice, the term falls into the category of untranslatable. The translated works of Negrón and Arenas compel me to tackle the significance of *bugarrón* sexual practice's untranslatability. For Apter, untranslatables challenge prevailing "logics of history," including literary history, that support current disciplinary models (64). By focusing on explicit literary passages ranging from the compressed representations of tropes to dialectically complex narratives, this chapter proposes a *bugarrón* literary thread for understanding the many narrative strategies depicting a nonidentitarian sexual practice.

THE ANTINOMIES OF REALISM IN PATRICIA POWELL'S *A SMALL GATHERING OF BONES*

Powell's *A Small Gathering of Bones* (1994) tells the story of a Jamaican gay community's struggle for acceptance and inclusion during the 1980s, when AIDS began to be conceived as a "punishment from God" for "love between men" (106, 107). Set in Kingston, Powell's account of male sexuality is shaped by the emergence of a new epidemic affecting the lives of queer and gay Jamaicans. Dale, the protagonist of the story, takes care of his friend Ian Kaysen, who is living with AIDS. The novel opens with an ominous description of Ian's illness: "When Ian Kaysen first come down with the offensive dry cough, Dale did have to finally tell him one Saturday morning, as him watch Ian stumble into the kitchen rubbing his chest, back hunched over . . . 'that rattle in that back of your throat not any little play-play cold'" (1). Unable to stop the disease's progress, Ian's body succumbs to the invading pathogen. The narrator states, "Ian was giving up, losing himself to this unknown disease that had grown roots and was flourishing rapidly eating away at Ian, little little, destroying him" (105).

The world depicted in Powell's novel is bifurcated into two realisms: the realism of the body wasting with AIDS and the realism of *bugarrón* sexual practice. The realism of wasting is typical of a literature of consciousness-raising at the time of the AIDS crisis when the public and the government had to be convinced to take care of an epidemic that was disproportionately affecting gay communities.[3] Descriptions of the wasting body of AIDS patients chronicled the "now" of the epidemic and served as consciousness-raising scenes. The description of wasting bodies takes the form of detailed accounts of the

---

3. Exemplary works of this epoch such as Andrew Holleran's *Chronicle of a Plague, Revisited: AIDS and Its Aftermath* (2008), previously published as *Ground Zero* (1988), Emmanuel Dreuilhe's *Mortal Embrace* (1988), and Paul Monette's *Borrowed Time* (1988) provided incisive accounts of the gay community's transformation during the AIDS crisis that resonate with descriptions of Powell's wasting male body and the killing of those infected subjects who were terminally ill.

affected body. In most cases, detailed narrative descriptions evoke a realism of social conditions that can be traced back to nineteenth-century realist novels, novels such as George Eliot's *Middlemarch* and Eugene Balzac's *Pere Goriot*. In *Antinomies of Realism* (2013), Jameson makes us aware of the antinomy between the narrative strategies of a brief account (*récit*) and longer, detailed descriptions. The antinomies of these two narrative strategies for portraying two types of realism become useful in understanding the structure of Powell's novel. In *A Small Gathering of Bones*, we encounter an antinomy between two main realist tropes: the representation of *bugarrón* sexual practice as *récit* and the gay body with AIDS as longer realist description. Whereas the realism of *bugarrón* sexual practice takes the form of brief narrative moments, the realism of illness in AIDS writing adds gravity to the situation. Over time, longer realist descriptions developed into conventions of an emerging subgenre of AIDS writing. If in the nineteenth century, longer narrative descriptions centered on the conventions of detailed accounts of contemporary social life and characterization of ordinary people, they also revealed aspects of social life that are "normally not known or confronted" (Shumway, "What" 192).

Powell's text is conditioned by developments such as the rise of AIDS politics on the US mainland, the absence of Caribbean literary accounts of the AIDS crisis, and the delayed appearance of an anomalous sexual practice in West Indian literature. Her tale is one of the few works of literature that attend to these developments directly. *A Small Gathering of Bones* establishes links between the Caribbean diaspora writer and the moment when the Caribbean became an epidemic hot zone, intervening in a nexus of discourses and subgenres in the diaspora. Whereas in the Anglo-American context, the HIV/AIDS crisis and the writing of AIDS began almost simultaneously, in Caribbean writing there is a substantial time lag between the spread of HIV in communities and its emergence in fiction.[4]

---

4. At the time, edited collections such as Timothy Murphy and Suzanne Poirier's *Writing AIDS: Gay Literature, Language, and Analysis* (1993) and Judith Laurence Pastore's *Confronting AIDS through Literature: The Responsibilities of Representation* (1993) provided venues for the dissemination of prose fiction representing AIDS and also presented criticism that questioned the absence of AIDS representation in literary canons. Today, in the early decades of the twenty-first century, this line of inquiry remains valid, if only because communities in general rely on history to construct their national identity. For the first generation of AIDS writers in the US, just as in Powell's novel, the portrayal of the body with AIDS became a key feature for the representation of physical and emotional pain. My discussion of Powell's novel addresses conventions that *A Small Gathering of Bones* shares with gay writing of the period, especially the representation of a gay body suffering with AIDS-related diseases, because they set the conditions for the appearance of *bugarrón* sexual practice in the novel's background. The tracing of the conventions of gay literature of AIDS inevitably leads to thorny passages that merit careful inspection. AIDS representation in Caribbean writing brings along with it unexpected anomalous sexual subjects.

For these reasons, Powell's emphasis on the wasted body anchors her work in a realist literature of AIDS that developed in the US years earlier. For instance, compare the chapter of Andrew Holleran's *Ground Zero* entitled "Bedtime Manners," where Holleran confronts us with an image that haunts the reader as much as Powell's depictions of Ian. While visiting a close friend, "Eddie," at the quarantine ward of a New York City hospital, the first-person narrator observes his friend's afflicted body in detail.

> His face is emaciated and gaunt, his hair longer, softer in appearance, wisps rising above his head. But the one feature the visitor cannot get over are his friend's eyes. His eyes are black, huge, and furious. Perhaps because his face is gaunt or perhaps because they really are larger than usual, they seem the only thing alive in his face; as if his whole being were distilled and concentrated, poured, drained, into his eyes. (31–32)

Like Holleran, Powell's realist accounts of Ian's physical deterioration abound: "Each time Dale visit, all that greet him is a pair of eyes, the colour of curry, sitting inside the darkness, shoulders slumped down into his belly. His entire left side was as stiff as a piece of board. Nothing atall moved, except for the rolling of his eyeballs, an occasional bobbing of the Adam's apple. Drops of saliva curdle themselves by the edges of his mouth" (90). The intensity of the eyes in Holleran's detailed account is Caribbeanized in Powell's descriptions of Ian's eyeballs. In *A Small Gathering of Bones,* Ian's cough dominates a section of the narrative and is depicted as if "the devil from hell inside him want to come out but the walls of his throat it seems just too narrow" (1). The realism reminiscent of *Ground Zero* infuses the general climate in Powell's novel. In an atmosphere where there is a strong "smell of antiseptic and illness," Powell's Ian fails to recover and suffers from a "constant cough-cough and vomit-vomit" (80, 81). Powell's realist depictions of a wasted body follow the descriptive style of earlier novels. Still, she adds the local dialect, thereby ensuring that cultural difference and place matter when we read phrases such as "atall" for "at all" and sonorous repetitions like "vomit-vomit." Caribbeanizing the conventions of a subgenre emphasizes cultural differences. The title *A Small Gathering of Bones* summarizes in a phrase the wasted body of the AIDS patient. It makes explicit the body's decimation under a virulent disease. In Powell's tale, "a small gathering of bones" is that which remains of the AIDS-infected body in the Caribbean.

In *A Small Gathering of Bones,* bugarrón sexual practice as *récit* functions in contrast to the subgenre's realist conventions. Suppose the wasted body is one antinomy of realism in these narratives, where the narrative expands on describing the reality of infection during an epidemic. The other side of the antinomy in Powell's narrative is the condensed segments on the realism of *bugarrón* sexual practice. Amid her descriptions of AIDS-infested bones and wasted bodies, Powell inserts the supporting character of Alexander Pilot. This minor character represents an oasis of calm, care, and love amid the horror, death, and desolation that saturate the novel. Alexander is Dale's lover, and Dale seeks refuge in memories of being together when he is stressed and desperate. As it happens, anxiety and fear are a consistent presence in this novel, and Alexander represents a key antidote to Dale's situation: "Dale's mind run on Alexander Pilot and calmness engulf him. It loosen the knots from inside his stomach and lift the heavy weight from off his back" (26).

Alexander is a forty-nine-year-old married man who has been with his wife for eight years. They have two children. He is described as not particularly fit: "His body, round and loose, and well out of form, slosh every which way when him walk" (26). But those traits did not matter to Dale, for what he cared about was Alexander's "broad shoulders," "heavy chest," and "pale green eyes" (26). He reminisces on his encounters with Alexander and how he used to "pin him against the fridge" (26). For Dale, these sexual escapades with a married, mostly straight man allowed him to regroup. As is typical for representations of *bugarrón* practice, Alexander does not speak; what we know of him is filtered through Dale's speech acts. Alexander's anomalous sexuality raises the specter of *bugarrón* practice, as his marital situation is consistent with accounts of the behavioral traits of traditional *bugarrón* practitioners. No more is said about Alexander in this novel, but his brief appearance functions as a sharp contrast.

The critical reception is aware that Powell's account of a community's disappearance into a "small gathering of bones" echoes motifs present in gay writing on the AIDS epidemic during the first decades of the outbreak.[5] Yet the novel also invokes the emergence of another Caribbean realism: that of a *bugarrón* sexual practice. The presence of *bugarrón* sexual practice is circum-

---

5. This is the reason behind literary critic Timothy Chin's claim that Powell's novels insert into Caribbean history "subjects that have been largely 'unspeakable' within Caribbean discourse—homosexuality and AIDS" ("Novels" 537). Critic Adele Newson shares Chin's perspective and points out that Powell's novel immerses us in a sidelined world where "AIDS is the experimental unknown . . . the disease for which doctors have no answers, the disease that plagues man-lovers, the disease that will claim many of the characters—who, at the time of the novel, remain unaware of its existence" ("A Small Gathering" 631). Concurring with Chin and Newson, Aparagita Sagar points out that even when AIDS is disavowed, its impact is "beginning to transform the social, cultural and physical landscape of Kingston" ("AIDS" 29). What these critics find in Powell's novel is a connection to gay literature on AIDS that was published in the US during the early years of the pandemic.

scribed, appearing as a reality that has already taken place, a temporal past that is not open to change. In other words, Alexander is a revisited memory remembered nostalgically. If at first glance *bugarrón* sexual practice appears to have emerged merely as a brief memory, its function as *récit* realism reveals a Jamesonian antinomy at work in Powell's novel. This *bugarrón* realism is often hidden from view in Caribbean sexual cultures, and likewise scholarship on the novel misses the antinomy of relations informing the narrative and its biopolitical implications. The Ian/Alexander antinomy is not explicit; only by determining which kind of realism each character represents can critics clarify the distinction between the realism of letting die via illness and the realism of nonexclusive heterosexuality.

As if informed by Kinsey, *bugarrón* sexual practice emerges as a potentiality in Powell's fiction. Nevertheless, representation in Powell's novel is complicated since the term *bugarrón* is not mentioned; likewise, AIDS remains nameless. True to its 1980s setting, *A Small Gathering of Bones* duplicates the historical unknowns affecting the community when a killer scourge ran uncontained. Even if Powell's particular historical contextualization of the epidemic is informed by the literature of AIDS writing, the other voices in her work belong to sexually indeterminate characters not typically found in US gay representation.

Powell's novel represents a challenge in putting together a genealogy of *bugarrón* sexual practice in Caribbean and Latin American literature. This is because constructing a preliminary genealogy of *bugarrón* sexual practice's literary representation requires untangling key instances of homoeroticism from gay identity. Is Alexander an example of *bugarrón* practice or of a closeted gay subject? In order to locate the literary thread of a *bugarrón* sexual practice, I have found useful not only Jameson's theory of antinomies of realism but also a body of scholarship that has disappeared from current academic discussions, namely, the gay literary histories written during the 1980s and 1990s. During this period, literary critics grappled with classifying, accounting for, and historicizing an array of representations of same-sex practices in fiction. An account of this thorny process is found in *A History of Gay Literature* (1998), by Gregory Woods, who explains that the formation of a modern gay literary history began to take shape in the late 1960s at a moment when "we can unproblematically speak about a certain kind of text as 'gay literature': that is to say, literature about being gay, by men who identify themselves as being gay" (Woods 9). Despite the fact that such clarity was only visible from the 1960s onward, keen gay literary historians of the 1990s looked backward to pre-1960s fiction to find more examples. The literary history of modern homosexuality tended to appropriate and relabel as gay (and later queer) "different types of men, boys and cultural texts . . . often without much attention to historical nuance" (Woods 6).

Woods himself acknowledged that "unproblematic" was an imperfect standard that did not resolve questions about where to draw boundaries: "It is easy to tell where gay literature begins—in openly gay authors' writing explicitly about the experience of being gay—but where does it end?" (12). With reference to gay readings of canonical texts such as Joseph Conrad's *Typhoon*, Woods explains,

> this is not a novel by a homosexual writer, as far as we know; nor is it explicitly about homosexual characters. Neither of these facts prevents its being amenable to gay readings. . . . It is not a mere option for gay critics to attempt to do so . . . it is incumbent on us to do so. You might call this the process of queering the canon. It works in parallel with canonizing queers. That, after all, is our job. (*History* 14)

This practice of "queering the canon" did not end in the 1990s but survives in queer literary histories written during the early decades of the twenty-first century.[6] If previous gay literary histories are not sufficiently discerning and end up categorizing a variety of instances of same-sex representations as belonging to modern sexual "identities" (gay, lesbian, etc.), then what are the challenges in making use of these histories for a genealogy of nonidentitarian practices? Gay literary histories become useful because, in their determination to construct their histories, they include "problematic" representations under the guise of "unproblematic" examples. Because *bugarrón* sexual practice involves heterosexually identified men who have sex with other men, it is imperative to disentangle this representation from that of homosexuality in gay literary histories. Yet, when approached from a *bugarrón* perspective, the task becomes more complex than merely reclassifying characters that have been "problematically" assumed to be gay in fiction.

---

6. Even today, gay and queer literary critics continue to reinterpret textual examples of mourning and loss as codes of sexual identity. Notice the repetition of the 1990s gay literary histories in a recent book on the subject: "My aim is to create an image repertoire of queer modernist melancholia in order to underline both the losses of queer modernity and the deeply ambivalent negotiation of these losses within the literature of the period" (Love, *Feeling* 5). For this particular critic, melancholia signifies backwardness, that is, an inability to move past the suffered losses ("a stubborn attachments to lost objects"), and this particular feeling represents "a key feature of queer culture" (7). These texts proved difficult "to integrate into a queer literary genealogy" or to make fit into "our sense of queer identity" (8). *Feeling Backwards* looks backwards in time to detect "a shared feeling of backwardness" in order to expand the "archive of feeling" of a "modern homosexual identity" (4, 8).

This decades-long misclassification further impoverished accounts of male heterosexual flexibility. Jameson's theory of the antinomies of realism showed how narrative structures function when they represent dual and competing realities that appear in the texts not only in tandem but, more importantly, in tension. In Powell, *bugarrón* sexual practice is positioned in the past, as a temporal anteriority, and the present belongs to the body with HIV/AIDS. But the analysis of the *bugarrón* practitioner in fiction also requires tools for engaging the literary representation of sexual practices. To that end, the 1990s gay literary histories help us understand the challenges of this kind of representation. But unlike most gay literary histories—where looking backward was a technique for recovering instances of gay identity—this chapter looks at Latin American and Caribbean fiction to reveal antinomies of realism in which one of the components shows the potential of nonidentitarian *bugarrón* sexual practice. In this context, reclassification raises thorny issues of untranslatability, polysemy, and the politics of nonidentitarian genealogical writing. Whereas gay literary critics searched for instances of gay representation to assimilate into an expanding literary history of gay identity, this chapter identifies representations of a sexual practice that are problematic, that is to say, homoerotic yet unassimilable to a gay identity. Their untranslatability into identitarian critical language muddles the scholarly terrain and challenges our ability to apprehend *bugarrón* sexual practice. *Bugarronizing* the literary canon becomes a logistical minefield.

Whereas Jameson addresses the antinomies of realism in a dialectical understanding of forms in forward motion, gay literary histories tend not to address dialectics. Instead, they provide tools for analyzing the literary representations of sexual practices in fiction. Moreover, gay literary histories of the 1990s were published when Caribbean writing began to chronicle the spread of HIV/AIDS in Jamaica. The 1990s mark this coincidence between the genres of gay literary historical writing in the US mainland and AIDS writing in Caribbean fiction. At the time, writing about AIDS and writing about gay identity shared a discursive ideology of survival. In the middle of this confluence of genres and discourses, *bugarrón* sexual practice emerges in literature. Yet at this moment, its emergence also leads to textual instances of occlusion, distortion, and demystification. Drawing attention to a thread is not writing a history. For this reason, *bugarronizing* literary production is limited to a series of genealogical encounters with *bugarrón* sexual practice as it emerges in the fictional writings of the Americas. The writing of *bugarrón* sexual practice in literature is complicated by many factors, one of which is that no self-identified *bugarrón* practitioner has written it. This paradox becomes intensified when *bugarrón* sexual practice is represented in diary form.

NEOBUGARRÓN ANTINOMIES IN FICTIONAL AND NONFICTIONAL DIARIES

While the previous section examined the antinomies of realism between wasted bodies and *bugarrón* sexual practice in the narrative dyad Ian/Alexander, this section addresses the antinomies of realism in fictional and nonfictional diaries in Hugo Villalobos's novel *Diario de un Chichifo Ilustrado* (2007) and David Caleb Acevedo's *Diary of a Common Whore*. These works contribute literary examples of life writing and ethnographic accounts of *bugarrón* sexual practice. Given each work's complexity, I first engage Villalobos's fictional diary, which provides a dual ethnographic representation of urban and rural *neobugarrón* practitioners and sex workers. If in Powell's novel, the antinomy Ian/Alexander framed the narrative, in Villalobos's novel, the tension between two main types of *chichifos* produces antinomies that structure the novel.

Chichifo, in the novel's title, is the epithet for a male sex worker who has relations with other men without necessarily having a particular preference for same-sex contact. Apparently, this term originates from a Mexican rendering of the Italian *cicisbeo* (with Italian pronunciation), meaning a male escort or kept man. Villalobos's novel is written in a personal diary style by Josué, a middle-aged sex worker, who is coping with aging and adjusting to the technological changes affecting the "pleasure industry." Innovations in the sex work industry, such as internet sites geared to advertise young sex workers, have forced him to seek new clients in less than desirable urban locations.

Diario, a recent work of literature set in the 1980s, narrates the exploits of Josué, whose clientele had been exclusively members of Latin America's wealthy elite. But as his regular customer base dwindles, he ventures into other areas of the city. Josué's visits to sketchy urban spaces allow him to notice particular details of the "pleasure industry." Written with an ethnographic component, the novel introduces readers to the world of hustlers or *neobugarrones*. Josué describes the underground world of hell's angels in a specific entry. Unlike the infamous motorcycle gang in Hunter Thompson's notorious novel *Hell's Angels* (1967), Villalobos's angels are none other than displaced Indigenous men from the countryside who are selling their bodies in the urban marketplace.

> Hell's angels are indigenous youngsters who, confronted with extreme poverty, migrated from the Mexican states of Michoacan, Guerrero, Hidalgo, Veracruz, and Oaxaca. . . . They know each other by the language they speak: Mazahua, Nahuatl, Otomi, Zapotero, and smile at each other when

they encounter one another in the streets.... They have experimented with everything and their sexual practice conforms to the agreed payment but in general they accept only an active role, it could be humiliating if their peers knew otherwise; however, at the moment of intimacy any monetary transaction could always take place. (*Diario* 90–91)[7]

Conveying that angels "accept only an active role," Josué indicates that these young men are selling *bugarrón* sexual practice. Of course, the fact that they are *selling* traditional *bugarrón* practices would make them *neobugarrones*. When describing the angels, Josué adopts a role reminiscent of a "participant informer/observer," the ethnographic methodology popularized by Bronislaw Malinowski.[8] In the Mexican context, anthropologist Oscar Lewis adopted Malinowski's method in his accounts of the urban underclass. Lewis's *The Children of Sánchez* (1961) provided an ethnographic study of urban poverty written in the style of multiple autobiographies. The "I" that we find nonfictionalized in Lewis reverberates in Villalobos's use of "I." Whereas Villalobos uses a fictional diary, Lewis uses a "tape recorder" to capture "a new kind of literature of social realism" (*Children* xii). For Lewis, this method of observing and writing in the form of multiple autobiographical writings/transcripts ensures that he avoids two "common hazards in the study of the poor, namely, oversentimentalization and brutalization" (xi–xii). By contrast, Villalobos's *Diario* is not a transcription of a tape recording but rather the act of observing and putting down on paper the narrator's experiences in the *bugarrón* sexual field.

Following Malinowski and Lewis, Villalobos's *Diary* chronicles Josué's surroundings and provides an impression of cultural life at the margins. The protagonist speaks from a perspective where he can describe the structural patterns of urban sexual cultures. As he tells us, hell's angels are determined to "signify their masculinity" ["significar su masculinidad"], an act that reinforces their active role in a sexual practice (91). Hell's angels represent for the protagonist a distinct group, who share similar physical types, hairstyles, and an overall look.

> Hell's angels are short, dark, and thin. They wear their hair short and simple clothing. They live in groups and have learned to interpret each other's codes, they have a particular way of looking, and they have developed a complicit smile when they discreetly touch their crotch to attract clients. (91)

---

7. All translations of Villalobos's *Diario* and Acevedo's *Diario* are my own.
8. See Malinowski's *Argonauts*, esp. 7–8.

Observing, learning, and recording their customs and behavior, Josué decodes their habits. It is essential for him to learn every detail of this organized group of *neobugarrones*, so he pays very close attention:

> After agreeing on a price, they meet their clients in a motel or in a public restroom where they have sex quickly, at most for an hour . . . their days are of fleeting encounters where almost everything is financial gain. They have to compete with other prostitutes that arrive before dusk: mechanics, soldiers, construction workers, some gays, and isolated cases of a transsexual worker. (92)

He explains that *chichifos* are one group among many who share the Mexican urban sex work underworld. The urban space has been stratified in a tacit agreement where hell's angels rule the streets by day and transsexual workers and gays rule by night. On occasion, their worlds overlap, but only slightly.

Still, there is a difference between two types of *chichifos*—the protagonist-observer-participant and his subjects of observation. The novel's title conveys that Josué is a *chichifo ilustrado* (schooled); Villalobos's categorization places the protagonist in a different social class altogether from other *chichifos*. Class difference is a cultural marker separating the newly arrived rural *chichifo* from the learned or schooled *chichifo* that Josué represents. This distinction is key, as Josué's schooling makes a dramatic difference in Villalobos's novel, where *chichifos* are represented as struggling for their daily survival. By contrast, Josué comes from an upper-middle-class background and his education sets him apart. He has traveled abroad and lived for a few years as a kept *neobugarrón* in Copenhagen with a Danish tourist who visited Latin America. Although Josué decided to make sex work his profession and now has fallen into financial duress, his education sets him apart from other *neobugarrones*. In the novel, Josué's distinction is marked by keeping a diary and his voracious reading of contemporary fiction and Western literary classics.

Villalobos's *Diario* distinguishes between the modern *neobugarrón* and the hell's angels. *Ilustrado* (enlightened, learned), signifying "modern," is the marker of that distinction. Villalobos's novel provides two contributions: the fictionalizing of an ethnographic account of a sexual underworld and the addition of a class distinction to understanding a *chichifo* practice. The *neobugarrón* marketplace expands with neoliberalism, and readers encounter the proliferation of *neobugarrones* as economic displacement becomes the rule for those at the mercy of globalizing forces.

In *Diario* a fictional *neobugarrón* decodes the culture of other *neobugarrones* and distinguishes between the realism of modern *neobugarrones* and uncultured (unschooled) *neobugarrones*. This fictionalized dualism takes place under the specter of neoliberalism, a theme not developed in the narrative. Villalobos's *Diario* addresses neither neoliberal economic practices nor lust directly. The protagonist's erudition seems to have precluded more explicit details about his sexual performances. As a result, the novel's insights about this dichotomy *chichifo / chichifo ilustrado* are written in a style consistent with nonfictional ethnographic writings. The antinomies of fiction and non-fiction (within the fictional space) and *neobugarrón* realism within a fictional *neobugarrón* narrative create a structure that shapes *bugarrón* sexual practice in Villalobos's fictional diary. Therefore, we turn to Acevedo's *Diario* for an unfettered account of lust with *bugarrones*.

Whereas Villalobos's *Diario* is a work of literature peppered with scenes written in the style of nonfiction, Acevedo's *Diario de una puta humilde* [*Diary of a Common Whore*] (2012) is a work that claims to be "non-fiction" but that reads as a work of erotic fiction. Acevedo describes his *Diary* as an "autobiography of his horniness or lust" (back cover).[9] *Diary of a Common Whore* provides an ethnographic account of gay cruising in Puerto Rico that shares similarities with Villalobos's work. Although Acevedo engaged in sex work for a couple of years, his identification with gay identity is unambiguous. In a candid narrative style, Acevedo's *Diary* begins on August 28, 2008, with a straightforward confession: "I'll begin my diary in all honesty: I am a male whore" (11). Acevedo correlates "whoring" with licentiousness. The author claims that an autobiography of lust describes "the demands placed on him by his prostate, his cock, his ass, his butthole, cum, shit, and blood . . . a chronicle of the virus on his skin and blood" (back cover). *Diary of a Common Whore* does not seek to paint an unblemished self-portrait; rather, it candidly chronicles his daily thoughts and narrates in detail his sexual encounters. Due to its matter-of-fact descriptions, the diary provides detailed evidence of his participant-observations similar to those available in accounts of anthropological value. At the same time, we can see how Acevedo's *Diario* shares the creative space used by writers such as Sam Steward in works written under the pseudonym Phil Andros.

Close in style to Steward's pornographic novels such as *Shuttlecock* (1984) and *Roman Conquests* (1971), Acevedo's *Diary* provides a particular pornographic series of "non-fictional" sexual accounts of his conquests all over Puerto Rico. Justin Spring argues that Sam Steward's works contribute an obscene "sexual record keeping" and a "radical form of self-documentation" (*Obscene*

---

9. It would be misguided to think that a diary or an autobiography is a genre of "truth." As deconstruction critic Paul de Man had argued, when analyzing Rousseau's memoirs, autobiography as literary form amounts to an exercise in defacement. For de Man, the "I" of memoirs consistently fails to provide an accurate description of him- or herself.

Diary 1–2). Concurring with Spring, Tim Dean explains that "inspired by Kinsey, Steward redoubled his efforts at sexual documentation and archiving" ("Steward's Pornography" 34). Acevedo's obscene diary delivers accounts of his sexual encounters with vivid imagery and photographic detail. Unlike Steward, Acevedo's *Diario* is written in a mixed style, including elements of an auto-da-fé (a written public penance) ("Soy puta" ["I am a male whore"] [*Diario* 11]), a blog-narrative on Facebook ("Luego de tantas peticiones, rogativas y hasta amenazas por Facebook decidí continuarlo" ["After so many requests, pleadings, and threats on Facebook I decided to continue writing the diary"] [*Diario* 134]), and an open letter to Benji, his ex-partner ("Comencé este diario por tí, Benji" ["I began writing this diary for you, Benji"] [*Diario* 133]). Whereas in some entries, the narrative seems to be intended to confess to Benji his peccadilloes after their abrupt breakup, at other times the text responds indirectly to online feedback on his latest conquests, thus establishing a dialogue between Acevedo and his potential Facebook "followers."

Openly gay and HIV-positive, Acevedo reveals his sexual contacts with mostly straight men who have sex with men (or *bugarrones*). He tells us that on one occasion a *bugarrón* practitioner confessed to him about his sexual contact with gays and how "they always ended smearing his cock with fecal matter after he penetrated them" (17). Seizing the opportunity, Acevedo asks him point-blank about his sexual identification: "Then, what are you?" (17). The *bugarrón* practitioner answered, "Heterosexual, of course" (17). Another entry chronicles his sexual contact with Slevin, of whom he says, "He fucked me . . . and today he tells me that he has a girlfriend" (19). Tormented by the news, Acevedo states, "I couldn't help feeling jealous, as if the world of heterosexuality would be stealing away a precious jewel from my world" (19). A separate entry informs us that Wilbert, his ex-con roommate at college, said to him, "Once out of prison, sex is only with women" (122). These anecdotes of sex with heterosexual men (e.g., traditional *bugarrón* sexual practice) pepper the diary.

Acevedo writes as if he is not withholding information about his encounters with *bugarrón* sexual practice. The entries on his interaction with *neobugarrones* (e.g., male sex workers, mostly heterosexual) in San Juan's metropolitan area are more graphic than the previously quoted examples. His interactions with *neobugarrones* merit closer inspection. After he met two "bugarroncitos" [young sex workers] waiting at the street corner, Acevedo proposed to have sex with one of them, the "older, with the face of a rascal, a bit of a beard, and a thug look" (98). This sexual encounter is described in great detail:

> Ten minutes later, I had lowered my pants, my blue bikini underwear had been ripped apart, and the dude had me on all fours fucking me while talk-

ing dirty at the same time: Hurry, slut! Slide that stinking hole down my pole you dirty faggot! Fucking fag! . . .

    That night at my apartment, I didn't shower. I wanted to hold on to the smell of the night's adventure in Rio Piedras, to the smell of a *bugarrón* junkie's cum in my hole. (99)

In chapter 1, we discussed Schifter's idea that the erosion of a traditional *bugarrón* sexual practice was due to the increasing demand for drugs. Acevedo revels in being penetrated by a *neobugarrón* and is even more aroused by the added stigma of having been "bred" by one with a junkie status.

If anthropologists like James Clifford use the tools of literature to address ethnographic concerns, then Villalobos's and Acevedo's writings used ethnographic techniques to provide us narratives that complicate *neobugarrón* representation even further. Diary writing becomes a venue for erotic tales but also for chronicling incidents of *bugarrón* sexual practice. The nonerotic accounts of *chichifos* in the literary form (Villalobos) contrast the erotic accounts of the nonfictional writing (Acevedo). Reality belongs to fiction as Villalobos's narrative replicates the discourse of ethnography. By contrast, Acevedo's nonfictional diary reads as a fictional narration reminiscent of Schifter's imaginary Luis, discussed in chapter 1. Two sets of binaries were developed in these works, one consisting of *chichifo ilustrado* / *chichifo* and the other of gay whore / *neobugarrón*. Moreover, the binaries fiction/nonfiction and informative / sexually graphic become parallel dualities in these works. The following sections segue from a discussion of supporting characters to works of fiction where the *bugarrón* practitioner takes center stage as protagonist and where the meaning of *bugarrón* sexual practice shrinks to a single definition: sex worker.

THE CRUEL WORLD OF *BUGARRÓN* SEXUAL PRACTICE

Bugarrón sexual practice becomes visible in Negrón's *Mundo Cruel,* a collection of tales that narrates the interaction among gays, lesbians, and *bugarrón* practitioners in an impoverished neighborhood of Santurce, Puerto Rico. Negrón recounts the intimate sexual activities taking place in an urban area where migrants from the Dominican Republic reside and where mostly Afro-Caribbean working-class people live. Santurce is transformed in Negrón's tales into a complex web of intimacies. The metropolitan location epitomizes a space of constant migration streaming from rural areas and other Caribbean islands. From there, some continue their migration to the US mainland. Effectively a borderland, Santurce becomes the ideal setting to represent urban love, social change, violence, pleasure, and despair. In the nine short stories that make up *Mundo Cruel*, Negrón exposes us to a transcultural microcosm where "homosexuality and homoeroticism are everywhere" (Cruz Malavé, "Mundo" 310). This is why literary critic Arnaldo Cruz Malavé argues that with the publication of *Mundo Cruel*, Negrón "expanded the range and depth of Puerto Rican and Latin American literary canon's portrayal of sexual cultures" (312).

For other critics, the novel's essential contribution to Caribbean literary studies lies in its engagement "with a particular constellation of identities through a somewhat realistic aesthetic" (Gutierrez Negrón, "Cruel" 173). These critics argue that *Mundo Cruel* offers "routes which might lead to a thematization of queerness beyond abjection" (175). What's consistent in the scholarship on *Mundo Cruel* is the recognition of an "inherent diversity" at the heart of Negrón's Santurce (Locane, "Interseccionalidad" 33). *Mundo Cruel* portrays a community that acknowledges racial, sexual, and class diversity. In Moisés Agosto Rosario's view, Negrón provides a story about the "diversity within a diversity," that is, about the "vast repertoire" of sexualities shaping sexual cultures in the contemporary Caribbean (qtd. in Locane 37, 34).

At the heart of *Mundo Cruel*, we find "Botella," the short story referenced at the beginning of this chapter. From the perspective of *bugarrón* sexual practice, "Botella" is *Mundo Cruel*'s most significant story. Although the collection is titled after the gay-centered short story "Mundo Cruel," "Botella" is the most complex and original. Whereas "Mundo Cruel" provides a humorous critique of gay life in Santurce, "Botella" deploys the *bugarrón* practitioner as a de facto sexual subject in Puerto Rican letters. "Botella," or "bottle," the short story's title, does not refer to the name of the main character, who remains nameless. Instead, "bottle" is the nickname of a secondary character framed by the male protagonist for the accidental murder of one of his customers. The protagonist's nickname for this secondary character becomes the short story's title. As the lead character states: "His name isn't Botella, but I gave him that nickname because he always had a little bottle full of bleach on him to wash up after fucking and kill any weird shit" (57). The story is written as a first-person narrative from the perspective of a male hustler, or as he is known in San Juan's metropolitan area, a *bugarrón*. His client's suicide after oral and anal sex makes the *neobugarrón* panic, and he decides to erase all traces of his DNA from his dead customer's body. He pours bleach over his lips and mouth, his penis, and inside his anus. Scared to death, the protagonist cannot help thinking, "I wonder if fingerprints stick to hair because I grabbed Caneca by the hair when he was blowing me" (53). The anonymity of personal identities and the proliferation of nicknames augments the story's sexual borderland between homoeroticism and homosexuality.

Caneca, another nickname, refers to a glass flask usually filled with whiskey, rum, or spirits. The protagonist tells us, "His name is Paco but I call him Caneca, like a bottle of rum, even though he doesn't know it" (51). The nickname indicates Caneca's regular drunkenness, and the protagonist describes him as "the old man, who pays good but stinks of rum no matter how much he bathes" (51). Negrón's writing technique doubles his use of synecdoche and displacement. The john is reduced to a bottle of rum; that is to say, his characteristics are narrowed down to his most salient flaw. Adopting the same process, where a part of his personality stands for the whole, Botella is reduced to a bottle (of bleach), signifying his obsessive-compulsive behavior. Because of his popular nickname and character trait, Botella becomes the primary suspect in what now has been interpreted by the police as a murder.

The protagonist tells us that his wife kicked him out of the house because she suspected he had been unfaithful: "In the middle of the night she wakes me up and asks me where I got those flip-flops and the shirt and she says she's not fucking stupid and kicks me out" (56). Only then does he begin to plan his escape from the island. He attempts to flee via plane but lacks the identification papers necessary to board a flight. Instead, he gives Botella his plane ticket. Once overseas, Botella manages to escape from the misguided efforts of the island's justice system. Having traded places with Botella, the protagonist assumes yet another change. In an ironic twist of fate, the *neobugarrón* ends up trading symbolic places with Caneca, the john he despised ("I fucked him and I said I was coming, but I wasn't, and I screamed and said he was mine and the old man came and I laughed because it was funny that he was such a faggot" [51–52]). At the story's end, the *neobugarrón* finds himself at the beach, homeless and drunk, holding a *caneca* in his hand.

By narrating a story from the perspective of a *neobugarrón* character, Negrón has led us into a new territory. The collection of short stories not only introduces the first *neobugarrón* protagonist in Puerto Rican fiction but also invigorates the writing of a gay Puerto Rican literary history.[10] *Mundo Cruel*'s literary representations of the *bugarrón* add to its impressive impact on Puerto Rican literary studies (*Mundo Cruel* won the prestigious Lambda Award for Gay Fiction in 2014). However, the critics missed the repositioning of the *neobugarrón* from the sidelines to center stage. *Mundo Cruel*'s publication makes it possible to trace a *neobugarrón* trajectory from literary represen-

---

10. As Arnaldo Cruz Malavé explains, "there are no lesbians or gay representations in Puerto Rican literature prior to the 1970s. . . . That is, there is prior to the 1970s no poetic persona or writing subjects for whom homosexuality is seen as the key factor that determines his or her being, as the source (or one of the sources) of his or her identity" ("Transvestism" 137–38).

tation as a supporting character's brief story (or *récit*) to protagonist. If there is no *bugarrón* literary history to date, *Mundo Cruel* serves as a resource for studying anomalous sexual cultures in the Caribbean. Yet this absence should not be interpreted as a repressive silence, the way Eve Sedgwick and James Creech claimed deconstructive readings had repressed sexual tropes in their interpretations (Creech, *Closet* 15). Instead, the *bugarrón* lacunae show a scholarship challenged by a logistic problem of grasping gradations in a male sexual continuum (*bugarrón* heteroflexibility) against the impulse to interpret all male same-sex acts as unproblematically gay. The tendency to overreach in interpreting nonidentitarian practices as signs of gayness becomes even more complicated when a translation of literary works normalizes *bugarrón* sexual practice by stripping away the practitioner's anomalous nonidentitarian characteristics.

A SEXUAL CULTURE LOST IN TRANSLATION: LEVINE'S ACCURATE REDUCTION

Mundo Cruel's popularity made possible its publication in English by Seven Stories Press with the work of award-winning translator Suzanne Jill Levine. Levine's edition illustrates the challenges that *bugarrón* sexual practice as a concept represent for translators seeking accuracy across languages and indeed across different styles of sexual reasoning. Levine translates the word *bugarrón* as "hustler," which is consistent with the use of *bugarrón* in San Juan and nearby areas. I referred to this use of *bugarrón* as a sex worker in chapter 2, where I coined the term *neobugarrón*. Levine's translation illustrates how *bugarrón* sexual practice has been reduced to a labor practice in the form of sex work.

> Me encuentro a Conejo y me dice . . . que la policía está buscando al que fue, que fue un *bugarrón* de seguro. (*Mundo* 70; italics applied)

> I run into Rabbit and he tells me . . . the police are looking for the guy who did it and that it was a *hustler* for sure. (*Cruel* 57; italics applied)

This narrowing of meaning, where the richness of the concept is reduced to one of its uses, is found in other stories in *Mundo Cruel*. For instance, in the story "Vampire of Moca," the protagonist is misled by a straight-acting young man who has moved from the town of Moca to Santurce. The protagonist tells us that the vampire "had a daughter named Yomaira and was easygoing and a hard worker" (25). The protagonist was surprised when one evening he witnessed "the Vampire" being anally penetrated by one of the protagonist's more effeminate gay friends named La Carlos ("Miss Carlos"). Distraught that straight-acting men prefer to get fucked, the protagonist decides to go bar-crawling every evening. He marvels at the demographic rise of *bugarrones* in Santurce.

> Una noche me di par de cervezas de más en la barra y como dos *bugarrones* se acercaron a ofrecerme sus ocho y nueve pulgadas, respectivamente, se me bajó la nota. Siempre me deprimo cuando se me acerca un *bugarrón*. (*Mundo* 40; italics applied)

> One night I had too many beers at the bar and as two *hustlers* came over to offer me their eight and nine inches, respectively, I quickly came down from my high spirits. (*Cruel* 26–27; italics applied)

And again,

> En eso pasó un *bugarroncito* . . . (*Mundo* 38; italics applied)

> And then a little macho *hustler*, a bit like my tenant, came by . . . (*Cruel* 25; italics applied)

Whereas Levine is constrained by Negrón's use of the metropolitan definition of *bugarrón* as a hustler, this usage prioritizes functionality (performance, accuracy) over nuance. This is the case, for instance, in Acevedo's book of poetry *Hustler Rave XXX* (2013) published in English, where *bugarrón* as a Spanish word has disappeared and instead we find only the word *hustler*. Because this volume of poems was initially written in English and has not been translated into Spanish, it is worth pondering whether *hustler* would translate as *bugarrón*. The prospect of regaining a lost multiplicity of meaning is one of the complications of translation. As if the obfuscation of multiple meanings were not problematic enough, the imposition of cultural models of sexual identity adds to the challenge.

THE USES OF GENEALOGY AND THE FORMATION OF A *BUGARRÓN* DIALECTIC

The discourse of 1990s gay literary history became useful in spotting thorny representations of sexual ambiguity, but it ultimately translated them into homosexuality and gayness. This identity horizon limits the usefulness of such histories when unpacking representations of *bugarrón* sexual practice.

Genealogy becomes handy for thinking through thorny terms such as the untranslatable *bugarrón* practice. Also, minor genealogies effectively assemble a historical account that considers semantic changes and variations in cultural terms. When putting together a minor genealogy, scholars may spot instances where literary examples correct cultural beliefs taken as historical facts once they become cultural norms. By thinking of *Mundo Cruel* in the context of a *bugarrón* genealogy in Puerto Rican letters, we can trace a shift in *bugarrón* meaning.

Beginning with Puerto Rican playwright Abniel Marat's *Dios en el Playgirl de noviembre* [*God in November's Playgirl*] (1986), *bugarrón* sexual practice is invoked and mobilized in Puerto Rican letters in surprising ways.[11] *God* is written in three parts: "God in November's Playgirl," "The History of the Madman Who Became Sane," and "Nocturne in Unicorn Sex." The first part, "God in November's Playgirl," is composed of five different monologues: "Isander," "Padre Miguel" ["Father Michael"], "El Ciego" ["The Blind Man"], "El Viejo tio Abniel constructor de arlequines" ["Old Uncle Abniel, Harlequin Maker"], and "La Tongo" ["Miss Tongo"]. These mini autobiographical performances are reminiscent in composition to those found in Oscar Lewis's *Children of Sánchez*, previously mentioned in the context of Villalobos's novel. However, in *God* we find a kaleidoscopic perspective on Puerto Rico's culture and a blistering critique of Puerto Rican society. The dissociative soliloquies emphasizing the most contemptuous perspective on Puerto Rican society challenge the idea of a community. For instance, the blind man ends his soliloquy by uttering in a "long, loud, shriek" that "Puerto Rico is like my life, a latrine full of murky black shit" (22). Similar in intensity is the first monologue in *God*. Isander, the lead character, is seated next to his bedridden mother. Suffering from the internal ravages of conscience, Isander fantasizes about condemning his mother to hell. In an inner monologue he tells her, "Die without the last rites and decompose in hell! Fucking bitch! Skanky whore!" (16). Here we find a son condemning his mother, an inverted image of the one found in Powell's *Small Gathering of Bones* where the mother condemns and kills her HIV-positive son, Ian. In *God*, we encounter the other side of the spectrum, the dark hour when a gay son condemns the diseased body of a hateful mother. The dissociated soliloquies that make up Marat's literary work dismantle a community mistakenly perceived as cohesive. And amid this breaking apart, we find a monologue by "La Tongo," a performance that Marat describes in the preface as a last "Fuck You!" ["un carajo"] (*God*, preface).

---

11. All translations of Marat's *Dios*, Ramos Otero's *Novelabingo* and "Loca la de la locura," and Laureano's *San Juan Gay* are my own.

La Tongo is a fifty-year-old male-to-female transvestite, "Me llamaban la Tongo, de Tongolele" ["People used to call me La Tongo, of Tongolele"] (26), whose monologue reveals surprising evidence of a traditional *bugarrón* usage in San Juan. "La Tongo" has plenty of complaints about Puerto Rican society, and her monologue opens with a series of utterances: "Ay, estoy fatigada" ["I am exhausted"] (26). In the middle of her complaints, La Tongo announces:

> En mis tiempos a los *bugarrones* se les salían las babas cuando me veian bailar [At the height of my beauty, *bugarrones* got immediately wet when they saw me dance on stage]. (26)

> La vida es un *bugarrón* que te abandona [Life is a *bugarrón* that dumps you]. (26)

In both instances, *bugarrón* refers not to a sex worker but to the traditional *bugarrón* practitioner. Marat's most crucial contribution to Puerto Rican letters is undoubtedly the inclusion of sexually marginalized voices condemning national culture. No other writer has so determinedly and openly criticized Puerto Rican society. But it is via those marginalized performances that readers can trace previous uses of *bugarrón*. Marat's powerful plays take us to a forced reckoning not only with the exclusion of sexual minorities but also with the inclusion in Puerto Rican letters of forgotten uses of *bugarrón* in San Juan.

If today, literary historians and cultural critics profess that *bugarrón* means only sex worker in San Juan, then a minor genealogy of literary works proves that this was not the case in the recent past. Literary references correct today's impression that *bugarrón* has always meant "hustler" in San Juan. The metropolitan area is highly susceptible to the normalizing tendencies of *scientia sexualis* from abroad and is especially receptive to US mainland cultural trends and norms. In *San Juan Gay* (2016), Javier Laureano explains that the local idea of gay life and gay citizenship in San Juan began during the 1970s, "from the activism directed from New York and Washington" (73). Gay subcultures in San Juan follow the trends set by US gays on the mainland. Genealogies thus become helpful when examining the layered semantic history of the term *bugarrón* in cultural production.

In the literature of the mainland passage, we find another example of traditional *bugarrón* use.[12] This literary production took place because of the great migration of Puerto Rican islanders to the US mainland that began in

---

12. For an in-depth study of the literature of the mainland passage, see Soto-Crespo, *Mainland Passage*, esp. xi–22.

the 1940s and extended to the 1970s. In Manuel Ramos Otero's untranslatable *La novelabingo* (1976), more literary evidence of the traditional *bugarrón* usage may be found. Written in an avant-garde style, *La Novelabingo* is composed of concentric chapters that experiment with narrative structure and language. By designing the chapters in the form of a bingo game's numbered balls, Ramos Otero brings a popular game into an avant-garde/borderland composition. Written in New York City in 1976, *La novelabingo* is a border narrative whose main character is language itself. In the preface, Ramos Otero states, "*La Novelabingo* fucks with language, jerks off old Castilian Spanish and the Royal Academy of Letters to construct the most impenetrable labyrinth yet: Puerto Rican Spanish" (*Novelabingo* 12). Using the *bugarrón* as metaphor, the novel's preface adds, "bugarronísimo Azar en los callejones de la fortuna" ["a *bugarrón*-like chance in the alleys of fortune"] (106).[13] Also important is the novel's very first line, which uses *bugarrón*, "hoy día de Santa Pitusa de los Pederastas desde los callejones lácteos de bugarrones de la perla" ["Today, the day of St. Pitusa of Pederasts and from the *bugarrón* practitioner's cum-covered alleys of la Perla" (a neighborhood in Old San Juan)] (21). "Bugarronísimo Azar" is used again later in the novel. In these examples, *bugarrón* marks sex and desire (desire for younger men) in spaces like alleys where enjoyment (oral sex, penetration) takes place. Missing here is the explicit component of moneymaking transactions that seems a negotiating rule in *neobugarrón* sex acts.

Ramos Otero's contribution is even more starkly evident in "Loca la de la locura," a short story with a polysemic title that means something like "Crazy is the one who is insane" (but that also could mean "Queen of a crazy life"). The drag-performer protagonist has fallen in love with a *bugarrón* practitioner nicknamed Nene Lindo (gorgeous dude), who admired her act at the local drag show. Concerned that he would get tired of her and her "fake eyelashes from Woolworth's," our protagonist consults her friends, who warn her that "he is a terrible *bugarrón*," "he is going to abandon you when you become bald," and "straight men are not worth the trouble" (234). Paying no heed to her friends' advice, our protagonist gets further involved with the *bugarrón*. But she shares the common gay misconception that *bugarrón* practitioners are closeted homosexuals and cannot stop herself from attempting to cross the erotic boundaries of a *bugarrón* sexual practice. First, she hints that he is not a *bugarrón* practitioner but a *maricón* by convincing him that "*maricón* is the one that fucks and faggot is the one that is fucked" (235). A quick smack in the face silences that line of argument (235). Undeterred, our protagonist

---

13. This phrase "bugarronísimo Azar" also repeats as *récit* in *Novelabingo* on pp. 141 and 142.

maneuvers to "eat the *bugarrón*'s asshole": "I ate his *bugarrón*'s fried-chicken-tasting asshole (I delved into his hole like ivy onto a crack on a brick wall and tried to turn him over) but Nene Lindo pulled out his gun. I never tried again" (236). Unable to shake her interest in discovering the true nature of a *bugarrón* practitioner, and haunted by her friend's ominous comment, our lead character became increasingly "afraid of going bald" (237). This fear predisposes her to satisfy her *bugarrón*'s every sexual need, even when awoken from sleep—"Jerk me now will you" (237). The "Caribbean *bugarrón*," "the Boricua *bugarrón*," persistently requests that she satisfy him (235). Not wanting to be abandoned, she decapitates the *bugarrón* ("degollé a Nene Lindo") (237). As she explains: "I, a jibarita from the countryside, and Him, a fucker from the ghetto" are now eternally connected, "seguirá poseyéndome desde el mas allá" ["he will continue to possess me from the beyond"] (237). This story of lust, murder, and *bugarrón* cements the traditional *bugarrón* in Puerto Rican letters years before *Mundo Cruel*'s *neobugarrón* protagonist. In Ramos Otero's works, *bugarrón* sexual practice has not yet become calcified as sex work. Accordingly, the polysemic *bugarrón* term has not been narrowed to today's monosemic *neobugarrón*.

However, Ramos Otero's short story has suffered from the misapprehensions and erasures of cultural ambiguities that can occur when translating sexual practices. For instance, Arnaldo Cruz Malavé translates Ramos Otero's short story title as "Queen of Madness," a clever and catchy title that nonetheless misses the play with nearness and distance that "Loca la" introduces in the potential phrases "the one who" or "that one who" ("Transvestism" 158). Cruz Malavé's smooth translation takes other liberties that sacrifice depth for simplicity. He transposes the protagonist from "Loca la" to "La loca," which reduces the meaning to an identity, "The queen or queer." Instead of holding the phrase's structure "Loca la que . . ." ["Crazy is the one who"], an avant-gardist linguistic play, Cruz Malavé's translation simplifies it to something like "the queeny or faggoty one." If in "Transvestism" (1995), Cruz Malavé argues that the story is important because it tells of a "transvestite cabaret bolero singer" who murders "the macho, the penetrating male, the *bugarrón* . . . the wielder of the phallic '*machete*,'" he later modifies this assessment in "Transnationalism" (2015), where he claims that the transvestite murdered her "trade" ("La Loca" killed the "straight trade man" ["Transvestism" 158; "Transnationalism" 2]). In Cruz Malavé's essays on Ramos Otero, we find that between "Transvestism" (1995) and "Transnationalism" (2015), *bugarrón* sexual practice has been made to disappear. Despite Cruz Malavé's impoverishment of Puerto Rican sexual cultures, I agree with his judgment that "Loca la" is Ramos Otero's "most emblematic" short story ("Transvestism" 158). However, for different reasons: it discloses the complexity of a traditional *bugarrón* sexual practice.

Of greater concern are instances in criticism where a less troubling option has replaced traditional *bugarrón* practice. Take, for example, Radost Rangelova's analysis of "Loca la" as the story of "a transvestite imprisoned for killing her lover" ("Nationalism" 79). Rangelova claims that Nene Lindo is one of those "marginalized" voices that are excluded. For her, Nene Lindo represents a political location within the state; that is, he "represents the state of not being included in the nation-state" (82). Asserting that Nene Lindo "does not belong to the national imaginary," Rangelova effectively impoverishes the historical legacy of sexual cultures in Puerto Rico (81). By erasing the term *bugarrón*, she loses one of the most distinctive differences in Puerto Rico's sexual ecology. Rangelova's *debugarronizing* of *bugarrón* sexual difference in Ramos Otero's story transforms the practitioner into a "state," a "lover," and a "ghost." In this account, *bugarrón* difference vanishes (82).

When the layers of signification are not dismissed and are taken seriously, the short story challenges the identitarianism that too often erases the text's sexual complexity and makes facile the reading of literary works. The denomination "lover" is always easier to explain than *bugarrón*. Whereas Negrón brings the *neobugarrón* to center stage, Ramos Otero places traditional *bugarrón* at a central point in Puerto Rican literary history. Genealogy pays close attention to those instances where the terms emerge in texts long read through an identitarian framework. The way in which literary evidence can substantiate a now outmoded *bugarrón* is another attribute of genealogy. Puerto Rican literary history misses these nuances in language and cultural change.[14] Minor genealogies make us aware of metaphoric intricacies and inconsistencies in scholarship on borderland and Caribbean writing. Minor genealogies revealed not only the problem of translation but also the development of an unexpected Puerto Rican *bugarrón* sublation. In the Puerto Rican context, we find not only two meanings of *bugarrón* (traditional) and *bugarrón* (sex worker) but also the fact that a sublation has taken place and the traditional *bugarrón* has been replaced by a dominant meaning of *bugarrón* (sex worker). This unexpected dialectical move cancels (that is, no longer uses) and preserves (in literature) the traditional meaning as negativity ("not-gay") at the heart of the *neobugarrón* ("not-gay"-for-sale). This "not-gay"-for-sale at the core of a *bugarrón* dialectic makes it interesting. In Reinaldo Arenas's work, the

---

14. The theatrical performance adaptation of Ramos Otero's "Loca la" by the New York–based *Pregones* misses this genealogy and portrays the Nene Lindo in a different light. See La Fountain-Stokes, *Translocas*, for this account, esp. 180–81.

bugarrón dialectic that underlies Puerto Rican polysemy and shift in usage assumes a predominant role.

REINALDO ARENAS AND THE *BUGARRÓN/SUPERBUGARRÓN* DIALECTIC

Arenas introduces a new term, *superbugarrón*, as a parody of the *bugarrón*. I analyze his use of *bugarrón, superbugarrón,* and the problem of translating *bugarrón* across linguistic and cultural borders. This problem of translating *bugarrón* becomes even more present in the English translation of Reinaldo Arenas's works. A problematic situation, akin to Levine's translation of *Mundo Cruel* and Rangelova's *debugarronizing* of the *bugarrón* practitioner in Ramos Otero, arises in Andrew Hurley's translation of *bugarrón* in Arenas's novel *El Color del Verano* [*The Color of Summer*] (1991), where the chapter "Del Bugarron," the third vignette in the novel, is translated as "HM Top Seeking Same . . ." thus once again erasing the word *bugarrón* for an English-speaking audience and adding an undefined "HM Top" as replacement. This erasure effects a conceptual effacement. In other words, the description "top," which is used instead of *bugarrón,* carries with it a meaning that is the conceptual opposite of the original. Unlike *hustler,* one of the current meanings of *bugarrón* in San Juan's metropolitan area, *top* is a misleading categorization. This is because "top" and "bottom" are terms commonly used in gay culture to articulate a preference for a sexual position during sex. Saying he is a "top" does not mean he is "not gay." As a result, these terms obfuscate even further the distinction between *bugarrón* and gay, and between homoeroticism, heterosexual flexibility, and gay identity. Arenas's example is significant because in "Del Bugarron" we find the *bugarrón* as protagonist and, at the same time, a demystification of *bugarrón* as a legitimate sexual category. At stake in this ambiguity, between presence and defacement, is an anomalous sexual practice represented in a key text foregrounding the *bugarrón* in Caribbean literature.

In "Del Bugarron," Arenas tells the story of a *superbugarrón,* that is to say, a *bugarrón* who only penetrates *bugarrones. Superbugarrón* is Arenas's own term. His story is pure irony, attempting to undo a sexual category that he sees as fundamentally problematic. The *superbugarrón* is a tragic figure because "he could only get hard when he was about to fuck a bugarron" (64).[15] This condition of erectile dysfunction prevented him from having intercourse with gay

---

15. All translations of Arenas's "Del Bugarron" and *El Color* and of Stéphanie Panichelli-Batalla's *El Testimonio en la Pentagonía de Reinaldo Arenas* are my own.

men: "I have never been able to fuck a gay man" (64). After a long life of sexual exploits, the old *superbugarrón* wants one last fuck but discovers there are no *bugarrones* left. All the so-called *bugarrones* have been exposed as "*bugarrones maricones*," a new category concocted by Arenas to mean something like a closeted bottom who has masqueraded as heterosexual while secretly craving to be anally penetrated (67). Arenas ventriloquizes his critique of the *bugarrón* by using his *superbugarrón* character's point of view as critic.

> Pero, cuál no sería su sorpresa al descubrir que todos aquellos bugarrones eran maricones pues se dejaban encular por otros bugarrones, bugarrones que no eran tales, pues a la ves se dejaban encular por otros bugarrones y asi *ad infinutus*. De manera que el viejo bugarrón descubrió, con pavor, que en el mundo solamente había maricones. Maricones de todos los tipos; algunos disfrazados de bugarrones; otros absolutamente tapados o tapiñados (estos eran los peores), casados, con mujeres, queridas, hijos y nietos, pasaban el tiempo singándose entre ellos o, . . . gastaban sus vidas delante del televisor mirándole los bultos a los negros jugadores de baloncesto. En fin, gastaban sus vidas en una gran mariconería visual. (64–65)

> But imagine his surprise to realize that all those supposed tops were really just a bunch of pansy faggots, because they would allow their butts to be stuffed by other tops—tops, in turn, who weren't really tops because they would allow their butts to be stuffed by other tops, and so on, ad infinitum. In fact, *ad nauseum*. Because to his horror, the old bull macho had finally realized that the world contained no men at all—there was nothing but pansy faggots. Faggots of all kinds—some, of course, passing themselves off as tops, but others totally and absolutely in the closet (those were the worst), married men with wives, mistresses, children and grandchildren, closet queens who got off by screwing each other or, in the majority of cases, not even that—. . . wasting their lives sitting in front of the TV secretly fantasizing about the baskets on the black basketball players, spending their lives in one long stupor of eyes-only faggotry. ("HM Top" 58)

Notice that Arenas shifts from describing the *bugarrón* to describing types of gay men who impersonate the *bugarrón* in an effort to attract the *superbugarrón*. The extensive list of gay types prompts the protagonist to wonder whether only two types of men are left in Caribbean sexual culture: *maricones* (gays) and *superbugarrones*.

Arenas is more explicit in the section of *El Color del Verano* titled "Las Cuatro Grandes Clasificaciones de los Bugarrones" ["Four Principal Categories of *Bugarrón*"], translated by Hurley as "The Four Major Categories of Tops." A dialogue occurs between "La Chelo" and "la superchelo" about *bugarrón* types. Reminiscent of Kinsey's 0–6 scale, Arenas explains his proposed scale of *bugarrón* variation. In his scale Arenas replaces heterosexuality for *bugarrón* in a parodic series of in-between categories of male sexual practices over the border. His first category, "*bugarrón de ocasión o dormido*" ["sleeper *bugarrón*"], is a man who lives a "normal life," is married with children, and does not desire other men, with the exception that once in a full moon he craves to fuck a homosexual. Similar to a sleeper cell in the context of lust, the *bugarrón* inside him awakens (*El Color* 207–8). Arenas closes his discussion of the "sleeper *bugarrón*" by stating that this kind could easily be "cualquier hombre" ["any man"] (208).

The second category is the "*bugarrón acomplejado*" or "*bugarrón* with a complex" (*El Color* 208). This type is married with children but feels guilty for lusting after another man's ass. Unable to contain his urge, every so often he fucks "un aro de carne" ["any man's butt hole"] (208). For Arenas, this category includes "boxers, kick boxers, practitioners of karate and judo, and, from antiquity, Jesus" (208).

The third category is the "*bugarron nato*" or "natural born *bugarrón*" (*El Color* 208). This third type is not interested in women. His sole interest is in fucking gay men. As Hurley translates: "The natural-born bull macho can screw up to thirty fairies in one day; he can also be married to one, though that doesn't keep him from screwing every queen on the block, and all the 'real men,' too" (*The Color* 190). The fourth category is the "*superbugarrón*" (*El Color* 208). Arenas describes him as "a rare type, now nearing extinction if not already extinct" (209). He is interested in "screwing only another man—that is another *superbugarrón* like himself" (209). With this categorization, Arenas *bugarronizes* Kinsey. He inverts the Kinsey scale in order to make it conform with the *bugarronacy* of the tropics. This political and ideological overturning of *scientia sexualis* gets lost in translation.

Hurley translates the categories of *bugarrón* as follows: "THE OCCASIONAL, OR SLEEPING, TOP," "THE TOP WITH A COMPLEX," "THE NATURAL-BORN TOP," and "THE SUPERBUGGER" (*The Color* 189–91). "Top" as a translation continues to be problematic, but "bugger" is no better. *Bugger*'s primary use in England today is as a mild insult; its use as "sodomizer" or "practitioner of anal intercourse" has fallen out of fashion. "Bugger" is an interesting choice, as etymologically it is an English cognate of *bugarrón*. However, its obsolete definition makes it imprecise for *bugarrón* because it does not specify the gender of the penetrated partner (men, women).

The problem of translating the term *bugarrón* across languages involves the difficulty in capturing accurately a specific cultural concept. Confronted with the lack of an exact equivalent, translators exacerbate the confusion. And literary critics have not been immune to misleading characterizations of the *bugarrón*; even critics who are born and raised in the Caribbean perpetuate a vague understanding of *bugarrón* practice. Like "white trash" in the US, *bugarrón* falls into the category of those everyday terms that everybody recognizes without grasping their specificity.[16] For instance, in *El Testimonio en la Pentagonía de Reinaldo Arenas* (2016), literary scholar Stéphanie Panichelli-Batalla writes that Arenas introduces the *bugarrón* as "a macho man with homoerotic tendencies" ["hombre machista con tendencias homoeróticas"] (292). Panichelli-Batalla's definition is neither completely incorrect nor entirely clear. Is "macho" synonymous with heterosexual? Are there not gay machos? Are "homoerotic tendencies" a euphemism for same-sex practices?

Translation becomes complicated further in *El Color del Verano* by the fact that Arenas is conjuring a hyperbolic metaphor, the *superbugarrón,* to demystify the concept of *bugarrón* in Cuban culture. The terminological complexity is intensified by Arenas's ironization. Here we find a dialectical representation of a conflicting relationship between two *bugarrón* nonidentities. The *bugarrón/superbugarrón* conflict assumes center stage, with the *superbugarrón* serving as a corrective to the fallacious manipulations of the *bugarrón*. Accordingly, the *superbugarrón*'s narrative provides ironic examples of the duplicitous nature of the *bugarrón* concept. For example, in "Del Bugarron," Arenas highlights this point by telling the story of Cuquejo, an old *bugarrón* who was surprised by the protagonist in the act of inserting a "huge plastic dildo up his ass"; "Still unsatisfied," he then "manage[s] to push inside his butt hole the dildo's two appended cojones" (*El Color* 66). Arenas provides an account of how the *superbugarrón* interrupts what could be called a "fuck train," where Fidel Castro (nicknamed Fifo) is on his back in a hospital bed with his legs raised, Che Guevara is penetrating him, and Che in turn is being penetrated by Camilo Cienfuegos (65).[17] The insertion of Che Guevara in the middle of this segment echoes Elio Rodríguez's painting of a Che Guevara look-alike (discussed in chapter 2), where Che is illustrated showing his ass to an American tourist while on stage. Here, Che is located in the middle wagon, so to speak, of a "fuck train," penetrating and being penetrated, thereby doubling his pleasure.

At a crucial juncture in "Del Bugarron," the *superbugarrón* realizes that "there are no more men, the Bugarronacy has been abolished or has always been a fallacy" (67). Astonished, he claims, "everything is just a representation, a continuous mask" (67). Whereas the *bugarrón* as a closet case is a

---

16. On this subject, see Soto-Crespo, *White Trash Menace,* esp. 1–12.

17. Camilo Cienfuegos (1932–59) was a Cuban revolutionary under the direction of Fidel Castro.

staple of Caribbean gay writers, as they cannot contain the impulse of reading homoeroticism as an indication of a repressed gay identity, Arenas's playfulness reaches a different height as unmasking a simulation by reaching its logical extreme. In Arenas, it is also a move of the dialectic where one concept seeks to unmask the fallacy of its opposing concept, thus ensuring that, as Theodor Adorno argues, the concept is free from "conceptual manipulation" (*Introduction* 2). The negative dialectical dynamic between *bugarrón/superbugarrón* leads not to an idealist Hegelian totality (a third term that sublates the previous two, a sort of identity) but to an unproductive culmination. Arenas is performing in fiction Adorno's revision of dialectics as a way "to think nonidentity" (*Introduction* 6). *Superbugarrón* is conjured as a counterterm, that is, as an antidote to the "truth" of *bugarrón* sexual practice. In this narrative, *superbugarrón* is realer than the real and *bugarrón* is fake. If, in dialectics, the truth of a concept is its identity, then nonidentity is revealed when "concept and thing are not simply equivalent" (*Introduction* 8). *Bugarrón* as concept reveals itself as an illusion, as a thing non-*bugarrón* (a simulation). Accordingly, "Del Bugarron" tells a tale of dislocation in which the *bugarrón* as thing and *bugarrón* as concept are revealed to be in a nonequivalent relationship. The *superbugarrón* unveils this condition of failed equivalency and interprets it as a farce. From the perspective of Arenas's *superbugarrón*, the *bugarrón* turns out to be the simulation of a "real" thing. The *bugarrón*'s "truth" is revealed only via his confrontation with the invented *superbugarrón* counterexample. But this confrontation takes place in the imaginative world of fiction, where truth is only an invented "truth." The real *bugarrón* identity, where concept matches thing, is a construct, another cultural ideal.

"Del Bugarron" ends with the *superbugarrón* attempting to anally penetrate the only other *bugarrón* left in Cuba, the president of the Royal Academy of Letters, who fights back, resulting in the demise of both *bugarrones*. Arenas's text reaches a crescendo in which both concepts, *bugarrón* and *superbugarrón*, cancel each other. They are both *superbugarrones* and, as such, fictional constructs. Yet, with the *superbugarrón*, Arenas gets closer to the fact that identity is unveiled as nothing more than a fictional construct. The *superbugarrón* is, after all, a narrative parody devoid of any reference outside the literary imagination of a gay Cuban writer. Parodying Kinsey, Arenas replaces exclusive heterosexuality with *bugarronacy,* a hierarchical system governing the desires of the living. In Arenas, exclusive heterosexuality disappears as a cultural ideal so unrealistic that it does not even merit demystification: exclusive heterosexuality seems inconsequential, *bugarrón* is a mask, and *superbugarrón* is an imaginative construct.

If, in the world of Arenas's "Del Bugarron," there is no resolution or synthesis to the conflict between *bugarrón* and *superbugarrón*, then there is also no uniting of "identity with non-identity," an outcome typically sought in a Hegelian dialectic. In the end, for Arenas, *bugarrón* is useful not as an "identity" category but as a nonidentitarian sexual practice, one that is performed in a larger order of cultural signification. There, on that conceptual plane, *bugarrón* sexual practice inserts a geopolitics of untranslatability into the cultural practice of nonidentity. Whereas Foucault seeks a "different economy of bodies and pleasures" to counter the deployment of *scientia sexualis,* Arenas *bugarronizes* key tenets of *scientia sexualis;* he *bugarronizes* Kinsey and "overturns" his knowledge across the border (Foucault, *History of Sexuality, Vol. 1,* 159).

A GEOPOLITICAL *BUGARRÓN*

The confusion about how to translate *bugarrón* accurately is a sign of a lack of clarity on what a *bugarrón* is. This problem is not confined to the realm of fiction but extends to the realm of memoir writing, where translators such as Dolores M. Koch provide a questionable account of *bugarrón* in her translation of Arenas's *Antes que Anochezca [Before Night Falls].*[18]

> I do not know what to call the young Cuban men of those days, *whether homosexuals who played the male role or bisexuals.* The truth is that they had girlfriends or wives, but when they came to us they enjoyed themselves thoroughly, sometimes more than with their wives, who often would refuse to suck or had inhibitions that made love-making less pleasurable. (*Before* 107; italics applied)
>
> No sé cómo llamar a aquellos jóvenes cubanos de entonces; *no sé si bugarrones o bisexuales.* Lo cierto es que tenían sus novias y sus mujeres, y cuando

---

18. The connection between *El Color del Verano* and *Antes que Anochezca* is strong and has not been lost on the criticism on Arenas. In "Strategic Rebellions: Reinaldo Arenas Has the Last Word" (2015), Del Risco characterizes this connection by asserting that "Arenas' own autobiography and *El Color del Verano* . . . function as parallel texts" to one another (53). Other critics find a similar correspondence between the texts. For further analysis, see Kate Mehuron, "Queer Territories" (1994); Robert Richmond Ellis, "Gay Lifewriting" (1995); Steven Clark, "*Antes que anochezca*" (1995); Francisco Soto, *Arenas* (1994); Ricardo L. Ortiz, "Docile Bodies" (1998); Benigno Sánchez-Eppler, "Arenas" (2000); Emilio Bejel, *Gay Cuban* (2001); and Rafael Ocasio, *Outlaw* (2003).

iban con nosotros gozaban extraordinariamente: a veces más que con sus mujeres, que muchas veces se negaban a mamar. (*Antes* 132; italics applied)

In the passage above, the English word *homosexual* for *bugarrón* is problematic. Koch misses the cultural difference between *bugarrón* and homosexuality, despite the fact that Arenas is highlighting that precise difference. In literature, criticism, and translation, the *bugarrón* continues to be erased, replaced, or made gay.

For all of the confusion Arenas generated by erasing the divide between homosexuality and *bugarrón* practices, and for all the further confusion added by translators and critics, his works provide the best representation of how Latin American writers have used the term *bugarrón* as a marker of cultural difference between Anglo-American gay culture and that of Latin American sexual cultures. More than an indication of a hybridized culture, *bugarrón* indicates the untranslatability of a sexual practice across borders. On this subject, Arenas elaborates:

no había que ser homosexual para tener relaciones con un hombre; un hombre podía tener relaciones con otro como un acto normal . . . al que le gustaran los hombres de verdad, también podía alcanzar a ese macho que quería vivir con él o tener con él una relación amistosa que no interrumpía para nada la actividad heterosexual de aquel hombre. Lo normal no era que una loca se acostara con otra loca, sino que la loca buscara a un hombre que la poseyera y que sintiera, al hacerlo, tanto placer como ella al ser poseída (*Antes que anochezca* 133).

You did not have to be a homosexual to have a relationship with a man, a man could have intercourse with another man as an ordinary act. In the same way, a real gay who liked another gay could easily go out and live with him. But the gay who liked real macho men could also find one who wanted to live or be friends with him, without in any way interfering with the heterosexual life of that man. It was not the norm for one queer to go to bed with another queer, "she" would look for a man to fuck "her" who would feel as much pleasure as the homosexual being fucked (*Before* 108).

For Arenas, *bugarrón* cultural practice has geopolitical implications, as it marks a difference in the understanding of sexuality between identity-driven Western societies and those in Latin America. Emily Apter has argued that untranslatables are "geopolitical configurations that overturn Western assumptions" (*Against* 39). She contends that literary history gains new insight when it "recognizes the importance of non-translation, mistranslation, incomparability, and untranslatability" (4).[19] There is a political dimension in untranslatable terms that conceptualize regimes of sexual practice differently from our own. In this sense, untranslatability is "knowledge transmission," as it points to the limits of what can be readily known. Whereas Foucault had argued for a constellation of concepts to make sense of the elements that constitute knowledge in their discursive diversity, Apter proposes a "galaxy of micro-mondes" in a new theoretical fulcrum that redraws the map of "language geopolitics" (7).

Apter's "micro-mondes" and Foucault's "constellations" underscore geopolitical distinctions at the heart of the works by Arenas and other writers of *bugarrón* practice. In those "micro-mondes," we find a "constellation of concepts" critical to unaccommodating cultures of sexual identity. Writing in 1992, Arenas critiques the balkanization of sexual cultures in advanced societies:

> En Cuba, cuando uno iba a un club o a una playa, no había una zona específica para homosexuales; todo el mundo compartía junto, sin que existiera una división que situara al homosexual en una posición militante. Esto se ha perdido en las sociedades más civilizadas, donde el homosexual ha tenido que convertirse en una especie de monje de la actividad sexual y ha tenido que separarse de esa parte de la sociedad, supuestamente no homosexual que, indiscutiblemente, también lo excluye. Al no existir estas divisiones, lo interesante del homosexualismo en Cuba consistía en que no había que ser un homosexual para tener relaciones con un hombre; un hombre podía tener relaciones con otro como acto normal. . . . La militancia homosexual ha dado otros derechos que son formidables para los homosexuales del mundo libre, pero también ha atrofiado el encanto maravilloso de encontrarse con una persona heterosexual o bisexual, es decir, con un hombre que sienta el deseo de poseer a otro hombre y que no tenga que ser poseído a la vez. (*Antes que anochezca* 133)

> In Cuba gays were not confined to a specific area of a club or beach. Everybody mingled and there was no division that would place the homosexual on the defensive. This has been lost in most advanced societies, where the homosexual has had to become a sort of sexual recluse and separate himself from the supposedly nonhomosexual society, which undoubtedly also

---

19. Apter's world-system of untranslatables, her mapping of incompatible terms in world literature, includes concepts from ancient and modern philosophy as well as contemporary theory from all over the world. But whereas her study is rich with literary examples, it does not include terms associated with the conceptualization of sexual practice. Apter makes clear that her study is not exhaustive, but the absence of cases concerning the sexually untranslatable in literature raises questions about the segregation of studies of literary translation from studies of sexual practice. *Bugarrón* brings these two seemingly unrelated approaches into conversation.

excludes him. Since such divisions did not exist in Cuba, the interesting aspect of homosexuality there was that you did not have to be a homosexual to have a relationship with a man; a man could have intercourse with another man as an ordinary act. . . . Homosexual militancy has gained considerable rights for free-world gays. But what has been lost is the wonderful feeling of meeting heterosexual or bisexual men who would get pleasure from possessing another man and who would not, in turn, have to be possessed. (*Before* 107–8)

Here Arenas draws attention to the duality of an identity-constrained "free world" and the more flexible experiences found in cultures with graded degrees of heteroflexibility. There is irony in the contrast drawn by Arenas where freedom, in a "free world," makes sense only in the context of limits accepted by an identity-driven culture. There is a hint in Arenas of Foucault's sense of self-surveillance techniques unwittingly adopted by identity groups in Western societies.

The untranslatability of the word *bugarrón* reflects the obstacles to making sense of specific sexual practices outside the cultural milieu that shapes them. It would have been challenging to translate these practices into societies where *scientia sexualis* dominates how sexuality is apprehended. Against current epistemes, a minor genealogy uncovers that *bugarrón* was used in a context other than that of "hustler." This phenomenon is what surprises in Marat's and Ramos Otero's examples. However, the untranslatability of *bugarrón* represents further difficulties. Kinsey's insights into nonexclusive sexual gradation are helpful as a conceptual translation of traditional *bugarrón* practices. Still, the idea of a nonexclusive sexual gradation is no longer applicable when *bugarrón*'s modern meaning of sex worker is considered. Because *bugarrón* in Spanish stands for a traditional sexual practice *and* the current sex-working practices of a *neobugarrón* subject, its polysemic characteristics make it fundamentally contradictory and indeterminate. The *bugarrón*'s conflictive polysemy underlies the problem of translation and ends up shaping a sexual practice's unconventional genealogy. Yet it is through thinking about sexual practices, in this case, *bugarrón* practices, that we discover that they have a historical trajectory of their own. This particular type of knowledge can stem only from the geopolitical margins.

CONCLUSION

This book has examined the emergence of the figure of the *neobugarrón* during the time of neoliberalism. It began by elucidating the surveillance of *bugarrón* sexual practice in anthropological studies of sexuality. It then proceeded to explore representations of *neobugarrón* in cinema and fiction, two discourses that showed a more sophisticated production of *neobugarrón* representation in visual and written works. All these discursive components do not render a complete picture or tell the full story of *neobugarrón* representation in Latin America, but they constitute a start.

This project delineates a series of parameters in the study of *bugarrón* sexual practice and of a *neobugarrón* subject. From sexual tourism, social photos, and visual art, this study apprehends the connection between neoliberalism and the emergence of a *neobugarrón* subject. From cinema, NEOBUGARRÓN uncovers an ecology of techniques used to make visible a sexual anomaly on screen. From literature, it traces the polysemic use of the term *bugarrón*, a polysemy threatened by cultural pressures pushing *bugarrón* toward a single meaning.

The claims of my argument are these:

1. The traditional *bugarrón* practitioner is a heteroflexible man who has sex with other men.

2. In considering himself neither queer nor gay, the *bugarrón* practitioner violates a fundamental taxonomic division through which Westerners understand adult sexuality, that is, the homosexual/heterosexual divide.
3. By violating the homo/hetero division, *bugarrón* sexual practice shows a continuum from homosociality to nongay sexual desire between men.
4. *Bugarrón* practitioners have never claimed to identify as *bugarrón*. Instead, they identify as *hombres normales* or normal men. We may think this is due to simple denial, selfishness, fear, or privilege; however, their consistency in answering this question suggests their deep conviction that a sexual practice does not change their identification with *hombres normales*. This contradiction at the heart of their self-image indicates their complicated location in the homo/hetero divide.
5. Scholarship in gay studies, queer studies, and trans studies has failed to recognize the particularity of *bugarrón* sexual practice on its own merits.
6. The *bugarrón/neobugarrón* transformation has gone unnoticed, given that the nomenclature *bugarrón* continues to be used when referring to Caribbean male sex workers targeting gay tourists.
7. *Bugarrón* as sex worker is neither the original meaning nor the deployment of a dehistoricized new "normal." Rather, it is the old term used to name a newly transformed cultural practice.
8. Neoliberal simulation has given a new lease on life to an almost extinct *bugarrón* sexual practice.
9. In neoliberalism, a thriving market for everything *neobugarrón* superimposes itself on a disappearing *bugarrón* sexual practice.
10. *Neobugarrón* is a subject of capital.

Bugarrón/neobugarrón concepts have a rich cultural history of their own. Their genealogical trajectory is worth thinking with, exploring, and knowing. To *bugarronize* heteroflexibility is to provide an account of neoliberalism's impact on the Global South and to confront the anomalous sexual practices on its geopolitical margins.

BIBLIOGRAPHY

Abramson, P. R. "Sexual Assessment and Epidemiology of AIDS." *The Journal of Sex Research* 25 (1988): 323–46.

Acevedo, David Caleb. *Diario de una puta humilde*. San Juan: Erizo Editorial, 2012.

Acevedo, David Caleb, and Charlie Vázquez. *Hustler Rave XXX: Poetry of the Eternal Survivor*. Maple Shade, NJ: Lethe Press, 2013.

Adorno, Theodor. *An Introduction to Dialectics*. 2010. Translated by Nicholas Walker. Cambridge, UK: Polity, 2017.

Andros, Phil. [Sam Steward]. *Roman Conquests*. New York: Alyson Books, 1971.

———. *Shuttlecock*. New York: Alyson Books, 1984.

Appe, Susan. "NGO Networks, the Diffusion and Adaptation of NGO Managerialism, and NGO Legitimacy in Latin America." *Voluntas* 27 (2016): 187–208. https://doi.org/10.1007/s11266-015-9594-y.

Apter, Emily. *Against World Literature: On the Politics of Untranslatability*. London: Verso, 2013.

Arenas, Reinaldo. *Antes que anochezca*. Barcelona: Tusquets Editores, 1992.

———. *Before Night Falls: A Memoir*. Translated by Dolores M. Koch. New York: Penguin, 1994.

———. *El Color del Verano*. Miami: Ediciones Universal, 1991.

———. *The Color of Summer, or The New Garden of Earthly Delights*. Translated by Andrew Hurley. New York: Viking, 2000.

———. "Las Cuatro Grandes Clasificaciones de los Bugarrones." In *El Color del Verano*, 207–9.

———. "Del Bugarron." In *El Color del Verano*, 64–68.

———. "The Four Major Categories of Tops." In *The Color of Summer*, 189–91.

———. "HM, top, seeking same . . ." In *The Color of Summer*, 57–61.

Barnshaw, John, and Lynn Letukas. "The Low Down on the Down Low: Origins, Risk Identification and Intervention." *Health Sociology Review* 19:4 (2010): 478–90. https://www.tandfonline.com/doi/abs/10.5172/hesr.2010.19.4.478.

Barry, Andrew, Thomas Osborne, and Nikolas Rose, eds. *Foucault and Political Reason: Liberalism, Neo-Liberalism, and Rationalities of Government*. Chicago: University of Chicago Press, 1996.

Barthes, Roland. *Camera Lucida: Reflections on Photography*. Translated by Richard Howard. New York: Noonday Press, 1981.

Baudrillard, Jean. *Screened Out*. Translated by Chris Turner. London: Verso, 2002.

———. *Simulacra and Simulation*. Translated by Sheila Faria Glaser. Ann Arbor: University of Michigan Press, 1994.

Bayly, Jamie. *La mujer de mi hermano*. Bogotá: Editorial Planeta, 2002.

———. *No se lo digas a nadie*. Lima: Peisa, 1998.

Bejel, Emilio. *Gay Cuban Nation*. Chicago: University of Chicago Press, 2001.

Bennett, Jane. *Vibrant Matter: A Political Ecology of Things*. Durham: Duke University Press, 2010.

Bersani, Leo, and Ulysse Dutoit. *Caravaggio's Secrets*. Cambridge, MA: MIT Press, 1998.

———. *Forms of Being: Cinema, Aesthetics, Subjectivity*. London: British Film Institute Publishing, 2004.

Bleek, Wolf. "Lying Informants: A Fieldwork Experience from Ghana." *Population and Development Review* 13:2 (1987): 314–22.

Bolton, Ralph. "Rethinking Anthropology: The Study of AIDS." In *Culture and Sexual Risk: Anthropological Perspectives on AIDS*, edited by Han ten Brummelhuis and Gilbert Herdt, 285–313. London: Taylor and Francis Books, 1995.

Brinkema, Eugenie. *The Forms of the Affects*. Durham: Duke University Press, 2014.

Brown, Wendy. *In the Ruins of Neoliberalism: The Rise of Antidemocratic Politics in the West*. New York: Columbia University Press, 2019.

Burchell, Graham. "Liberal Government and Techniques of the Self." In Barry, Osborne, and Rose, 19–36.

Cabezas, Amalia L. *Economies of Desire: Sex and Tourism in Cuba and the Dominican Republic*. Philadelphia: Temple University Press, 2009.

Cáceres, Carlos F. "HIV among Gay and Other Men Who Have Sex with Men in Latin America and the Caribbean: A Hidden Epidemic?" *AIDS* 16:S3 (2002): S23–S33.

Cáceres, Carlos F., and Ana Maria Rosasco. "The Margin Has Many Sides: Diversity among Gay and Homosexually Active Men in Lima." *Culture, Health & Sexuality* 1:3 (1999): 261–75. https://www.tandfonline.com/doi/abs/10.1080/136910599301012.

Carbone, Mauro. *The Flesh of Images: Merleau-Ponty between Painting and Cinema*. Translated by Marta Nijhuis. Albany: State University of New York Press, 2015.

Carrillo, Héctor. *The Night Is Young: Sexuality in Mexico in the Time of AIDS*. Chicago: University of Chicago Press, 2002.

Carrillo, Héctor, and Amanda Hoffman. "'Straight with a pinch of bi': The Construction of Heterosexuality as an Elastic Category among Adult US men." *Sexualities* 21:1–2 (2018): 90–108. https://doi.org/10.1177/1363460716678561.

———. "From MSM to Heteroflexibilities: Non-Exclusive Straight Male Identities and Their Implications for HIV Prevention and Health Promotion." *Global Public Health* 11:7–8 (2016): 923–36. https://doi.org/10.1080/17441692.2015.1134272.

Chauncey, George. *Gay New York: Gender, Urban Culture, and the Making of the Gay Male World, 1890–1940.* London: HarperCollins, 1995.

Chibber, Vivek. *Postcolonial Theory and the Specter of Capital.* London: Verso, 2013.

Chin, James. *The AIDS Pandemic: The Collision of Epidemiology with Political Correctness.* Oxford: Radcliffe Publishing, 2007.

Chin, Timothy. "The Novels of Patricia Powell: Negotiating Gender and Sexuality across the Disjunctures of the Caribbean Diaspora." *Callaloo* 30:2 (2007): 533–45.

Chomsky, Noam. *Profit over People: Neoliberalism & Global Order.* New York: Seven Stories Press, 1999.

Clark, Steven. "*Antes que anochezca*: Las paradojas de la representación." *Revista del Ateneo Puertorriqueño* 5:13–15 (1995): 209–25.

Cleland, John. "Review of *The Wisdom of Whores.* E Pisani." *International Journal of Epidemiology* 37:1 (2008): 1441–42. https://doi.org/10.1093/ije/dyn199.

Clifford, James. *The Predicament of Culture: Twentieth-Century Ethnography, Literature, and Art.* Cambridge, MA: Harvard University Press, 1988.

Connolly, William. *The Fragility of Things: Self-Organizing Processes, Neoliberal Fantasies, and Democratic Activism.* Durham: Duke University Press, 2013.

Cook, Deborah. *Adorno, Foucault, and the Critique of the West.* London: Verso, 2018.

Creech, James. *Closet Writing/Gay Reading: The Case of Melville's Pierre.* Chicago: University of Chicago Press, 1993.

Cruz Malavé, Arnaldo Manuel. "Mundo Cruel." *Review: Literature and Arts of the Americas* 87. 46:2 (2013): 310–12.

———. "Toward an Art of Transvestism: Colonialism and Homosexuality in Puerto Rican Literature." In *¿Entiendes?: Queer Readings, Hispanic Writings,* edited by Emilie L. Bergmann and Paul Julian Smith, 137–67. Durham: Duke University Press, 1995.

———. "Transnationalism and Manuel Ramos Otero's 'Traveling Theater' of Return." *emisférica* 12:1 (2015): 1–5. https://hemisphericinstitute.org/en/emisferica-121-caribbean-rasanblaj/12-1-dossier/e-121-dossier-cruz-malave-transnationalism-and-manuel-ramos.html.

Dardot, Pierre, and Christian Laval. *Never Ending Nightmare: The Neoliberal Assault on Democracy.* Translated by Gregory Elliott. London: Verso, 2019.

———. *The New Way of the World: On Neo-liberal Society.* 2009. Translated by Gregory Elliott. London: Verso, 2017.

Davidson, Arnold I. *The Emergence of Sexuality: Historical Epistemology and the Formation of Concepts.* Cambridge, MA: Harvard University Press, 2001.

de la Mora, Sergio. *Cinemachismo: Masculinities and Sexuality in Mexican Film.* Austin: University of Texas Press, 2006.

de Man, Paul. "Autobiography as De-facement." In *The Rhetoric of Romanticism,* 67–81. New York: Columbia University Press, 1984.

de Moya, Antonio E., and Rafael García. "Three Decades of Male Sex Work in Santo Domingo." In *Men Who Sell Sex: Interpersonal Perspectives on Male Prostitution and HIV/AIDS,* edited by Peter Aggleton, 127–39. Philadelphia: Temple University Press, 1999.

Dean, Mitchell, and Daniel Zamora. *The Last Man Takes LSD: Foucault and the End of Revolution.* London: Verso, 2021.

Dean, Tim. "Sam Steward's Pornography: Archive, Index, Trace." In *Samuel Steward and the Pursuit of the Erotic: Sexuality, Literature, Archives,* edited by Debra A. Moddelmog and Martin Joseph Ponce, 25–43. Columbus: The Ohio State University Press, 2017.

Decena, Carlos Ulises. *Tacit Subjects: Belonging, Same-Sex Desire, and Daily Life Among Dominican Immigrant Men*. Durham: Duke University Press, 2011.

Del Risco, Enrique. "Strategic Rebellions: Reinaldo Arenas Has the Last Word." Translated by Stacey Van Dahm. *Latin American Literary Review* 44:87 (2017): 53–64.

D'Emilio, John. "Capitalism and Gay Identity." In *The Lesbian and Gay Studies Reader*, edited by Henry Abelove, Michèle Aina Barale, and David Halperin, 467–78. New York: Routledge, 1993.

Delany, Samuel R. *Times Square Red, Times Square Blue*. New York: New York University Press, 1999.

Diamond, Lisa M. *Sexual Fluidity: Understanding Women's Love and Desire*. Cambridge, MA: Harvard University Press, 2008.

Dinshaw, Carolyn. *Getting Medieval: Sexualities and Communities, Pre- and Postmodern*. Durham: Duke University Press, 1999.

Domínguez-Ruvalcaba, Héctor. "Mayate: The Queerest Queer." In *Modernity and the Nation in Mexican Representations of Masculinity: New Concepts in Latino American Cultures*, 131–47. New York: Palgrave Macmillan, 2007. https://doi.org/10.1057/9780230608894_8.

Dreuilhe, Emmanuel. *Mortal Embrace: Living with AIDS*. Translated by Linda Coverdale. New York: Farrar, Straus and Giroux, 1988.

Drucker, Donna J. *The Classification of Sex: Alfred Kinsey and the Organization of Knowledge*. Pittsburgh: University of Pittsburgh Press, 2014.

Dunphy-Blomfield, Jocelyn. "Harmony in a Dislocated World." In *Merleau-Ponty and Environmental Philosophy: Dwelling on the Landscape of Thought*, edited by Suzanne L. Cataldi and William S. Hamrick, 217–34. Albany: State University of New York Press, 2007.

Ellis, Robert Richmond. "The Gay Lifewriting of Reinaldo Arenas: *Antes Que Anochezca*." *a/b: Auto/Biography Studies* 10:1 (1995): 126–44.

Finn, Jonathan. *Capturing the Criminal Image: From Mug Shot to Surveillance Society*. Minneapolis: University of Minnesota Press, 2009.

Foucault, Michel. *The Archaeology of Knowledge*. New York: Pantheon Books, 1972.

———. *The Birth of Biopolitics. Lectures at the Collège de France, 1978–1979*. Edited by Arnold I. Davidson. Translated by Graham Burchell. New York: Palgrave, 2008.

———. *The Birth of the Clinic: An Archaeology of Medical Perception*. 1963. Translated by Alan Sheridan. New York: Pantheon, 1973.

———. *Discipline and Punish: The Birth of the Prison*. 1975. Translated by Alan Sheridan. New York: Pantheon, 1977.

———. *Essential Works of Foucault (1954–1984), Vol. 1: Ethics: Subjectivity and Truth*. Edited by Paul Rabinow. Translated by Robert Hurley et al. New York: The New Press, 1997.

———. *Essential Works of Foucault (1954–1984), Vol. 2: Aesthetics: Method, and Epistemology*. Edited by James D. Faubion. Translated by Robert Hurley et al. New York: The New Press, 1998.

———. *The History of Sexuality, Vol. 1: An Introduction*. Translated by Robert Hurley. New York: Pantheon Books, 1978.

———. "Nietzsche, Genealogy, History." In *Essential Works of Foucault (1954–1984), Vol. 2: Aesthetics: Method, and Epistemology*, 369–91.

———. *The Order of Things: An Archaeology of the Human Sciences*. 1966. New York: Pantheon Books, 1970.

———. *Psychiatric Power: Lectures at the College de France, 1973–1974*. Edited by Jacques Lagrange. Translated by Graham Burchell. New York: Palgrave Macmillan, 2006.

———. "Sex, Power, and the Politics of Identity." In *Essential Works of Foucault (1954–1984), Vol. 1: Ethics: Subjectivity and Truth*, 163–73.

———. "Sexuality and Solitude." In *Essential Works of Foucault (1954–1984), Vol. 1: Ethics: Subjectivity and Truth*, 175–85.

———. *Sexuality: The 1964 Clermont-Ferrand and 1969 Vincennes Lectures*. Translated by Graham Burchell. Edited by Claude-Oliver Doron. New York: Columbia University Press, 2021.

———. *Subjectivity and Truth. Lectures at the Collège de France, 1980–1981*. Edited by Frédéric Gros. Translated by Graham Burchell. London: Palgrave, 2017.

———. *The Use of Pleasure*. Translated by Robert Hurley. New York: Pantheon Books, 1985.

Freud, Sigmund. "Mourning and Melancholia.'" 1917. In *Standard Edition*, 243–48. Translated by James Strachey. Vol. 14. London: Hogarth Press, 1957.

———. "A Note Upon the 'Mystic Writing Pad.'" 1925. In *Standard Edition*, 225–32. Translated by James Strachey. Vol. 19. London: Hogarth Press, 1961.

———. *Three Essays on the Theory of Sexuality*. In *Standard Edition*, 124–245. Translated by James Strachey. Vol. 7. London: Hogarth Press, 1953.

Freud, Sigmund, James Strachey, Anna Freud, and Carrie Lee Rothgeb. *The Standard Edition of the Complete Psychological Works of Sigmund Freud*. London: Hogarth Press and the Institute of Psycho-Analysis, 1953.

García Canclini, Néstor. *Hybrid Cultures: Strategies for Entering and Leaving Modernity*. Translated by Christopher L. Chiappari and Silvia L. Lopez. Minneapolis: University of Minnesota Press, 1995.

Green, Edward C., Melissa Farley, and Allison Herling Ruark. "Review of *The Wisdom of Whores: Bureaucracies, Brothels, and the Business of AIDS*." *Journal of the American Medical Association* 301:23 (2009): 2502–4. https://doi.org/10.1001/jama.2009.884.

Grugel, Jean. "Romancing Civil Society: European NGOs in Latin America." *Journal of Interamerican Studies and World Affairs* 42:2 (2000): 87–107. https://doi.org/10.2307/166283.

Gutiérrez Negrón, Sergio. "Cruel Dispositions: Queer Literature, the Contemporary Puerto Rican Literary Field and Luis Negrón's *Mundo Cruel* (2010)." In *Pierre Bourdieu in Hispanic Literature and Culture*, edited by Ignacio M. Sánchez Prado, 157–86. New York: Palgrave, 2018.

Gutmann, Matthew. *Fixing Men: Sex, Birth Control, and AIDS in Mexico*. Berkeley: University of California Press, 2007.

Halberstam, Jack. *Female Masculinity*. Durham: Duke University Press, 1998.

———. *The Queer Art of Failure*. Durham: Duke University Press, 2011.

Han, Byung-Chul. *Psychopolitics: Neoliberalism and New Technologies of Power*. Translated by Erik Butler. London: Verso, 2017.

Harvey, David. *A Brief History of Neoliberalism*. Oxford: Oxford University Press, 2005.

———. *Spaces of Global Capitalism: Towards a Theory of Uneven Geographical Development*. London: Verso, 2006.

Herdt, Gilbert. *Sexual Cultures and Migration in the Era of AIDS: Anthropological and Demographic Perspectives*. Oxford: Oxford University Press, 2007.

Herdt, Gilbert, and Shirley Lindenbaum. *The Time of AIDS: Social Analysis, Theory, and Method*. London: Sage Publications, 1992.

Herring, Scott. *Queering the Underworld: Slumming, Literature, and the Undoing of Lesbian and Gay History*. Chicago: University of Chicago Press, 2007.

Hodge, Derrick G. "Colonizing the Cuban Body." In *The Cuba Reader: History, Culture, Politics*, edited by Aviva Chomsky, Barry Carr, and Pamela Maria Smorkaloff, 628–34. Durham: Duke University Press, 2003.

Hoff, Benedict. *Reprojecting the City: Urban Space and Dissident Sexualities in Recent Latin American Cinema.* Oxford: Legenda, 2016.

Holleran, Andrew. *Chronicle of a Plague, Revisited: AIDS and Its Aftermath.* New York: Da Capo Press, 2008.

———. *Ground Zero.* New York: Plume, 1988.

Irvine, Janice M. *Disorders of Desire: Sexuality and Gender in Modern American Sexology.* Philadelphia: Temple University Press, 2005.

Jameson, Fredric. *Antinomies of Realism.* London: Verso, 2013.

Jurgenson, Nathan. *The Social Photo: On Photography and Social Media.* London: Verso, 2019.

Kahan, Benjamin. *The Book of Minor Perverts: Sexology, Etiology, and the Emergences of Sexuality.* Chicago: University of Chicago Press, 2019.

Kempadoo, Kamala. *Sexing the Caribbean: Gender, Race, and Sexual Labor.* New York: Routledge, 2004.

Kickbusch, Ilona. "Foreword: Governing Interdependence." In *Global Health Governance and the Fight Against HIV/AIDS,* edited by Wolfgang Hein, Sonja Bartsch, and Lars Kohlmorgen, x–xv. New York: Palgrave, 2007.

King, J. L., and Karen Hunter. *On the Down Low: A Journey into the Lives of 'Straight' Black Men Who Sleep with Men.* Easton, PA: Harmony, 2005.

Kinsey, Alfred J., Wardell B. Pomeroy, and Clyde E. Martin. *Sexual Behavior in the Human Male.* 1948. Bloomington: Indiana University Press, 1975.

Klein, Naomi. *The Shock Doctrine: The Rise of Disaster Capitalism.* New York: Picador, 2007.

Kunzle, David. *Che Guevara: Icon, Myth, and Message.* Los Angeles: UCLA Fowler Museum of Cultural History, 1997.

La Fountain-Stokes, Lawrence. *Translocas: The Politics of Puerto Rican Drag and Trans Performance.* Ann Arbor: University of Michigan Press, 2021.

Lacan, Jacques. *The Four Fundamental Concepts of Psychoanalysis.* 1973. Edited by Jacques-Alain Miller. Translated by Alan Sheridan. London: Penguin, 1987.

Lancaster, Roger N. "Tolerance and Intolerance in Sexual Cultures in Latin America." In *Passing Lines: Sexuality and Immigration,* edited by Brad Epps, Keja Valens, and Bill Johnson González. Cambridge, MA: Harvard University Press, 2005. 255–74.

Laplanche, Jean, and Jean-Bertrand Pontalis. "Fantasy and the Origins of Sexuality." In *Formations of Fantasy,* edited by Victor Burgin, James Donald, and Cora Kaplan, 5–34. London: Methuen, 1986.

Laureano, Javier E. *San Juan Gay: Conquista de un Espacio Urbano de 1948 a 1991.* San Juan: Instituto de Cultura Puertorriqueña, 2016.

Lema-Hincapié, Andrés, and Debra A. Castillo, eds. *Despite All Adversities: Spanish American Queer Cinema.* Albany: State University of New York Press, 2015.

Levine, Martin P. *Gay Macho: The Life and Death of the Homosexual Clone.* Edited by Michael S. Kimmel. New York: New York University Press, 1998.

Lewis, Oscar. *The Children of Sánchez: Autobiography of a Mexican Family.* New York: Vintage, 1963.

Locane, Jorge Joaquín. "Interseccionalidad y Polifonía: Para Una Approximación a la Narrativa de Luis Negrón" *Revista Iberoamericana* 83:258 (2017): 31–39.

Lorey, Isabell. *State of Insecurity: Government of the Precarious*. Translated by Aileen Derieg. London: Verso, 2015.

Love, Heather. *Feeling Backwards: Loss and the Politics of Queer History*. Cambridge, MA: Harvard University Press, 2007.

Malebranche, Jack. *Androphilia: A Manifesto. Rejecting the Gay Identity, Reclaiming Masculinity*. Baltimore: Scapegoat Publishing, 2006.

Malinowski, Bronislaw. *Argonauts of the Western Pacific*. 1922. Prospect Heights, IL: Waveland Press, 1984.

Marat, Abniel. *Dios en el Playgirl de noviembre [God in November's Playgirl]*. Río Piedras: Editorial Edil, 1986.

Marcus, Sharon. *Between Women: Friendship, Desire, and Marriage in Victorian England*. Princeton: Princeton University Press, 2007.

Marx, Karl. *Capital: A Critique of Political Economy*. Vol. 1. 1887. Edited by Frederick Engels. New York: International Publishers, 1992.

Mehuron, Kate. "Queer Territories in the Americas: Reinaldo Arenas' Prose." *Prose Studies* 17:1 (1994): 39–63.

Mercado, Gustavo. *The Filmmaker's Eye*. London: Routledge, 2017.

Merleau-Ponty, Maurice. "Eye and Mind." In *The Merleau-Ponty Aesthetic Reader: Philosophy and Painting*, 121–50. Evanston, IL: Northwestern University Press, 1993.

———. *Signs*. 1960. Translated by Richard C. McCleary. Evanston, IL: Northwestern University Press, 1964.

———. *The Visible and the Invisible*. Translated by Alfonso Lingis. Evanston, IL: Northwestern University Press, 1968.

Mirandé, Alfredo. *Hombres y Machos: Masculinity and Latino Culture*. Boulder, CO: Westview Press, 1997.

Mnookin, Jennifer L. "The Image of Truth: Photographic Evidence and the Power of Analogy." *Yale Journal of Law and the Humanities* 10:1 (1998): 1–74. https://digitalcommons.law.yale.edu/yjlh/vol10/iss1/1.

Molinero, Rita. "Arenas en el jardín de las delicias." In *Reinaldo Arenas: Recuerdo y Presencia*, edited by Reinaldo Sánchez, 129–38. Miami, FL: Ediciones Universal, 1994.

Molloy, Sylvia. "The Politics of Posing." In *Hispanisms and Homosexualities*, edited by Sylvia Molloy and Robert McKee Irwin, 141–60. Durham: Duke University Press, 1998.

Monaco, James. *How to Read a Film: The World of Movies, Media, and Multimedia*. Oxford: Oxford University Press, 2000.

Monette, Paul. *Borrowed Time*. London: Collins Harvill, 1988.

Murphy, Timothy, and Suzanne Poirier, eds. *Writing AIDS: Gay Literature, Language, and Analysis*. New York: Columbia University Press, 1993.

Negrón, Luis. *Mundo Cruel*. 2010. San Juan: Agentes Catalíticos, 2011.

———. *Mundo Cruel: Stories [Cruel World]*. Translated by Suzanne Jill Levine. New York: Seven Stories Press, 2010.

Nesvig, Martin. "The Complicated Terrain of Latin American Homosexuality." *Hispanic American Historical Review* 81:3–4 (2001): 689–729.

Newson, Adele. "*A Small Gathering of Bones.*" *World Literature Today* 69:3 (1995): 630–31.

Ocasio, Rafael. *Cuba's Political and Sexual Outlaw: Reinaldo Arenas*. Gainesville: University of Florida Press, 2003.

Ong, Aihwa. *Neoliberalism as Exception: Mutations in Citizenship and Sovereignty.* Durham: Duke University Press, 2006.

Ortiz, Ricardo L. "Docile Bodies, Volatile Texts: Sexual Politics in Cuban-Exile Prison Texts." *Annals of Scholarship* 12:3-4 (1998): 91-111.

Padilla, Mark. *Caribbean Pleasure Industry: Tourism, Sexuality, and AIDS in the Dominican Republic.* Chicago: University of Chicago Press, 2007.

Panichelli-Batalla, Stéphanie. *El Testimonio en la Pentagonía de Reinaldo Arenas.* Rochester, NY: Boydell and Brewer, 2016.

Parker, Richard. *Beneath the Equator: Cultures of Desire, Male Homosexuality, and Emerging Gay Communities in Brazil.* New York: Routledge, 1999.

Parker, Richard, Shivananda Kahn, and Peter Aggleton. "Conspicuous by Their Absence? Men Who Have Sex with Men (MSM) in Developing Countries: Implications for HIV Prevention." *Critical Public Health* 8:4 (1998): 329-46.

Pastore, Judith Laurence, ed. *Confronting AIDS through Literature: The Responsibilities of Representation.* Urbana: University of Illinois Press, 1993.

Pathela, Preeti, Anhum Hajat, Julia Schillinger, Susan Blank, Randall Sell, and Farzad Mostashari. "Discordance between Sexual Behavior and Self-Reported Sexual Identity: A Population-Based Survey of New York City Men." *Annals of Internal Medicine* 145:6 (2006): 416-25.

Pearl, Raymond. *Introduction to Medical Biometry and Statistics.* Philadelphia: W. B. Saunders, 1940.

———. *Man the Animal.* Edited by Maud M. De Witt Pearl. Bloomington, IN: Principia Press, 1946.

Pérez-Bonilla, Lauren M. "Dominican *Bugarrones*: (in)Visibility, Masculinities, and Same-Sex Performances." In *Gender, Health, and Society in Contemporary Latin America and the Caribbean,* edited by Ronnie Shepard and Shir Lerman Ginzburg, 33-58. London: Lexington Books, 2019.

Phillips, Layli. "Deconstructing 'Down Low' Discourse: The Politics of Sexuality, Gender, Race, AIDS, and Anxiety." *Journal of African American Studies* 9:2 (2005): 3-15. https://www.jstor.org/stable/41819081.

Pisani, Elizabeth. *The Wisdom of Whores: Bureaucrats, Brothels, and the Business of AIDS.* New York: W. W. Norton, 2008.

Prieur, Annick. *Mema's House, Mexico City: On Transvestites, Queens, and Machos.* Chicago: University of Chicago Press, 1998.

Powell, Patricia. *A Small Gathering of Bones.* Oxford: Heinemann, 1994.

Ramírez, Rafael L. *What It Means to Be a Man: Reflections on Puerto Rican Masculinity.* Translated by Rosa E. Casper. New Brunswick: Rutgers University Press, 1999.

Ramírez, Rafael L., Victor I. García-Toro, Myriam L. Vélez-Galván, and Ineke Cunningham. "Masculine Identity and Sexuality: A Study of Puerto Rican Blue-Collar Workers." In *Caribbean Masculinities: Working Papers,* edited by Rafael L. Ramírez, Victor I. García-Toro, and Ineke Cunningham, 83-104. San Juan: University of Puerto Rico Press, 2002.

Ramos Otero, Manuel. *La novelabingo.* 1976. Rio Piedras: Instituto de Cultura Puertorriqueña, 2011.

———. "Loca la de la Locura." In *Cuentos de buena tinta,* 233-40. San Juan: Instituto de Cultura Puertorriqueña, 1992.

Rancière, Jacques. *The Intervals of Cinema.* Translated by John Howe. London: Verso, 2014.

Rangelova, Radost. "Nationalism, States of Exception, and Caribbean Identities in *Sirena Selena vestida de pena* and 'Loca la de la locura.'" *Centro Journal* 19:1 (2007): 74-88.

Rechy, John. *City of Night.* New York: Grove Press, 1963.

Robinson, Paul. *The Modernization of Sex: Havelock Ellis, Alfred Kinsey, William Masters, and Virginia Johnson.* Ithaca, NY: Cornell University Press, 1989.

Rocchi, Vince. *Gay for Pay: How I Went Queer for Cash with Craigslist.* Lulu.com, 2021.

Rose, Jacqueline. *Sexuality in the Field of Vision.* 1986. London: Verso, 2006.

Rose, Nikolas. "Governing 'Advanced' Liberal Democracies." In Barry, Osborne, and Rose, 37–64.

Rubin, Gayle. "Sexual Traffic. Interview with Judith Butler." *differences* 6:2–3 (1994): 62–99. https://doi.org/10.1215/10407391-6-2-3-62.

Ryan, Chris, and C. Michael Hall. *Sex Tourism: Marginal People and Liminality.* London: Routledge, 2001.

Sagar, Aparagita. "AIDS and the Question of Memory: Patricia Powell's *A Small Gathering of Bones.*" *Small Axe* 7 (2000): 28–43.

Sánchez-Eppler, Benigno. "Reinaldo Arenas, Re-Writer Revenant, and the Re-patriation of Cuban Homoerotic Desire." In *Queer Diasporas*, edited by Cindy Patton and Benigno Sánchez-Eppler, 154–82. Durham: Duke University Press, 2000.

Savin-Williams, Ritch C. "An Exploratory Study of Exclusively Heterosexual, Primarily Heterosexual and Mostly Heterosexual Young Men." *Sexualities* 21:1–2 (2018): 16–29. https://doi.org/10.1177/1363460716678559.

Savin-Williams, Ritch C., and Zhana Vrangalova. "Mostly Heterosexual as a Distinct Sexual Orientation Group: A Systemic Review of the Empirical Evidence." *Developmental Review* 33 (2013): 58–88. https://doi.org/10.1016/j.dr.2013.01.001.

Schifter, Jacobo. *From Toads to Queens: Transvestism in a Latin American Setting.* New York: Haworth Press, 1999.

———. *Latino Truck Driver Trade: Sex and HIV in Central America.* New York: Haworth Press, 2001.

———. *Lila's House: Male Prostitution in Latin America.* New York: Haworth Press, 1998.

———. *Macho Love: Sex behind Bars in Central America.* New York: Haworth Press, 1999.

———. *Mongers in Heaven: Sexual Tourism and HIV Risk in Costa Rica and the United States.* Lanham, MD: University Press of America, 2007.

———. *Public Sex in a Latin Society.* New York: Haworth Press, 2000.

Sedgwick, Eve Kosofsky. *Between Men: English Literature and Male Homosocial Desire.* New York: Columbia University Press, 1985.

———. *Epistemology of the Closet.* Berkeley: University of California Press, 1990.

———. *Tendencies.* Durham: Duke University Press, 1993.

Sheller, Mimi. *Consuming the Caribbean.* London: Routledge, 2003.

Shumway, David R. "What Is Realism?" *Storyworlds: A Journal of Narrative Studies* 9:1–2 (2017): 183–95.

Silverman, Kaja. *Threshold of the Visible World.* New York: Routledge, 1996.

Smallman, Shawn. *The AIDS Pandemic in Latin America.* Chapel Hill: University of North Carolina Press, 2007.

Smith, Paul Julian. *Vision Machines: Cinema, Literature and Sexuality in Spain and Cuba, 1983–1993.* London: Verso, 1996.

Sontag, Susan. *On Photography.* 1973. New York: Picador, 1977.

Sosa-Velasco, Alfredo J. "The Construction of the Bisexual Subject in *No se lo digas a nadie* (Francisco Lombardi, 1998)." In *Despite All Adversities: Spanish American Queer Cinema,* edited by Andrés Lema-Hincapié and Debra A. Castillo, 185–202. Albany: State University of New York Press, 2015.

Soto, Francisco. *Reinaldo Arenas: The Pentagonía*. Gainesville: University Press of Florida, 1994.

Soto-Crespo, Ramón E. *Mainland Passage: The Cultural Anomaly of Puerto Rico*. Minneapolis: University of Minnesota Press, 2009.

———. *The White Trash Menace and Hemispheric Fiction*. Columbus: The Ohio State University Press, 2020.

Spring, Justin. *An Obscene Diary: The Visual World of Sam Steward*. Norwich, VT: Elysium Press, 2010.

Stewart, Christine. "*The Wisdom of Whores: Bureaucrats, Brothels and the Business of AIDS*, by Elizabeth Pisani." *Culture, Health & Sexuality* 11:7 (2009): 743–45. https://www.jstor.org/stable/27784499.

Stoler, Ann Laura. *Carnal Knowledge and Imperial Power: Race and the Intimate in Colonial Rule*. Berkeley: University of California Press, 2010.

Subero, Gustavo. *Queer Masculinities in Latin American Cinema: Male Bodies and Narrative Representations*. London: I. B. Tauris, 2014.

———. *Representations of HIV/AIDS in Contemporary Hispano-American and Caribbean Culture*. Surrey, England: Ashgate Publishing, 2014.

Tanke, Joseph J. *Foucault's Philosophy of Art: A Genealogy of Modernity*. London: Continuum, 2009.

———. *Jacques Rancière: An Introduction. Philosophy, Politics, Aesthetics*. London: Continuum, 2011.

Thompson, Hunter S. *Hell's Angels: A Strange and Terrible Saga*. 1967. New York: Modern Library, 1999.

Toro-Alfonso, José. "Vulnerability of Gay Men and Other Men Who Have Sex with Men to the HIV/AIDS Epidemic in Latin America: The Other Side of Masculinity." In *AIDS and Male-to-Male Sex in Latin America: Vulnerabilities, Strengths, and Proposed Measures*, edited by Carlos F. Cáceres, Mario Pecheny, and Veriano Terto Júnior, 77–97. Lima, Peru: Universidad Peruana Cayetano Heredia, 2003.

Venkatesh, Vinodh. *New Maricón Cinema: Outing Latin American Film*. Austin: University of Texas Press, 2016.

Villalobos, Hugo. *Diario de un Chichifo Ilustrado*. Mexico City: Fontamara, 2007.

Wanner, Rene. "Web Poster Exhibition—La Cubanidad! Cuban Posters, 1940–2004." http://www.posterpage.ch/exhib/ex110cub/ex110cub.htm.

Ward, Jane. *Not Gay: Sex between Straight White Men*. New York: New York University Press, 2015.

Watney, Simon. *Policing Desire: Pornography, AIDS and the Media*. London: Methuen, 1987.

Whyte, Jessica. *The Morals of the Market: Human Rights and the Rise of Neoliberalism*. London: Verso, 2019.

Woloch, Alex. *The One vs. the Many: Minor Characters and the Space of the Protagonist in the Novel*. Princeton: Princeton University Press, 2003.

Woods, Gregory. *A History of Gay Literature: The Male Tradition*. New Haven: Yale University Press, 1998.

Wright, Timothy. "Gay Organizations, NGOs, and the Globalization of Sexual Identity." In *Same-Sex Cultures and Sexualities: An Anthropological Reader*, edited by Jennifer Robertson, 279–94. Oxford: Blackwell, 2005.

Youde, Jeremy. *Global Health Governance*. Cambridge, UK: Polity Press, 2012.

FILMOGRAPHY

Absent. Dir. Marco Berger. Instituto Nacional de Cine y Artes Audiovisuales (INCAA). 2011. 91 min.

The Blonde One. Dir. Marco Berger. Universidad del Cine. 2019. 108 min.

Brokeback Mountain. Dir. Ang Lee. Focus Features. 2005. 134 min.

Hawaii. Dir. Marco Berger. La Noria Cine. 2013. 102 min.

Horseplay. Dir. Marco Berger. Sombracine. 2022. 102 min.

Kiss of the Spider Woman. Dir. Hector Babenco. HB Filmes. 1980. 120 min.

Men of Hard Skin. Dir. José Campusano. Compañia de Cine. 2019. 96 min.

La mujer de mi hermano. Dir. Ricardo de Montreuil. Cinefarm. 2005. 89 min.

Plan B. Dir. Marco Berger. Rendez-vous Pictures. 2009. 106 min.

Por Allá [From Afar]. Dir. Lorenzo Vigas. Factor RH Producciones. 2015. 93 min.

Sexual Tension Volatile. Dir. Marco Berger and Marcelo Monaco. Swift Productions. 2012. 101 min.

Taekwondo. Dir. Marco Berger. Cinemilagroso. 2017. 112 min.

Undertow. Dir. Javier Fuentes-León. Elcalvo Films. 2009. 97 min.

Young Hunter. Dir. Marco Berger. Sombracine Producciones. 2020. 101 min.

Y tu mamá también. Dir. Alfonso Cuarón. Anhelo Producciones. 2001. 106 min.

INDEX

Absent (Berger), 14, 85, 88, 89, 94, 98–102, 118
Acevedo, David Caleb, 14, 123, 131, 134–36, 140
Adorno, Theodor, 123, 150
AIDS, 16–18, 34; literature of, 124, 124n3, 125, 125n4, 126–27, 127n5
Androphilia (Malebranche), 91–92
Andros, Phil, 134. See also Steward, Sam
anthropology, 4, 5, 13, 16, 17, 27, 49, 58, 62; and HIV/AIDS, 16–18, 34. See also ethnography
Appe, Susan, 26n3
Apter, Emily, 123–24
Arenas, Reinaldo, 5, 123, 124; *Before Night Falls*, 14, 151–54; "Del Bugarron," 149–51; *The Color of Summer*, 146–51; "Four Principal Categories of Bugarrón," 147–49. See also *superbugarrón*
Argentina, 47n2, 91, 91n4, 92, 94, 97, 98, 119

Babenco, Héctor, 106. See also *Kiss of the Spider Woman*
Baker, Josephine, 77–78
Barnshaw, John, and Lynn Letukas, 10
Barthes, Roland, 64–65
Baudrillard, Jean: *Screened Out*, 114; *Simulacra and Simulation*, 59–60, 60n7, 68, 79

Bayly, Jamie: *La mujer de mi Hermano*, 108–12; *No se lo digas a nadie*, 111
Bejel, Emilio, 151
Bennett, Jane, 101n8
Berger, Marco, 84, 85, 87, 96, 98, 98n6, 99, 114, 118. See also *Absent*; *The Blond One*; *Hawaii*; *Horseplay*; *Plan B*; *Sexual Tension Volatile*; *Taekwondo*; *Young Hunter*
Bersani, Leo, and Ulysse Dutoit, 105, 116n13
biopolitics, 33; and Foucault, 2; and Schifter, 27
bisexuality, xii, xiii, 7, 10n12, 20, 28, 31, 88, 90, 111, 111n12, 112
Bleek, Wolf, 38
Blonde One, The (Berger), 14, 85, 86, 87, 88
Bolton, Ralph, 41
Brinkema, Eugenie, 93n5
Brokeback Mountain (Lee), 90–91
Brown, Wendy, 12n13
bugarrón, xi–xv, 1, 2, 3–6, 72; and AIDS, 13; and anthropology, 18–19; and cinema, 85, 113; "cinematic bugarrón" definition, 85n2, 102, 118, 120–21; and disappearance, 83; and extinction, 46, 72, 74; and "gay-for-pay," 11; and geopolitics, 86, 151, 154; and heteroflexibility, 98n6; and non-reciprocity, 81; perception of sexual risk,

169

1, 2, 5, 17, 19, 21, 23, 25–26, 27, 29, 32–33, 35–43, 46, 55; and subjectivity, 55, 58, 83, 104; and visibility, 19–20, 31–33, 85, 118; and visual representation, 85, 114, 121. See also *cachero*; *hombre normal*; *mayate*; *neobugarrón*
bugarronizing, 83, 112, 130, 151; and *debugarronizing*, 145

Cabezas, Amalia L., 50, 52
cachero, 18–19, 92; and compartmentalization, 23, 113; and drug culture effects, 21–22; and economic development, 19; and modernity, 20; and premodernity, 20; safe sex practices, 25–26. See also *bugarrón*; *hombres normales*; *mayate*; Schifter, Jacobo
Campusano, José, 14, 85, 88, 119. See also *Men of Hard Skin*
Carbone, Mauro, 96
Carrillo, Héctor, 17, 28, 43; *The Night Is Young*, 29–30
Carrillo, Héctor, and Amanda Hoffman, 7; "From MSM to Heteroflexibilities," 10, 10n12; "'Straight with a pinch of bi,'" 10
Chauncey, George, 3, 8, 53–54
Chibber, Vivek, 14, 49
chichifo, 131–34. See also *neobugarrón*
Chin, James, 18, 41–42
Chin, Timothy, 127n5
Chomsky, Noam, 47n2
City of Night (Rechy), 67
Clark, Steven, 151n18
Cleland, John, 42
Clifford, James, 136
Colombia, xiii
Connolly, William, 47
Cook, Deborah, 44
Costa Rica, xiii, 1, 19, 20, 21, 23, 24, 39
Creech, James, 139
Cruz Malavé, Arnaldo Manuel, 137, 138n10, 144
Cuarón, Alfonso, 93. See also *Y tu mamá también*
Cuba, xiii, 1, 2, 44, 47, 76–83, 86, 149–54

Da Vinci, Leonardo, 85
Dardot, Pierre, and Christian Laval, 12–13, 13n14
Davidson, Arnold I., 3, 57
de la Mora, Sergio, 85, 88
de Man, Paul, 134n9

de Montreuil, Ricardo, 14, 85, 88, 89, 107–13. See also *La mujer de mi hermano*
de Moya, Antonio E., and Rafael García, 3, 3n2, 46n1, 50, 62n10
Dean, Mitchell, and Daniel Zamora, 13n14
Dean, Tim, 135
Decena, Carlos Ulises, xiii, 74, 85
Del Risco, Enrique, 151n18
Delany, Samuel R., 3n1
D'Emilio, John, 52–53
Diamond, Lisa M., 6
dialectic, 123, 145, 150; and antinomy of realism, 123, 125, 128, 131; binary, 123, 136
Diary of a Common Whore (Acevedo), 131, 134–36
Dinshaw, Carolyn, 3n1
Domínguez-Ruvalcaba, Héctor, xiii
Dominican Republic, xiii, 1, 50, 54, 55, 58, 62, 63, 65, 68, 72, 73, 74, 75, 76, 136
down low, 8, 9–10
Dreuilhe, Emmanuel, 124n3
Drucker, Donna J., 7n6
Dunphy-Blomfield, Jocelyn, 89

ecology, 89, 98n6, 101, 107, 117–18; ecological connections, 98; ecological relatedness, 118–21
ecosystem, 89, 94
Ellis, Robert Richmond, 151n18
ethnography: and lust, 18–19; and male prostitution, 20–22; and North American Free Trade Agreement, 23; post-Padilla, 74–76; and US-Mexico border, 23. See also Schifter, Jacobo

Finn, Jonathan, 70–71
Foucault, Michel: *The Archaeology of Knowledge*, xv, 57, 153; on biopolitics, 2, 36, 44; *The Birth of Biopolitics*, 12, 36, 37; *The Birth of the Clinic*, 94; and confession, 106; and constellation of concepts, 153; and Dardot and Laval, 12; and Dean and Zamora, 13n14; on disciplinary regime of visibility, 71, 94; *Discipline and Punish*, 30, 71, 154; on emergence, xiv, 57; and governmentality, 36–37; *The History of Sexuality, Vol. 1: An Introduction*, xi, xiii, 6, 8, 9, 13, 16n1, 36, 43–44, 55, 55n4, 57, 106, 151; and neoliberalism, 12, 36; "Nietzsche, Genealogy, History," xiv; *The Order of Things*, 65n12; on power/knowledge, 15, 15n1, 18–19, 26n3, 55, 58;

INDEX • 171

Psychiatric Power, 8n8, 60n7; on *scientia sexualis,* 55, 71, 109, 154; "Sex, Power, and the Politics of Identity," 12; *Sexuality,* 16n4; "Sexuality and Solitude," 12; and simulation, 60n7; *Subjectivity and Truth,* 3; and surveillance, 43–44; *The Use of Pleasure,* xii; on visibility and invisibility, 65n12, 94
Freud, Sigmund, 61n8; "Mourning and Melancholia,'" 101; "A Note Upon the 'Mystic Writing Pad,'" 88–89, 95; *Three Essays on the Theory of Sexuality,* 6n4, 56n5, 85n1
Fuentes-León, Javier, 14, 85, 88, 89, 102. See also *Undertow*

García Canclini, Néstor, 5–6
global health governance, 16, 17, 18, 19, 26, 26n3, 38, 43, 44
governmentality, 36–37; and nongovernmental organizations, 38; and politics of double concealment, 37. See also Foucault, Michel; neoliberalism
Green, Edward C., et al., 41
Grugel, Jean, 26n3
Guevara, Che, 78–81
Gutiérrez Negrón, Sergio, 137
Gutmann, Matthew, 13, 17, 43; *Fixing Men,* 33–38

Halberstam, Jack, 3n1
Han, Byung-Chul, 12n13
Harvey, David: *A Brief History of Neoliberalism,* 47n2; *Spaces of Global Capitalism,* 51n3
Hawaii (Berger), 14, 85, 88, 89, 94–98, 113, 121
Herdt, Gilbert, 25–26
Herdt, Gilbert, and Shirley Lindenbaum, 16
Herring, Scott, 3n1
heteroflexibility, 6–7, 11, 103, 113, 117, 154, 155; and *bugarrón,* 10, 98n6; and cinema, 87, 88, 113; and down low, 10; exclusive heterosexuality, 97, 120; and film techniques, 87, 88, 89, 107, 109, 115, 118, 121; flexible heterosexuality, 92, 97; and homosociality, 88, 92–93; inclusive heterosexuality, 20, 57–58, 88, 112; and Kinsey, 7; nonheterosexually exclusive, 92, 102, 113, 154; and not-gay, 11–12, 88, 92; and trade, 8–9
Hodge, Derrick G., 2
Hoff, Benedict, 85
Holleran, Andrew, 124n3, 126

hombre normal, xi–xv, 1, 26, 31, 31n4, 56–57, 86, 156; and Arenas, 148, 152–53; and Chauncey, 8; and Pérez-Bonilla, 75
Horseplay (Berger), 98n6

identity, 58; and disavowal, 56; gay, 25–26, 49, 51–55, 70, 86, 88, 90, 91, 123, 130; identitarian, 27; nonidentitarian, 92–93; simulated market, 56, 74. See also *neobugarrón*: and commodification
Irvine, Janice M., 7n6

Jameson, Fredric: *Antinomies of Realism,* 123, 125, 128, 130
Jurgenson, Nathan, 70–71

Kahan, Benjamin, 9n9
Kempadoo, Kamala, 50, 52
Kickbusch, Ilona, 43
King, J. L., and Karen Hunter, 10
Kinsey, Alfred J.: and *bugarrón* sexual practice, xii, 128; and *bugarronizing,* 148, 150, 151; on exclusive heterosexuality, xii; on Kinsey scale, xii, 148; and Sam Steward, 135; *Sexual Behavior in the Human Male,* xii; on sexual gradation, 154
Kiss of the Spider Woman (Babenco), 106–7
Klein, Naomi, 13
Kunzle, David, 79–80

La Fountain-Stokes, Lawrence, 145n14
La Leyenda del Macho (Rodríguez), 82–83
La mujer de mi Hermano (de Montreuil), 14, 85, 88, 89, 107–13, 121
Lacan, Jacques, 107n10
Lancaster, Roger N., 17, 18, 28–31, 43, 54
Laplanche, Jean, and Jean-Bertrand Pontalis, 88, 116n13; on enigmatic signifier, 115, 116n13
Laureano, Javier E., 141n11, 142
Lee, Ang, 90. See also *Brokeback Mountain*
Lema-Hincapié, Andrés, and Debra A. Castillo, 85
Levine, Martin P., 3n1
Lewis, Oscar, 132, 141
literary history, 139; as corrective, 142; and gay identity, 128–29, 140; and genealogy, 128–30, 141, 154
Locane, Jorge Joaquín, 137
Lorey, Isabell, 12
Love, Heather, 3n1, 129n6

Malebranche, Jack, 91–92. See also *Androphilia*
Malinowski, Bronislaw, 132, 132n8
Marat, Abniel, 123, 154; *Dios en el Playgirl de noviembre*, 141–42
Marcus, Sharon, 3n1, 86, 86n3
maricón, 86, 90, 144
Marx, Karl, 60–61
mayate, 31. See also *bugarrón*
memory, 95–96, 110–11; enigmatic, 96; inner world of mental images, 101; mnemonic traces, 95, 121
Men of Hard Skin (Campusano), 14, 85, 88, 119–20, 121
Mercado, Gustavo, 99n7
Merleau-Ponty, Maurice, 88–89, 101n8; "Eye and Mind," 67, 100, 104, 109; *Signs*, 96; *The Visible and the Invisible*, 119
Mexico, xiii, 1, 18, 23, 29, 30, 31n4, 32, 33, 34, 35, 37, 38, 108
Miranda, Carmen, 76, 77
Mnookin, Jennifer L., 70
Moca, Puerto Rico, 139
modernity, 19–20
Molloy, Sylvia, 105
Monaco, James, 87
Monette, Paul, 124n3
MSM (men-who-have-sex-with-men), 6, 10n12, 18; and AIDS, 18, 32–33, 37, 38, 42–43
Mundo Cruel (Negrón), 122–23, 122n1, 136–40, 145
Murphy, Timothy, and Suzanne Poirier, 125n4

Negrón, Luis, 14. See also *Mundo Cruel*
neobugarrón: and authenticity, 11–12, 61, 67; and capital, 2, 14, 60, 155; and commodification, 2, 8, 13, 50–51, 60, 61, 72, 76; definition, 1, 2; distinction from *bugarrón*, 2, 13, 64, 72, 75, 81, 122n1; emergence of, 59; and genealogy, 5, 123, 128, 154; and hybrid methodology, 5; and literary realism, 14, 124–30; and Marx, 60; and nonexclusive heterosexuality, 7, 88; non-identitarian, 91–93; and polysemy, 144–46, 154; and Schifter, 27; and sex work, 54, 136, 139; and simulation, 59, 68, 155; and subjectivity, 3, 4, 5, 7, 9, 12, 13, 13n14, 49, 55–58, 60n7, 62, 75, 105, 154, 155; and translation, 14–15, 139–40, 144–46, 148–49, 152, 152n19, 154; and visibility, 14, 50, 53, 65, 67, 82–83, 105. See also *chichifo*

neoliberalism, 2, 7, 8, 9, 12, 12n13, 13, 13n14, 14, 36, 43, 45, 47, 47n2, 49–51, 51n3, 53, 54, 55–59, 61, 64, 82–83, 134, 155, 156; and governmentality, 36, 44–45, 51
Nesvig, Martin, 25
Newson, Adele, 127n5
nongovernmental organizations (NGOs), 33, 36, 39–42
not-gay, 8, 10, 11, 61, 61n8, 88, 92, 94, 98n6, 145

Ocasio, Rafael, 151n18
Ong, Aihwa, 51
Ortiz, Ricardo L., 151n18

Padilla, Mark: *Caribbean Pleasure Industry*, 50–58, 61–62, 61n8, 69, 85; post-Padilla, 74–76
Panichelli-Batalla, Stéphanie, 149
Parker, Richard, 17, 18, 30, 39, 43, 54; *Beneath the Equator*, 8n7, 28–29, 32
Pastore, Judith Laurence, 125n4
Pathela, Preeti, et al., 32–33
Pérez-Bonilla, Lauren M., 74–76
Phillips, Layli, 9–10
Pisani, Elizabeth, 18, 39–42
Plan B (Berger), 14, 85, 87, 88, 89–98, 106, 113, 117, 121
Por Allá [From Afar] (Vigas), 14, 85, 88, 89, 114–21
Powell, Patricia, 5, 14, 123; *A Small Gathering of Bones*, 124–30
Prieur, Annick, 13, 17, 28, 39, 43; *Mema's House, Mexico City*, 30–32, 46
Puerto Rico, xiii, xiv, 1, 73, 74, 83, 134, 136, 137, 141, 145

queer, 85, 86, 88, 90; and theory, 3, 86n3

Ramírez, Rafael L., 3–4
Ramírez, Rafael L., et al., 3n2
Ramos Otero, Manuel, 123, 141n11, 146, 154; *La Novelabingo*, 15, 143–44; "Loca la de la Locura" 144–46, 145n14
Rancière, Jacques, 88, 89; *Intervals of Cinema*, 109–10
Rangelova, Radost, 145–46
Rechy, John, 67. See also *City of Night*
representation, 4, 5, 14, 55, 65n12, 155; literary, 122–23, 126–30; of sexual variance, 121; visual cinematic, 83, 85, 97, 104, 119

Robinson, Paul, 7n6, 112
Rocchi, Vince, 11
Rodríguez, Elio, 76, 77, 82, 149. See also *La Leyenda del Macho*; *Tropical*, 2
Rose, Jacqueline, 14, 84, 85n1; on Freud's Leonardo da Vinci, 105, 113
Rose, Nikolas, 36
Rubin, Gayle, 30
Ryan, Chris, and C. Michael Hall, 51

Sagar, Aparagita, 127n5
Sánchez-Eppler, Benigno, 151n18
Savin-Williams, Ritch C., 6, 7
Savin-Williams, Ritch C., and Zhana Vrangalova, xii
Schifter, Jacobo, 12, 17, 18–22; and biopolitics, 27; *Latino Truck Driver Trade*, 22–28; *Lila's House*, 12, 20–22; and new *bugarrón* (*neobugarrón*), 27–28
Sedgwick, Eve Kosofsky, 3, 139; *Between Men*, 88, 92; *Epistemology of the Closet*, xii, 9; *Tendencies*, 86n3
sex tourism, 45, 47, 49–50, 52, 155
Sexual Tension Volatile (Berger and Monaco), 114
sexuality: and confession, 106; and fluidity, 6; and globalization, 32, 47; and gradations, xii, xiv, 7, 88, 105, 113, 121, 154; and modernity in Latin America, 28–30; passive/active role, 28–29, 46, 55, 58; and truth-telling, 106. See also Foucault, Michel; heteroflexibility; Kinsey, Alfred J.
Sheller, Mimi, 52
Shumway, David R., 125
Silverman, Kaja, 104n9
simulation, 49, 58–60, 64, 65; and Baudrillard, 59–60, 60n7, 68, 79; and *bugarrón*, 150, 156; and Foucault, 60n7
Smallman, Shawn, 42
Smith, Paul Julian, 85
Sontag, Susan, 70
Sosa-Velasco, Alfredo J., 111–12
Soto, Francisco, 151
Soto-Crespo, Ramón E.: *Mainland Passage*, 142n12; *The White Trash Menace*, 149n16
Spring, Justin, 134–35
Steward, Sam, 134–35. See also Andros, Phil
Stewart, Christine, 41
styles of reasoning, 28–29, 54, 57, 61n8

Subero, Gustavo: *Queer Masculinities in Latin American Cinema*, 85, 111–12; *Representations of HIV/AIDS*, 38n5
superbugarrón, 5, 123, 147–51
surveillance, 1, 8, 9, 13, 16, 18, 26, 26n3, 33, 36, 37, 38–44, 46, 53, 58, 61, 154, 155

Taekwondo (Berger), 97, 98n6
Tanke, Joseph J.: *Foucault's Philosophy of Art*, 65n12; *Jacques Rancière*, 110
Thompson, Hunter S., 131
Toro-Alfonso, José, xiv
Tropical, 2 (Rodríguez), 76, 77, 149

Undertow (Fuentes-León), 14, 85, 88, 89, 102–7, 113, 118, 121
untranslatables, 123–24, 151–53, 153n19, 154. See also Apter, Emily

Venezuela, 114
Venkatesh, Vinodh: *New Maricón Cinema*, 85–87, 93–94, 93n5
Vigas, Lorenzo, 14, 85, 88, 89, 114. See also *Por Allá*
Villalobos, Hugo, 123; *Diario de un Chichifo Ilustrado*, 131–34, 136, 141
visibility, 19–20, 49, 50, 67, 82–83, 104, 113; and anthropology, 49; and biopolitics, 31–33; and discursive regimes, 94; and double concealment, 37; and invisibility, 53, 65, 65n12, 89, 94, 96; and Merleau-Ponty, 96–97, 100, 118; and surveillance, 42–44; and "visibilization," 83. See also Foucault, Michel; Merleau-Ponty, Maurice

Wanner, Rene, 79
Ward, Jane, 11, 61n8
Watney, Simon, 39–40
Whyte, Jessica, 36
Woloch, Alex, 122n2
Woods, Gregory, 128–29
World Health Organization, 19, 41; and *bugarrón* surveillance, 43–44
Wright, Timothy, 26

Y tu mamá también (Cuarón), 93
Youde, Jeremy, 26n3
Young Hunter (Berger), 84

ABNORMATIVITIES: QUEER/GENDER/EMBODIMENT
SCOTT HERRING, SERIES EDITOR

This series explores the embodiment of gender identity and queerness within national and global frameworks of deviance that challenge hetero- and homonormative constructions of the body. The scope of the series is global and transnational, its time frame broad, and its focus interdisciplinary—from literary and cultural studies to history and anthropology and beyond.

Neobugarrón: *Heteroflexibility, Neoliberalism, and Latin/o American Sexual Practice*
    RAMÓN E. SOTO-CRESPO

Diagnosing Desire: Biopolitics and Femininity into the Twenty-First Century
    ALYSON K. SPURGAS

Asexual Erotics: Intimate Readings of Compulsory Sexuality
    ELA PRZYBYLO

Prevention: Gender, Sexuality, HIV, and the Media in Côte d'Ivoire
    CHRISTINE CYNN